Cognitive Science Series, 4

Cognitive Science Series

Categories and Concepts

Edward E. Smith and Douglas L. Medin

Harvard University Press
Cambridge, Massachusetts
London, England
1981

Library of Congress Cataloging in Publication Data

Smith, Edward E., 1940–
    Categories and concepts.

    (Cognitive science series ; 4)
    Bibliography: p.
    Includes index.
    1. Concepts. 2. Categorization (Psychology) 3. Cognition.
4. Psycholinguistics. I. Medin, Douglas L.
II. Title. III. Series.
BF311.S58   153.2′3   81-4629
ISBN 0-674-10275-4   AACR2

To our parents, Harry and Bessie Smith, Kenneth and
Pauline Medin
To Linda Powers
and
To William K. Estes (who believes in the progress of
psychology)

Preface

This book had its inception at Rockefeller University in 1977. Medin was then on the faculty of Rockefeller; Smith was visiting there for a sabbatical year. We spent a lot of time talking about research on concepts and categories, and we both felt that the psychological literature in this area was extremely stimulating, yet thoroughly muddled. What was stimulating was that researchers, particularly Eleanor Rosch at Berkeley, were reporting findings that suggested the view of concepts we had inherited from Aristotle was severly lacking and needed to be replaced by a theory based on *prototypes*. What was muddling was that no two researchers seemed to mean the same thing by prototype, nor was there much agreement on exactly which findings impugned Aristotle's notion of concepts. We decided it would be worthwhile to try to get these issues straight (or straighter). We decided to "review the literature" systematically; the review grew into this book.

Along the way, several people have contributed to this book. Bill Estes provided a supportive environment that year at Rockefeller, and he has continued to encourage our efforts. Eric Wanner, our editor at Harvard Press, was the one who initially suggested that we turn our would-be literature review into a book. He provided valuable criticism on all our preliminary drafts, as well as needed encouragement when our progress was slowed by job changes (Medin moved from Rockefeller to Illinois, Smith from Stanford to Bolt, Beranek and Newman in Cambridge) and other inevitable exigencies.

Current and former colleagues also left their mark on this book. Carolyn Mervis, Andrew Ortony, and Ed Shoben, all colleagues of Medin at Illinois, read early drafts of some of the chapters and made helpful comments. And while at Stanford, Smith benefited from ideas about concepts from a host of colleagues — Gordon

Bower, Eve Clark, Herb Clark, Ellen Markman, Dan Osherson, Roger Shepard, and Amos Tversky. A particularly fertile source of ideas was an advanced seminar on categorization that Smith jointly taught with Tversky in 1978, where the "students" included no fewer than twenty-five distinguished faculty from various universities.

Many thanks are due to those who did the typing: Ruth Colwell at Illinois, Annie Edmonds at Stanford, and Norma Peterson at Bolt, Beranek and Newman.

We would also like to acknowledge the National Institute of Mental Health (Grants MH–19705 and MH–32370) and the National Institute of Education (Contract No. US–NIE–C–400–76–0116) for supporting our research efforts.

Figure 5 was originally published in L. J. Rips, E. J. Shoben, and E. E. Smith, "Semantic Distance and the Verification of Semantic Relations," *Journal of Verbal Learning and Verbal Behavior*, 12 (1973), 1–20, and is reproduced by permission of Academic Press.

Contents

Categories and Concepts

1 | Introduction

WITHOUT CONCEPTS, mental life would be chaotic. If we perceived each entity as unique, we would be overwhelmed by the sheer diversity of what we experience and unable to remember more than a minute fraction of what we encounter. And if each individual entity needed a distinct name, our language would be staggeringly complex and communication virtually impossible. Fortunately, though, we do not perceive, remember, and talk about each object and event as unique, but rather as an instance of a class or concept that we already know something about. When entering a new room, we experience one particular object as a member of the class of chairs, another as an instance of desks, and so on. Concepts thus give our world stability. They capture the notion that many objects or events are alike in some important respects, and hence can be thought about and responded to in ways we have already mastered. Concepts also allow us to go beyond the information given; for once we have assigned an entity to a class on the basis of its perceptible attributes, we can then infer some of its nonperceptible attributes. Having used perceptible properties like color and shape to decide an object is an apple, we can infer the object has a core that is currently invisible but that will make its presence known as soon as we bite into it. In short, concepts are critical for perceiving, remembering, talking, and thinking about objects and events in the world.

The point of this discussion is that a great deal in psychology hinges on how people acquire and use concepts, which in turn depends on the structure of concepts. And lately many psychologists seem to be changing their views about such structure. Until recently the dominant position — which we will call the *classical* view — held that all instances of a concept shared common properties, and that these common properties were necessary and sufficient to define the concept. This view, which dates back to Aristotle, has always had its critics, but in the past decade the criticisms have become more frequent and intense, and new views have emerged. Perhaps the most prominent of these assumes that instances of a concept vary in the degree to which they share certain properties, and consequently vary in the degree to which they represent the concept. This view has sometimes gone by the name of *prototype*, but since this label has been used to mean many different things, we prefer to call it the *probabilistic* view. Another emerging view, which offers an even more extreme departure from the classical one, holds that there is no single representation of an entire class or concept, but only specific representations of the class's exemplars. This we call the *exemplar* view.

The development of alternatives to the classical view has been accompanied by a bustle of research activity. Indeed, the activity has been so frenzied that we think it is time to take a hard look at what has been learned. This book attempts to provide that look. It offers a systematic analysis of the three views of concepts, the processing models they have generated, and the empirical findings that the views and models endeavor to capture. In particular, we will emphasize the major problems that are responsible for the recent shift away from the classical view, show how the newer views take account of these problems, and indicate some of the costs incurred by such an accounting. But before beginning such a survey, it will be useful to provide some introductory examples of the three views.

To illustrate the classical view, we can consider the geometric concept of squares. Suppose that people in general represented this concept in terms of four properties: (1) closed figure, (2) four sides, (3) sides equal (in length), and (4) angles equal. Since these four properties, or criteria, would be applied to any object whose squareness is at issue, we have a unitary description of the concept "square." Moreover, the four properties that make up this concept are precisely those that any square must have. Roughly, then, to have a classical-view concept is to have a unitary description of all class members, where this description specifies the properties that every member must have.

Generalizing this approach, let us try to come up with a plausible classical-view concept that people might have of a cup. Such a concept might consist of the following five properties: (1) concrete object, (2) concave, (3) can hold liquids, (4) has a handle, and (5) can be used to drink hot liquid out of. These properties offer a unitary description of cups, but are all the properties true of everything people would call a cup? Properties 1–3 seem to be, but 4 and 5 are debatable. The teacups commonly used in Chinese restaurants typically do not have handles, yet they are still cups; and one can certainly imagine a poorly manufactured cup which conducts heat and so is useless for drinking hot liquids, but which we would still call a cup. But if we give up the last two properties, we are left with properties 1–3, which are true of some non-cups — bowls, for example — and so do not uniquely describe cups. Considerations like these led Labov (1973) to argue that people's concept of a cup does not conform to the classical view because the properties that make up the concept are not common to all members. Then what kind of view would capture people's concept of cup? According to Labov and others, one needs a view that posits a unitary description of cups, but where the properties in this description are true of most though not all members. This is the probabilistic view. Given such a view, some instances of the class are going to have more of the critical properties than others, and those that do will seem more representative of the concept.

To illustrate a third possible concept, let us consider the class of all psychiatric patients who have suicidal tendencies. One could try to construct a classical-view concept that clinicians might have for this class, but years of futile effort suggests that this cannot be done. What about a probabilistic concept — can it capture a clinician's concept of the suicide-prone? No doubt a probabilistic concept would work better, but even it might fail to capture the knowledge that a clinician uses in deciding that a particular patient is suicidal. For a probabilistic concept provides a single description of all people with suicidal tendencies, yet clinicians may sometimes decide that a patient is suicidal by comparing him to other specific patients known to be suicidal (this suggestion is taken from Tversky and Kahneman, 1973). That is, the class of people with suicidal tendencies may be represented not by a single description, but rather by separate descriptions for various patients known to be members of the class. This corresponds to the exemplar view of concepts.

The examples given above suggest that the various views of concepts can be partly understood in terms of two fundamental questions: (1) Is there a single or unitary description for all members of the class? and (2) Are the properties specified in a unitary description true of all members of the class? The classical view says yes to both questions; the probabilistic view says yes to the first but no to the second; and the exemplar view says no to the first question, thereby making the second one irrelevant. These distinctions, which we will refine and augment later in the book, are summarized in Figure 1.

Though our principal concern in this book is with the three

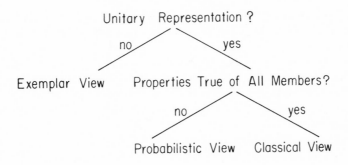

Figure 1   *Three views of concepts*

views, there are important preliminary matters to be considered first. Some of these have to do with what we consider a concept to be in the first place; others concern the nature of the properties that are used to describe concepts. These preliminary issues will be discussed in Chapter 2. In Chapter 3 we discuss the classical view. After describing it in detail, we review numerous arguments and experimental findings that have been offered as evidence against it. We will emphasize that the classical view is a theory about representations, and that to evaluate the view against experimental findings one must add processing assumptions to it, thereby converting a theory about concepts into a model about categorization. In Chapters 4, 5, and 6 we move on to the probabilistic view. These three chapters correspond to the method of describing concepts in the probabilistic view — by qualitative features, quantitative dimensions, or holistic patterns — for the three modes of description have somewhat different consequences. Again we will be concerned not only with the view itself, but with processing models that have been generated from it and with their ability to account for empirical findings. Chapter 7 deals with the exemplar view, again with an eye toward the specific models that instantiate the view and the findings they purport to explain. Finally, Chapter 8 summarizes our main conclusions and raises some unexplored issues.

What exactly are the empirical phenomena with which we intend to measure the views and models? Our major source of phenomena deals with *categorization*. Specifically, we will be concerned primarily with data on how adults use natural concepts with one-word names to classify things. Such "things" might be pictures of objects, say of a dog or a cup, and subjects might be asked if a pictured object belongs in a particular category. Or the things to be categorized might be denoted by words, as when subjects are asked, "Is a raisin a fruit?" and timed as they make their decisions.

(Our reasons for so emphasizing the categorization aspect of concepts will be discussed further at the beginning of the next chapter.)

In almost all cases we will be concerned with object concepts — animals, plants, human artifacts, and so on. Our main reason for choosing this domain is that it has been the most extensively studied in the last decade of experimental research. There is also an ancillary benefit of working with this domain — namely, it is a particularly interesting test case for the three views. That is, had we chosen geometric concepts, like "square," as a target domain, we might have prejudiced things in favor of the classical view; for we know that mathematicians have constructed classical-view descriptions of these concepts and have at least partially succeeded in inculcating these descriptions into many people's conceptual lives. Similarly, had we chosen as our domain abstract concepts, such as "love" or "brilliance," we might have prejudiced the case against the classical view; for no mathematician or metaphysician has come even close to constructing a classical-view description of such concepts. Thus natural objects and human artifacts offer an in-between case — between concepts that any schoolboy can define and concepts that no scholar can grapple with.

There is another rationale for concentrating on object concepts.[1] There are two questions we can ask about any potential psychological concept: (1) Can it be given a classical-view definition in *any* language? and (2) Can it be given a classical-view definition in the language of the mind — that is, do people have a mental representation that corresponds to a classical-view definition of the concept? While question 2 is clearly a psychological one, question 1 is more the province of philosophy and logic. However, question 1 has important implications for a psychological analysis of concepts, for a *no* answer to it virtually necessitates a *no* answer to question 2. (We hedge with "virtually" just in case all things in the world turn out not to have classical-view definitions but our minds impose classical-view structure on them.) It is for this reason that we ignore abstract concepts like love and brilliance: since there is good reason to doubt they can be classically defined in any language, to study whether they can be classically defined psychologically may be beside the point. In contrast, the object concepts that we will focus on seem more likely to be definable in some language, that is, more likely to provide a *yes* answer to question 1, thereby making question 2 a worthwhile topic of study.

In addition to work on natural concepts, we will also consider some studies of artificial concepts. By an artificial concept we mean an equivalence class constructed for a particular experiment, say a class of schematic faces that tend to have similar properties. There are two reasons why such artificial classes are particularly useful for testing proposals about concepts. First, if natural concepts are hypothesized to have a particular structure, one can build this structure into an artificial class and see if people use this class in the same way they use a natural one; if they do, we have added support for the hypothesized structure of natural concepts. Second, the use of artificial concepts allows the experimenter to have precise control over the experiences or instances that the learner is exposed to in acquiring the concept. There are also drawbacks to using artificial concepts, which we will discuss later in the book. But first we need some discussion of what a concept is all about.

2 | Preliminary Issues

Functions of a Concept

THOUGH ONE'S SPECIFIC NOTION of a concept depends on which of the views one endorses, there are some aspects or functions of a concept that seem generally agreed upon. Most would agree that people use concepts both to provide a taxonomy of things in the world and to express relations between classes in that taxonomy (Woods, 1981). The taxonomic function can itself be split into the following two generally agreed upon component functions:

1. *Categorization.* This function involves determining that a specific instance is a member of a concept (for example, this particular creature is a guppie) or that one particular concept is a subset of another (for example, guppies are fish).
2. *Conceptual combination.* This function is responsible for enlarging the taxonomy by combining existent concepts into novel ones (for example, the concepts pet and fish can be combined into the conjunction pet-fish).

Similarly, the notion of using concepts to express relations can be subdivided into the following two component functions:

1. *Constructing propositional representations.* This function is at the heart of language understanding. The concepts denoted by the words in a sentence are mapped into a representation of the proposition expressed by that sentence (for example, the sentence "fish are friendly" is mapped into a proposition in which the concept of "friendly" — or a token of it — is predicated of the concept "fish").

2. *Interrogating propositional representations.* Here a relation between concepts is typically used as a basis for drawing certain inferences from representations (for example, given that one knows that guppies are fish and that fish have scales, one can infer that guppies have scales).

Though this fourfold breakdown has its rough edges, it gives some idea of the various research areas that bear on the nature of concepts. It also clearly suggests that the last three functions of concepts involve combinatorial procedures that play no role in the categorization function.

In this book we will focus almost exclusively on what we have called the categorization function. The main reason for so limiting our inquiry is that most of the critical work in psychology that bears on a shift from the classical to the probabilistic and exemplar views is categorization research. True, one can find analyses of constructing and interrogating representations that explicitly opt for the probabilistic or exemplar views over the classical one (for example, Rips, 1975; Clark and Clark, 1977; Collins, 1978), but the rationale usually given for this move is based on categorization studies. This is not to say that things have to be this way. Indeed, it is quite possible that research on conceptual combinations and on the construction and interrogation of propositional representations will ultimately be essential for constraining a view of concepts; we will return to this possibility at the end of the book. But until then, we are mainly concerned with what research on categorization can tell us about the nature of concepts.

Categorization and Inference

To say that concepts have a categorization function is to acknowledge that concepts are essentially pattern-recognition devices, which means that concepts are used to classify novel entities and to draw inferences about such entities. To have a concept of X is to know something about the properties of entities that belong to the class of X, and such properties can be used to *categorize* novel objects. Conversely, if you know nothing about a novel object but are told it is an instance of X, you can *infer* that the object has all or many of X's properties; that is, you can "run the categorization device in reverse."

Consider the concept of a hat. Let us assume that you have two properties for this concept: (1) it has an aperture that is the size of a human head, and (2) it was manufactured with the intent of a human wearing it. If we give you a novel object and ask, "Is it a hat?" presumably you would try to determine if it has properties 1 and 2. While you can check property 1 by means of perceptual tests, you need more than that to establish whether property 2 applies. Hence, classification may require recourse to nonperceptual information, and when we say that a concept is a pattern recognition device we do not necessarily mean that it uses only perceptual information. Now suppose that instead of asking you to classify the novel object, we hide it from view, tell you that it is a hat, and ask you to tell us something about it. Presumably you would say something about an aperture that was head-sized, and something like "you're supposed to wear it." These statements would be inferences, activated by gaining access to your concept via the word that denotes it, and something like this may happen whenever you hear the word.

Our example neatly separates classification from inference, but this is an oversimplification; most classification situations involve some inferences as well. If you have a prior reason to believe an object is a hat (it is on a hat rack, for example), you might infer that it has a head-sized opening and then perform only minimal perceptual checks to confirm your inference. More generally, where context suggests that an unexamined object belongs to a particular concept, inferences may be drawn about that object's properties, and such inferences will reduce the effort that need be put into classification. A similar phenomenon can occur even without context. Having determined that an object has some perceptual properties of a hat, you might tentatively assume that the object is a hat and then infer the less perceptual properties. This is like the apple example we used earlier—having determined that an object is small, round, and red, you assume that it is an apple and infer that it has a core.

While all three views of concepts—classical, probabilistic, and exemplar—would acknowledge that concepts have the twin functions of categorization and inference, the views differ with respect to the confidence one can have in the accomplishments of these functions. According to the classical view, aside from perceptual limitations one can have complete confidence in any categorization that considers all relevant properties of the concept, for such properties offer sufficient conditions for class membership. The case is different with the probabilistic and exemplar views. In these views, one can never be certain about a categorization, for categorization is always probabilistic when there are no sufficient conditions. A similar story holds for inferences. In the classical view, the inferences are deductions because the inferred properties are necessary ones (if we tell you "it's a square," you can deduce that it has four sides); in the other two views, many of the inferred properties will be probabilistic inferences because they do not conform to necessary properties. These distinctions will become clearer when we consider the views in detail.

Stability of Concepts

A good deal of work presupposes that concepts are relatively stable mental representations. They are stable in two ways: within an individual and across individuals. A concept is stable within an individual to the extent that once a person has a concept, then, except for early developmental changes or physiological ones, that person will always have the same set of properties in mind. A concept is stable across individuals to the extent that when any two people have the same concept, they have the identical sets of properties in mind. If concepts are indeed stable in these two respects, it seems reasonable to think of a concept as a very bounded unit of knowledge, something of which we can say, "He has it completely, she has it partially, and this child doesn't have it at all." This kind of thinking seems to lie behind much of the literature on conceptual and semantic development, where researchers talk of a child's acquiring and mastering concepts.

It turns out that this way of thinking is view-dependent. Believing in the stability of concepts is more consistent with the classical view than with the other two approaches. To illustrate, if one believes that concepts are represented by exemplars rather than by necessary and sufficient conditions, then frequent experience with a new exemplar, say a derby hat, can alter one's concept of hats, which constitutes a breakdown in within-individual stability. Similarly, if one person has intensive experience with a particular exemplar while another person does not, they may end up with very different concepts, a breakdown in across-individual stability.

Because of this view-dependence, we caution the reader not to prejudge issues of concept stability. If in the next chapter we sound as if we are treating concepts as stable, bounded entities, it is because we are describing the classical view, which thinks of concepts in this way. If in Chapter 7 we sometimes sound as if we think concepts are capable of constantly changing with individual experience, again it is the view under consideration — this time the exemplar view — that is dictating our description.

Kinds of Properties for Concepts

Component versus Holistic Properties

In talking about the knowledge contained in a concept, we have thus far used the term *property* with no attempt to specify exactly what we mean. In our attempt to unpack some of the meaning of this term, we will rely heavily on distinctions previously drawn by Garner (1978) and Tversky (1977).

Following Garner (1978), we first distinguish between *component* and *holistic* properties of an object concept. A component property is, roughly, one that helps to describe an object but does not usually constitute a complete description of the object. Some examples should help to get this across. For one's concept of a car, the component properties might include the following: having wheels, having a motor, the average shape of a car, and the fact that its major function is transportation. Note that while some of these components refer to parts of the object (like wheels), others depict global aspects of the entire object (shape), or the purpose or function of the object (transportation). In contrast, a holistic property offers a complete description of the object. For example, your concept of a car might be represented by some sort of template of an ideal car.

Intuitive though it may be, there is a problem with this distinction—namely, how do we distinguish global component properties from holistic ones? What, for example, is the difference between a car's shape when it is treated as a global component and when it is given by a holistic template? We think there are two answers. First, usually when we talk about components there will be more than one of them, and we assume that each component is processed as a unit. This contrasts with a holistic property, like that given in a template, where one property suffices to represent the object class and that property is the only unit that gets processed. Second, when a global property like shape is treated as a component, we intend it as an abstraction from the object, not as a point-for-point isomorphism with the object. In contrast, when shape is given by a template, we often intend it more as a point-for-point isomorphism. Thus a component version of a property is usually more abstract than the corresponding holistic version.[1]

Rough as it is, we think the distinction between component and holistic properties is a useful one, and we employ it in what follows.

DIMENSIONS AND FEATURES

If we decide to represent object concepts in terms of components, we have a choice of how to characterize these components—either by quantitative components, called *dimensions*, or by qualitative components, called *features*. To illustrate this distinction, let us consider one's possible concepts of weapons. You could represent all weapons in terms of a few dimensions, like degree of potential damage, with, say, penknife near one end and atomic bomb near the other. Alternatively, you could represent each weapon by a set of features: for knife, such features might include (1) sharp, (2) has a handle, and (3) metallic. The key difference is that dimensions naturally capture quantitative variations, while features indicate qualitative ones. Thus if two concepts differ with respect to a particular dimension, one concept must have more of that dimension (a higher value) than the other; for example, one weapon is more damaging than the other. But if two concepts differ with respect to a feature, then one concept has "it" while the other does not. Or as Garner (1978) puts it, a feature is a component that either exists or does not exist.[2]

Each way of describing components appears to have a natural limitation: dimensions cannot handle qualitative variations while features will not work with quantitative variations. But these appearances are somewhat misleading. For featural descriptions can clearly be extended to cover quantitative variations, while a limiting case of what we mean by a dimension is extendable to qualitative variations. These ideas require some amplification.

Consider first the extendability of featural descriptions. As Atkinson and Estes (1963) pointed out some time ago, the values for any dimension may be expressed by a set of nested features. It is simplest to illustrate with the dimension of line length. Suppose that the shortest length you can detect is one millimeter; we can represent the length of this standard line by a single feature, call it F_1. Suppose the next shortest line you can detect as different from our standard is two millimeters long; that is, a just-noticeable-difference, or jnd, is one millimeter. We represent that jnd by another feature, F_2, and represent the second line by the feature set F_1 and F_2. Hence the feature representing the length of the first line is nested within the feature set representing the length of the second line. By continuing in this way — representing each successive jnd by a new feature, and nesting the feature sets of shorter lines in those of longer ones — we can represent any value of the dimension of length by a set of nested features. The same procedure will work for any quantitative dimension. And the resulting feature representation captures the important intuition that the closer two objects are on a supposed dimension, the more features they share and the fewer features there are to distinguish between them. So feature descriptions can clearly cover quantitative variations, and can do so in a manner that captures intuitions about quantitative similarity in terms of common and distinctive features (Tversky, 1977). (We note, though, that some implications of this extension of feature descriptions may prove incorrect; for example, since the descriptions of entities at the upper end of a continuum need to contain more features than those at the lower end, the former entities would be expected to be more complex.)

The case for the extendability of dimensions is more precarious. Note first that while dimensions are typically quantitative, they need not be continuous; discrete dimensions are still dimensions (Garner, 1978). To return to our weapon example, your dimension of potential damage may only include five discriminable values, but it is still quantitative as long as you can reliably judge one value to be greater than another. This raises the possibility of a dimension with only two values, where one value indicates some positive amount and the other, or zero value, indicates the absence of the dimension. Such a limiting case of a dimension captures something of what we mean by a feature, with the positive dimension value mapping onto the presence of a feature and the zero value mapping onto the absence of the feature. There are two problems with this extendability argument. First, a zero value on a dimension may not capture what people mean by the absence of a feature; thus it is one thing to say that the feature of "red" does not apply to the concept of truth, and quite another to say that truth has a zero value of redness. Second, our limiting case of a dimension may no longer constitute a "dimension" in any rigorous sense. Following Beals, Krantz, and Tversky (1968), it seems reasonable to insist that for something to be called a dimension it must have the property of *betweenness* — roughly that there exist some triple of values along the dimension such that one value appears (psychologically) to be between the others. Given this constraint, binary-valued contrasts are not dimensions, and true featural variations cannot be captured by dimensional descriptions. The upshot is that only a weak notion of dimensions can be fully extended to cover featural variations, and in this respect dimensional descriptions may be less powerful and more constrained than their featural counterparts.

Let us now return to differences between dimensions and features as they are typically used. In addition to the quantitative versus qualitative distinction, there is another difference in how dimensions and features are employed to represent objects. In describing a set of related objects in terms of dimensions, a person (1) typically uses a small number of dimensions and (2) assumes that every object has some value on each one. For example, a dimensional description of weapons might involve only three to five dimensions and assume that each weapon can be placed on each dimension. Feature descriptions, in contrast, are likely (1) to use many features and (2) to include features for some objects that are not applicable to others. One weapon, say a knife, might have dozens of features corresponding to the size, shape, and structure of its blade and handle, while another weapon, say a grenade, might be described in terms of fewer features that need not correspond to any of those used to describe the previous instance (what feature of a grenade can possibly correspond to the pointedness of a knife's blade?). The feature approach again seems less constrained than the dimensional one.[3]

Regardless of whether dimensions or features are used to describe concepts, the goal is the same: to make apparent the relations between concepts. There are numerous ways this can be done. With the dimensional approach, each concept may be represented by a list of the values it takes on a set of dimensions, and the relation between any pair of concepts is determined by the proximity of their values along all dimensions; alternatively, the concepts may be represented as points in a multidimensional space and the relation between concepts given by the distance between the corresponding points. With the featural approach, concepts are often represented by feature lists, and the relation between concepts is given in terms of common and distinctive features. Figure 2 illustrates the latter approach. It contains (partial) featural descriptions of the concepts of robin, chicken, collie, and daisy. The features are of various types — animate, feathered, furry, and so on — but they are all potentially useful in describing relations between concepts. For example, Figure 2 makes it apparent why robin and chicken are more similar than robin and collie: robin and chicken have more common features and fewer distinctive ones than robin and collie, and the similarity of any two items should increase with the number of shared features and decrease with the number of distinctive ones (Tversky, 1977). An alternative to simple feature lists is to depict not only the features of a concept but relations between them as well — for example, to indicate explicitly that the features "animate" and "feathered" are correlated. When this is done many of the features are interconnected, and a network (rather than a list) of features results.

Though all the alternatives discussed above can be used to represent concepts and their interrelations, the feature list approach has

Robin	Chicken	Collie	Daisy
F_1 animate	F_1 animate	F_1 animate	F_1 inanimate
F_2 feathered	F_2 feathered	F_2 furry	F_2 stem
F_3 flies	F_3 pecks	F_3 brown-grey	F_3 white

Figure 2 *Some featural descriptions*

been the most extensively used, particularly for classical-view representations of concepts. For this reason, the rest of this chapter focuses on features per se. Later, when we take up the probabilistic view, we will return to other kinds of descriptions.

Contents of Features

CONSTRAINTS ON FEATURES

If we are going to describe concepts in terms of features, we need some guidelines as to what can count as a feature. If any property, no matter how arbitrary or complex, could serve as a feature, we would soon be faced with all kinds of difficulties. For example, one could have a "concept" that consisted of the pseudofeatures "saw all of Tuesday Weld's movies in one week" and "prefers Bloody Marys that contain two parts Worcestershire sauce for one part Tabasco." Such a "concept" seems totally unnatural and points to the need to constrain features.

One constraint follows directly from the main purpose of features. If features make apparent relations between concepts, then a property is a useful feature to the extent that it reveals many relations between concepts. The feature of being male, for example, is useful because it brings out the relation between various classes of animate beings, like that between son and father, or between boy and colt. In contrast, neither of the pseudofeatures mentioned above would reveal many relations between concepts.

The above constraint can be strengthened. A set of features should not only make relations apparent but ideally should exhaust all potential relations between the concepts of interest. To illustrate, suppose someone postulated that young-male served as a single feature in describing concepts of animate beings. Although this would make apparent the relation between boy and colt (both contain the feature of young-male), it would not exhaust all potential relations of interest; for example, it would not show the relation between boy and girl. To capture the latter relation we obviously need to decompose young-male into the component features of (1) young (in the sense of a quality, not a quantity) and (2) male, where feature 1 can now be used to show the relation between boy and girl. To ask for features that exhaust all possible relations is to ask for features that are not themselves decomposable, that is, for primitives or all-or-none features. This is a difficult constraint to meet (we never really invoke it), but it is surely powerful since it unequivocally excludes a pseudofeature like "saw all of Tuesday Weld's movies in one week."[4]

As a second constraint we seek features with some generality, in the sense that a feature should apply to many concepts within a domain rather than to a few. (Of course, we would not want the feature to apply to every concept in the domain, for then it would have no discriminative value.) A kind of corollary of this generality constraint is that the number of features needed to describe a conceptual domain should be small relative to the number of concepts in that domain; that is, all other things being equal, the greater the applicability of a set of features, the fewer the features needed to characterize a domain. Although this constraint of generality rests on rough intuitions, it again seems sufficient to rule out properties like "saw all of Tuesday Weld's movies in one week." (Note that even though we seek features that are as general as possible, they still may be more numerous than the dimensions needed to describe the same conceptual domain.)

The two constraints discussed above deal with structural aspects of concepts. Consider now a processing constraint: the features posited should serve as the inputs for categorization processes. Thus, for the feature of male to be a useful one, it must not only reveal relations between concepts in an economical fashion (our two structural constraints), but it must also be used by people in reaching decisions about categorization. Though this constraint may carry little force with those interested in a purely structural approach to concepts (many linguists and philosophers), it is essential for psychologists interested in the processing of concepts. Indeed, it must take precedence over other constraints, as we will readily accept a nonprimitive and nongeneral property as a feature if there is convincing evidence that it is used in categorization.

It is instructive to illustrate these three constraints in relation to recent work on the perception of letters. This work essentially treats each letter of the alphabet as a separate concept and asks what features should be posited to define the concept. Introspection as well as early physiological evidence (for example, Hubel and Wiesel, 1962) suggested that the features may be line segments, angles, and curves. But exactly which lines, angles, and curves are posited as features depends on the three constraints. Just about everyone would agree that the features must account for why, under limited viewing conditions, a particular letter (for example, *P*) is confused with some letters (*B*, *R*) but not with others (*X*, *V*; see Gibson, 1969; Rumelhart and Siple, 1974; Townsend and Ashby, 1976). Since the probability of confusing a particular pair of letters is assumed to be a measure of the similarity of that pair, accounting for patterns of confusions amounts to making similarity relations apparent, which is our first constraint. Furthermore, all serious proposals in this domain posit features that apply to many letters —

a vertical line is a feature of *B, D, E, F,* and so on — and this is in keeping with our second constraint. Finally, researchers have tried to show that these features are the inputs to recognition processes by demonstrating, for example, that an estimate of the exact features extracted from a letter can be used to predict the accuracy, confidence, and speed with which a letter can be categorized (see Rumelhart and Siple, 1974; Townsend and Ashby, 1976). Failure to meet this third constraint would usually make researchers discard their featural definitions.

This example can also be used to address a fundamental issue about features, one that arises whenever any component properties are posited. The issue, in a nutshell, is that there are no a priori means for distinguishing between a concept and a feature, for any feature can itself be treated as a concept. In the letter perception work, for example, the concept for the letter *E* might include the feature of a vertical line, but a vertical line is also a possible concept, so what reasons are there for calling it a "feature" and reserving the term "concept" for *E*? Or to put it another way, do not all the problems we face in explaining how *E* is represented, accessed, and processed also apply to how a vertical line is represented, accessed, and processed? If so, explaining *E*'s in terms of vertical lines is simply begging the question, and the business of seeking constraints on features is beside the point.

There is a way out of this conceptual morass, we think, that is nicely demonstrated by the research on letter perception. In essence the solution is this: true, there may be no conceptual reasons for distinguishing between concepts and features, but there may well be empirical reasons for making this distinction. Thus, when it comes to explaining results in letter perception, there are many empirical reasons for assuming that a vertical line is a feature while the letter *E* is not. To restate a previously mentioned finding, treating a vertical line as a feature helps to explain why some letter pairs are more likely than others to be confused under limited viewing conditions; for example, *E* and *F* are more likely to be confused than *E* and *V* because the former pair shares a vertical line. No such account of confusions is forthcoming if one treats *E* and *F* as features here. This is just one example among many of how treating components such as vertical lines as features has led to an account of empirical findings about letter perception that might have remained a mystery had researchers not reduced the letters to their component properties.

These empirical successes in distinguishing visual features from visual concepts provides a rationale for thinking that the same kind of distinction can be supported with semantic concepts and their features. Indeed, we think there is already some evidence that describing concepts in terms of their component features will lead to accounts of empirical phenomena that would not be forthcoming otherwise.

One important caveat must be added to the foregoing discussion. If empirical results determine whether we should assign an entity the role of feature or that of concept, then a major change in the set of results to be accounted for can lead to a change in role assignment. To illustrate, if we change the empirical results of interest from findings on letter perception to findings on word perception, we may want to change the status of E from concept to feature. We may, for example, need to assume that E is a feature of word concepts in order to explain why certain words, such as *bed* and *ted*, are likely to be confused under limited viewing conditions. When such a change in role assignments occurs, it may indicate we are dealing with a system that has several levels, so that what is a concept at level n is best thought of as a feature at level $n + 1$.

PERCEPTIBILITY OF FEATURES

Perceptual versus Abstract Features

Even with the constraints mentioned above, the features of object concepts can vary a great deal. One particular source of variation, the perceptibility of features, will be of great concern to us. At one extreme are true perceptual features—those corresponding to outputs from the perceptual system; examples might include the presence of a line or the presence of some degree of curvature. At the other extreme are abstract features that have minimal connection to perceptual experience; as an example, a feature of the concept "clothing" might be "manufactured with the intent of human usage." And then there are a myriad of in-between cases, including the familiar features used with animal concepts like "animate" and "male," and functional features like "used for transporation."[5]

This perceptibility distinction raises a number of issues. The first is whether the features of object concepts should be restricted to more perceptual features, that is, whether perceptibility should be another constraint on features. This constraint has frequently been tried, particularly in conjunction with the classical view, for there is a long tradition in psychology to define stimulus objects in physical terms. This move always seems to end in failure, however. The most recent effort, and it is a valiant one, can be found in the work of Miller and Johnson-Laird (1976). After systematically reviewing what is known about the possible outputs of the human perceptual system, they attempt to use only these outputs in their feature description of certain object concepts (such as "table"). They convincingly argue that this enterprise is doomed.

Miller and Johnson-Laird first try to represent the concept of table by perceptual features like the following: (1) is connected and rigid, (2) has a flat and horizontal top, and (3) has vertical legs. They then spell out two serious drawbacks to this approach. First, some of these features are not true of all things we call tables (for example, many drafting tables do not have a horizontal top); this seems to be the case no matter how one alters the list of perceptual features. Second, if concept descriptions are confined to perceptual features, how can one ever explain that the same object may sometimes be treated as an instance of the concept "kitchen table" and other times as an instance of the concept "work table"? The solution to these problems, according to Miller and Johnson-Laird, is to include functional features in concept descriptions. For example, in the concept "table" if we replace the perceptual features "has a flat and horizontal top" with the functional feature "has a top capable of support," we can see how drafting tables can be included in the general concept of tables. And once we accept functional features, there is no problem in explaining how the same object can sometimes be subcategorized a kitchen table and sometimes a work table; the more specific concepts of kitchen table and work table have different functional features, and sometimes use of the object will match one of these functions, while other times its use will match the other function. Given arguments like this, we take it as a starting point that the features of an object concept can contain abstract and functional features as well as perceptual ones.

But now we have a new problem. How can one decide that a visually presented object is an instance of a particular concept, since features of the object must be true perceptual ones whereas some features of the concept may be abstract? The only solution is that one must have some knowledge that is capable of mediating between the features at the two levels; that is, to determine whether an abstract feature is perceptually *instantiated* in an object, one must have recourse to ancillary knowledge about the relation between abstract and perceptual features.

Let us illustrate with the concept of boy. Following traditional linguistic wisdom, we assume that people may represent this concept by three abstract features: human, male, and young (relative to some criterion). How can one use these features to determine that some particular person (a clothed one) is in fact a boy? To establish that the person is male, one would presumably check things like body proportions, dress, and hairstyle, which are more perceptual features. (Even these features are more abstract than outputs of the perceptual system, but we will ignore this complication in what follows.) To establish that the person is young, one would use perceptual features like height and weight. Hence, both male and young are instantiated by more perceptual features, and categorization therefore requires ancillary knowledge about which perceptual features instantiate which abstract ones.

The Core versus Identification Procedure of a Concept

In view of the foregoing discussion, let us distinguish between the *core* of the concept and the ancillary knowledge, which we will call the *identification procedure*. (A similar distinction is used by Miller and Johnson-Laird, 1976, and by Woods, 1981). The core of the concept "boy" would include the abstract features of human, male, and young, while the identification procedure would include perceptual features like height and weight as well as an indication that they instantiate the feature of young. The features of the core are primarily responsible for revealing certain relations between concepts, like that between boy and girl (both young and human) or that between boy and colt (both young and male), while the features of the identification procedure are used for categorizing real-world objects. To the extent that the features of a core are perceptual, there is no need for a separate identification procedure; for a geometric concept like "square," the core contains perceptual features like "four-sided" which can be used for categorizing real-world objects, thereby making an identification procedure superfluous. Perceptual features in the core, then, shrink the requisite identification procedure. There is also another way in which the core takes psychological precedence over the identification procedure: abstract features in the core determine the nature of the perceptual features in the identification procedure. To return to the boy example, being male (a core feature) is partly a matter of hormones, and these hormones produce secondary sex characteristics like body proportions (a feature in the identification procedure). From this perspective, if one wants to understand the nature of concepts, it is best to go for the core.[6]

The distinction discussed above is clearly related to Frege's classic distinction (1892) between *sense* and *reference*: the sense of a concept is given by its relation to other concepts, while the reference of a concept is given by its relation to objects and events in the world. Thus Frege's sense corresponds to our core, and Frege's reference to our identification procedure. Just as we have assumed that the core dictates the contents of the identification procedure, so Frege postulated that the sense of a concept determines its reference. We prefer our terms to Frege's because his distinction was intended as a philosophical rather than a psychological one, and hence it may be wrong to identify his notion of reference with the features people actually use in categorizing real-world objects.

Consider now how we can use our core versus identification distinction in evaluating experimental studies of concepts. As mentioned earlier, in some experiments subjects are asked to decide whether statements about subset relations (for example, "A raisin is a fruit") are true or false. In this kind of *semantic* task, subjects can answer just by consulting the cores of the relevant concepts (do the core features of the concept fruit match those of the concept raisin?). They might also consider the identification procedures of the two concepts, but there is no necessity to do so. In other experiments, however, subjects are asked to decide whether a pictured object is an instance of a target concept (for example, "Is this specific object a fruit?"). In such a *perceptual* task, subjects must consult the identification procedure of the target concept unless the core consists entirely of perceptual features. Since the views of concepts we are interested in, particularly the classical view, are mainly concerned with concept cores, we will emphasize experimental studies that either use a semantic task or use a perceptual one where there is good reason to believe the core consists entirely of perceptual features. Later, at the end of our discussion of the classical view, we will have occasion to question the wisdom of our decision.

3 | The Classical View

THE CLASSICAL VIEW is a psychological theory about how concepts are represented in humans and other species. In philosophy, the origins of this view go back to Aristotle, while in experimental psychology the view can be traced to Hull's 1920 monograph on concept attainment. In assembling our rendition of the classical view, however, we have relied mainly on contemporary sources. These sources include philosophically oriented studies of language (for example, Katz, 1972, 1977; Fodor, 1975); linguistic studies (Lyons, 1968; Bierwisch, 1970; Bolinger, 1975); psycholinguistics (Fodor, Bever, and Garrett, 1974; Miller and Johnson-Laird, 1976; Anglin, 1977; Clark and Clark, 1977); and psychological studies of concept attainment (Bruner, Goodnow, and Austin, 1956; Bourne, 1966; Hunt, Marin, and Stone, 1966).

While we think we have captured some common assumptions in these various sources, we are less sure that we have been faithful to the spirit of these works. For instance, the psychological studies of Bruner, Goodnow, and Austin (1956) were more concerned with the strategies people use in determining the relevant features of concepts than with supporting the classical view. Indeed, these authors even devoted one chapter of their influential book to concepts structured according to the probabilistic view. Still, the bulk of their effort employed artificial concepts structured according to the classical view, and there is no guarantee that the strategies that Bruner, Goodnow, and Austin turned up will be easily extendable to other views of concepts. Similar caveats apply to many of the other sources.

In terms of distinctions drawn earlier, we will be concerned here exclusively with feature descriptions, since all the sources given above (as well as many not listed) have analyzed concepts in terms of features. Also, it seems that practitioners of the classical view have been primarily interested in characterizing the core of concepts, not their identification procedures, and as mentioned earlier, our treatment of the view will focus on the core. Finally, a word about the role of process models is in order. The classical view is a proposal about representations, not about processes. Once we have described the representational assumptions that make up the classical view and the criticisms of these assumptions, we will give some consideration to process models that can be generated from the view.

Representational Assumptions

SUMMARY REPRESENTATIONS

The first assumption is as follows: The representation of a concept is a summary description of an entire class, rather than a set of descriptions of various subsets or exemplars of that class. To illustrate, in representing the concept of bird we would not list separate descriptions for different species (like robin and chicken) or for specific instances (like our pet canary Fluffy), but rather would give a summary representation for all birds. As Rosch (1978) has emphasized, condensing a concept into a single summary greatly reduces the amount of information we need to store.

This notion of a summary representation is sufficiently important that it is worth specifying some explicit criteria for it. A summary representation, then, (1) is often the result of an abstraction process, (2) need not correspond to a possible specific instance, and (3) applies to all possible test instances. Thus: (1) one's summary representation for fruit is often based on induction from specific instances (as well as on facts one has been told about fruits in general); (2) the representation might contain fewer features than would be found in the representation of any possible instance; and (3) whenever one is asked whether or not a test item designates an instance or subset of fruit, the same summary representation is always retrieved and examined.

NECESSARY AND SUFFICIENT FEATURES

The heart of the classical view is contained in its second assumption: The features that represent a concept are (1) singly necessary and (2) jointly sufficient to define that concept. For a feature to be singly necessary, every instance of the concept must have it; for a set of features to be jointly sufficient, every entity having that set must be an instance of the concept. It is convenient to illustrate with a geometric concept — squares again. Recall that the concept of square may be represented by some in terms of the following features: closed figure, four sides, sides equal in length, and equal angles. Being a closed figure is a necessary condition, since any square must have this feature; the same is true of the features of having four sides, the sides being equal, and the angles being equal; and these four features are jointly sufficient, since any entity that is a closed figure, has four sides equal in length, and has equal angles must be a square. We will sometimes refer to such necessary and sufficient features as *defining* ones.

Many scholars who have written about the classical view have emphasized that this assumption is about necessity or essentialism, not probability (see Cassirer, 1923; Katz, 1972). It is not just that all squares happen to have four sides, but rather that having four sides is essential to being a square. Or take another example: the defining features of bachelor — male and unmarried — are not only true of all bachelors (which is merely a statement about conditional probabilities), but are essential conditions for being a bachelor. To appreciate this distinction between probability and essentialism, suppose that the feature of "not wearing wedding bands" is also true of all bachelors. While this feature has the same conditional probability as being unmarried, only the latter would be essential.

It is important to note that this assumption about defining features implies that natural concepts are never disjunctive. To illustrate, let us consider first a *totally disjunctive* concept, which says that an instance either has features F_1, F_2, F_i, F_n or features F'_1, F'_2, F'_i, F'_n; that is, two instances need have no features in common. This means there are no necessary features, which violates the classical view's assumption about defining features. Now consider a *partially disjunctive* concept, which says that an instance either has features F_1, F_2, F_i, F_n or F_1, F_2, F_i, F'_n; that is, any two instances must have some features in common (F_1–F_i), but other features may differ (F_n versus F'_n). This means there is no set of necessary features that are jointly sufficient: F_1–F_i are necessary but not jointly sufficient, while either F_1–F_n or F_1–F'_n are sufficient but include at least one nonnecessary feature (F_n or F'_n). This too violates the assumption about defining features.

NESTING OF FEATURES IN SUBSET RELATIONS

The final representational assumption of interest is as follows: If concept X is a subset of concept Y, the defining features of Y are nested in those of X. It is again convenient to illustrate the assumption with geometric concepts. Suppose that people represent the concept of quadrilateral by two features: closed figure and four-sided. These two features are the ones we have included in our previous example of the concept square, along with the features of equal sides and equal angles. Hence a square is a subset of quadrilateral, and the defining features of quadrilateral are nested in those of square. Similarly, the defining features of bird (for example, animate and feathered) are nested in those of robin, since robins are a subset of birds. Of course the more specific concept — square or robin — must also include some defining features that are not shared by its superset; for example, robin must contain some features that distinguish it from other birds. This guarantees that the representation of a concept cannot be a realizable instance, since the concept must contain fewer features than any of its instances.

Although this nesting assumption is a common one among advocates of the classical view, some would not buy it wholesale. Fodor (1975) in particular questions the assumption, and suggests instead that related concepts may be defined by different sets of features. For example, the feature of bird that specifies "feathered" may not be identical to any specific feature of chicken. If we accept this possibility, the classical view is considerably weakened in the claims it makes about concepts. Given this, for the time being we opt for the version of the view that includes assumption 3.

SUMMARY

The three assumptions of the classical view are summarized in Table 1. Although they are not the only assumptions used by proponents of the classical view, they are the modal ones. Indeed, they are presupposed by most of the significant psychological work done on artificial concepts from 1920 to 1970 (for reviews, see Bruner, Goodnow, and Austin, 1956; Bourne, 1966; Bourne, Dominowski, and Loftus, 1979).

TABLE 1   THREE ASSUMPTIONS OF THE CLASSICAL VIEW

1. Summary representation
2. Necessary and sufficient (defining) features
3. Nesting of concept's defining features in it subsets

One last point: the three assumptions say nothing about possible relations between features — that is, the features are treated as if they were independent. This treatment may be adequate for certain semantic domains, called *paradigms;* an example would be kinship concepts, like mother, father, son, and daughter. Here the features — sex and age — seem to combine as independent entities. However, the idea of independent features does not fit with other semantic domains, called *taxonomies;* an example would be animal concepts, like robin, bird, animal, and organism. Here the features are clearly related; for example, the feature "living" (defining for organism) is implied by the feature "animate" (defining for animal). Though such relations are not mentioned in our three assumptions, we do not mean to exclude them from the classical view. Rather, we are trying to keep the assumptions down to a minimum, agreed-upon set. Even this small set will soon be shown to contain a great deal of debatable content.

General Criticisms of the Classical View

Throughout the years there have been various general criticisms of the assumptions of the classical view. In what follows we consider four criticisms that seem especially widespread, along with possible rebuttals.

FUNCTIONAL FEATURES

Some have argued as follows:

1 .   The classical view deals only with structural features — fixed properties (of varying perceptibility) that describe an entity in isolation, like the handle or concavity of a cup — and prohibits functional features, like the fact that a cup is used to hold something.
2.   But for many concepts, particularly those corresponding to human artifacts like cups and chairs, the defining features are functional ones.
3.   Therefore, the classical view cannot handle all concepts.

Cassirer (1923) put forth this argument some time ago, and Nelson (1974) and Anglin (1977) have recently reiterated it and suggested that it is devastating to the classical view.

Given our earlier discussion about the need to consider abstract, functional features in concept cores, it should come as no surprise that we think this argument is based on a faulty premise, namely premise 1. Nothing in our three assumptions excludes functional features. A functional feature, such as the fact that a cup can hold liquid, can be used in a summary description of an entire class, can be singly necessary and part of a jointly sufficient set, and can be nested in other feature sets. Furthermore, none of our constraints on features is inconsistent with functional features. A feature like "holdability" can bring out relations between concepts (for example, between cup and bowl), can apply to many different classes, and can be used as an input to categorization processes. In short, our rendition of the classical view is as hospitable to functional features as it is to structural ones.

Why, then, do so many psychologists think the classical view should be restricted to structural features? No doubt because such features are generally more perceptual than functional features. But then why do psychologists think the classical view should be restricted to perceptual features? We discussed one answer to this in the previous section — perceptual features greatly simplify the analysis of how people categorize perceptual objects. Another reason perceptual features have proved so attractive to psychologists is that such features are very easy to manipulate in experimental studies of concept attainment and utilization.

When Hull started his experimental study of the classical view in 1920, he used novel visual forms that were composed of multiple features. This allowed him to control precisely which features occurred in all instances of a concept, that is, which features were necessary. Had he used more abstract features, like functional ones, Hull would have had either to give his subjects real manipulable objects and let them discover the function (a messy task at best), or to give them pictures of objects that instantiated the function to varying degrees (which again is a relatively uncontrolled paradigm, though very likely a more ecologically valid one). Hull's emphasis on easily manipulable perceptual features proved so attractive that more than two generations of experimental psychologists have bought it, thereby making it seem that perceptual features are part and parcel of the classical view. It is only during the last fifteen years, with the influence of nonexperimental disciplines like linguistics and philosophy on psychology, that psychologists have begun to realize that some concepts may have functional features at their core.

DISJUNCTIVE CONCEPTS

A more powerful argument against the classical view is the following:

1. The classical view excludes disjunctive concepts.
2. But many concepts are clearly disjunctive, like that of a strike in baseball (which can be either a *called* or a *swinging* strike).
3. Therefore, the classical view cannot handle all concepts.

Certainly we agree with premise 1, for we noted earlier that the assumption of defining features excludes disjunctive concepts. Premise 2, though, is debatable. Specifically, how widespread are disjunctive concepts? Unfortunately, there is nothing resembling a clear-cut answer to this question. If we rely on intuitions (our own and those published by semanticists) and restrict ourselves to concepts about naturally occurring objects (flora and fauna), we can think of no obvious disjunctive concepts. Disjunctive concepts, then, may be rare, restricted to man-made concoctions (like a baseball strike), and constitute special cases that should not obscure the general conjunctive nature of concepts.

This reasoning may be too facile, however. There are alternatives to intuitive analyses of concepts, and at least one of these suggests that disjunctive concepts may be quite widespread. Rosch and her colleagues (1976) asked people to list the features of concepts, where the concepts varied in their level of inclusiveness (for example, kitchen chair, chair, and furniture). Their data suggest that the more inclusive or superordinate concepts may be disjunctive. For superordinate concepts like animal, plant, vehicle, furniture, clothing, and tool, people list few if any features; for concepts that are one level less inclusive, like bird, flower, truck, chair, hat, and hammer (what Rosch and colleagues call the *basic* level), people list a substantial number of features. This finding suggests that superordinate concepts are often disjunctive (and that basic-level concepts are the most inclusive level at which conjunctive concepts appear).

There is, however, an alternative interpretation of the data compiled by Rosch and her associates, one that can save the classical view from a plethora of disjunctive concepts. The features that people listed may well have been part of the identification procedure, not the core. But then why should identification procedures be disjunctive only for superordinate concepts? The reason is very likely that the cores of superordinate concepts contain abstract features (remember "intended to be worn by a human"), and such features can only be instantiated disjunctively at the perceptual level. Under this interpretation, concept cores are as conjunctive as the classical view claims they are, and those who mistakenly think otherwise have confused the identification procedure with the core. To illustrate further the flavor of this argument, let us consider the concept "extreme." Some might deem it disjunctive because it implies one pole or the other, but this may be an aspect of the identification procedure, not the core, where the latter may mean "a value far from the central tendency." Another example is the concept of split personality: doesn't this mean personality X or personality Y, but not both (an exclusive disjunction)? Perhaps it does at the level of an identification procedure, but the concept core may mean "manifests different personalities," which is not inherently disjunctive. (Anisfeld, 1968, has made a similar argument using the notions of sense and reference.)

The upshot is that we have no firm evidence, intuitive or otherwise, about the prevalence of disjunctive concepts. Without such evidence, it is difficult to say how damaging the disjunctive-concepts argument is to the classical view.

UNCLEAR CASES

A third argument against the classical view (see, for example, Hampton, 1979) takes the following form:

1. The classical view assumes that if concept X is a subset of concept Y, the defining features of Y are nested in those of X.
2. Given this, judgments about whether one concept is a subset of another should be clear-cut, since one merely has to compare defining features.
3. In fact, it is often unclear whether one concept is a subset of another. People disagree with one another about a particular subset relation, and the same person may even change his mind when asked the same question on different occasions (see McCloskey and Glucksberg, 1978). The classical view has no way of accounting for such unclear cases.

The weak part of this argument is premise 2, since a nesting of defining features does not guarantee that judgments about subset relations will be clear-cut. We can think of at least two reasons why this is so, and it is best to illustrate them by a specific example.

When asked, "Is a tomato a fruit?" many people, even college-educated ones, are unsure of whether this particular subset relation holds. One simple reason they may be uncertain is that their concepts of tomato and fruit may be faulty or incomplete—that is, they are missing some defining features of fruit and consequently cannot tell whether or not a tomato is a fruit. To put it more generally, the classical view does not stipulate that every adult has mastered every familiar concept; rather, it allows for the possibility that many of us are walking around with incomplete concepts, just as long as whatever features we do have are at least necessary ones. (Such incomplete concepts could not be *too* incomplete, however, since adults obviously do a good job of using their concepts in dealing with their environment.) A second way to reconcile the classical view with unclear cases is to assume that some concepts have two definitions, a common and a technical one (Glass and Holyoak, 1975). Thus one might be unsure about what concept a tomato belongs to because a tomato meets the technical definition of a fruit (for example, it has seeds) but the common definition of a vegetable (it plays a particular role in meals).

Specifying the Defining Features of Concepts

Of all the arguments against the classical view, the best-known one goes as follows:

1. The heart of the classical view is its assumption that every concept has a set of necessary and sufficient features.
2. Decades of analysis have failed to turn up the defining features of many concepts.
3. Therefore, many concepts simply do not have defining features.

It was essentially this argument that Wittgenstein (1953) pursued in his well-known critique of a classical-view approach to natural concepts. One of Wittgenstein's most famous examples was that of the concept of games, and we can use it to illustrate the flavor of his argument. What is a necessary feature of the concept of games? It cannot be competition between teams, or even the stipulation that there must be at least two individuals involved, for solitaire is a game that has neither feature. Similarly, a game cannot be defined as something that must have a winner, for the child's game of ring-around-a-rosy has no such feature. Or let us try a more abstract feature — say that anything is a game if it provides amusement or diversion. Football is clearly a game, but it is doubtful that professional football players consider their Sunday endeavors as amusing or diverting. And even if they do, and if amusement is a necessary feature of a game, that alone cannot be sufficient, for whistling can also be an amusement and no one would consider it a game. This is the kind of analysis that led Wittgenstein to his disillusionment with the classical view.

Although this argument clearly has merit, it is by no means ironclad, for its conclusion — that many concepts do not have defining features — is based on a lack of progress by the classical view. When Wittgenstein — or anyone else — asserts: "There are no defining features of concept X," it is equivalent to asserting: "No one has yet determined the defining features of concept X," since both assertions would be refuted by a cogent proposal of these features. Moreover, one could claim that part of the reason progress has been so slow is that we have been looking for the wrong kind of defining features — perceptual ones that are likely to be part of an identification procedure — when we should have been seeking abstract, relational, or functional features that may well make up the core of many concepts.

Thus the Wittgenstein argument is nothing like a principled disproof of the classical view; it is instead an empirical argument about the observed rate of progress of a theoretical approach to concepts. Once this is appreciated, one can acknowledge that the argument certainly has force (like any excellent empirical argument) but that it deals no death blow to the classical view.[1]

A Note on Scientific Concepts

It is worth pointing out that the last two criticisms of the classical view of psychological concepts — unclear cases and failure to specify defining features — have also been raised as criticisms of the classical view when it is used as a metatheory of scientific concepts. That is, in addition to its use as a psychological theory, the classical view has also served as a metatheoretical prescription of what scientific concepts should look like, and here it has run into problems similar to those we just described.

There are numerous unclear cases for classically defined biological concepts. For example, there is no uniform agreement among biologists as to whether *Euglena*, a mobile organism that manufactures chlorophyll, should be classified as an animal or a plant. Cases like this are occurring with sufficient frequency to lead scientists to question the validity of the classical view for biological classification (see Sokal, 1974).

Similarly, there has been substantial difficulty in specifying the defining features of biological species, at least in terms of structural features (Sokal, 1974; Simpson, 1961). Toward the end of the eighteenth century Linnaeus proposed that any biological species can be characterized by three kinds of features: (1) features that comprise the *essence* of the species, which are features that every member of the species must have and that correspond to what we have called defining features; (2) features called *properties*, which are common to all members of the species but are not part of the essence; and (3) features called *accidents*, which characterize some but not all members of a species. According to Linnaeus, only features comprising the essence should be used in classification. This classical-view approach has had great influence, but it now seems problematic as a guide to biological classification. For one thing, taxonomists have generally been unable to distinguish features comprising the essence from those called properties. For another, taxonomists have found that the so-called accidents, features not true of every species member, are sometimes genetically based and important for understanding and defining the species.

These developments in biological classification are relevant to a psychology of concepts. Recall that in the Introduction we noted that there was little hope for classically defined mental representations if there was little evidence that such concepts could be given a classical definition in some language. The most likely place to look for classical definitions of flora and fauna is the language of biology, and to the extent that the classical view fails here, it will likely fail as a psychological theory as well.

SUMMARY

Table 2 summarizes the four general criticisms we have discussed. How badly do they damage the classical view? In answering this, we must distinguish between an *in principle* criticism — one that shows that the view could never handle a particular problem — and an *empirical* criticism — one that shows that specific embodiments of the view have thus far failed to handle a particular problem. All four criticisms seem to be mainly empirical ones.

TABLE 2   FOUR GENERAL CRITICISMS OF THE CLASSICAL VIEW

1. Exclusion of functional features
2. Existence of disjunctive concepts
3. Existence of unclear cases
4. Failure to specify defining features

The first criticism — that the classical view excludes functional features — is clearly about typical applications of the view in psychology, and not about what this view can accomplish in principle. We showed that the assumptions of the classical view are as compatible with functional features as they are with structural ones. How successfully one can use the view with functional features, however, remains an open question. The work of Miller and Johnson-Laird (1976) at least suggests that one can develop a classical-view model of categorization that employs functional features.

The second criticism — that the view excludes disjunctive concepts — comes closest to offering an in-principle argument against the classical view. If some natural concepts are clearly shown to be disjunctive, they simply fall outside the domain of the classical view. Such convincing demonstrations, though, have been rare.

With regard to the third criticism, we argued that unclear cases are not necessarily inconsistent with a classical-view description of natural concepts because people may have incomplete, or multiple, definitions of a concept. Again, the criticism is hardly a proof against the classical view.

Finally, there is the criticism that the classical view has made little progress in specifying defining features. In discussing this criticism, we emphasized its empirical nature — it is a statement about what has happened so far, not about what can happen. Still, as an empirical criticism, it is one of the strongest arguments against the classical view.

We emphasize the empirical nature of these criticisms because we wish to dispel the popular notion that the classical view has been proved wrong by a priori arguments and consequently that no empirical work is needed. A more correct reading of the situation is this: serious empirical criticisms have been raised against the classical view of natural concepts — serious enough to make us have grave reservations about the view, but not serious enough to say that the view should be discarded at this point.

Experimental Criticisms of the Classical View

Though the general criticisms discussed above are telling, they are not the only reasons why psychologists are currently forsaking the classical view in droves. There are other criticisms of this view that stem from experimental findings about how people use natural concepts, such as how they decide that apples are fruit. Before delving into these findings, we would like to interject a cautionary note. Since the findings deal with how people use concepts, they reflect categorization processes as well as concept representations. This means that we cannot go directly from the findings to claims about how concepts are represented; instead, we must interpret these findings in terms of both representations and processes — in short, in terms of models. This point has been missed in a good deal of recent research on natural concepts, where it has often been assumed that categorization data directly inform us about the nature of concepts. The best way to document the need for a model in interpreting categorization effects is to consider some results of interest and then show that their implications for the classical view depend on the specific model used to instantiate this view. This is the procedure we adopt in the following discussion.

SIMPLE TYPICALITY EFFECTS

Experimental Results

Of all the experimental findings used as evidence against the classical view, perhaps the best known are the effects of *typicality* (also called *prototypicality*). The most critical result is that items judged to be typical members of a concept can be categorized more efficiently than items judged to be less typical. The details of this result are as follows: People find it a natural task to rate the various

TABLE 3.   TYPICALITY RATINGS FOR BIRD
           AND MAMMAL INSTANCES

Instance	Rating	Instance	Rating
Robin	3.00[a]	Deer	2.83
Sparrow	3.00	Horse	2.76
Bluejay	2.92	Goat	2.75
Parakeet	2.83	Cat	2.67
Pigeon	2.83	Dog	2.67
Eagle	2.75	Lion	2.67
Cardinal	2.67	Cow	2.58
Hawk	2.67	Bear	2.58
Parrot	2.58	Rabbit	2.58
Chicken	2.00	Sheep	2.58
Duck	2.00	Mouse	2.25
Goose	2.00	Pig	2.17

Source: After Rips, Shoben, and Smith (1973).
a. Higher numbers indicate greater typicality.

subsets or members of a concept with respect to how typical or representative each one is of a concept.[2] Such ratings were first reported by Rips, Shoben, and Smith (1973) and by Rosch (1973). Table 3 presents the ratings of Rips, Shoben, and Smith for the concepts of birds and mammals. As can be seen, robin and sparrow are considered typical birds, hawk and eagle less typical, and chicken and penguin atypical. Ratings like these have now been obtained for many noun categories in English, and have been shown to be highly reliable across raters (Rosch, 1973) and to be relatively uncorrelated with frequency or familiarity (Mervis, Catlin, and Rosch, 1976).

What is most important about these ratings is that they predict how efficiently people can categorize the various members of a concept in a semantic categorization task. One variant of this task is illustrated in Figure 3. On each trial, the subject is given the name of a target concept, like bird, followed by a test item; the subject decides whether the test item names a subset or member of the target concept, like robin or chicken, or a nonmember, like dog or pencil. The main data of interest are the times for correct categorizations. When the test item, or probe, in fact names a member of the target concept, categorization times decrease with the typicality of the probe (see Rips, Shoben, and Smith, 1973; Rosch, 1973). For example, when bird is the target concept, test items corresponding to robin and sparrow are categorized more quickly than those corresponding to eagle and hawk, which in turn are categorized faster

	Target Concept	Test Item	Correct Response
Trial n	Bird	Robin	Yes
Trial n + 1	Fruit	Cup	No
Trial n + 2	Bird	Chicken	Yes

Figure 3 *One variant of semantic categorization task (other variants require verification of sentences of form "A robin is a bird" or "All apples are fruit")*

than the probes of chicken and goose. Furthermore, to the extent that there is any variation in the accuracy of these categorizations, error rates also decrease with the typicality of the probe (see Rips, Shoben, and Smith, 1973). These effects are extremely reliable: they have been documented in more than 25 experiments that have used many different variants of the semantic categorization task (see Smith, 1978, for a partial review).

Though most studies of typicality have been concerned with categorization times, Rosch and Mervis have demonstrated a host of other typicality effects. For instance, the typical members of a concept are the first ones learned by children, as judged by either a semantic categorization task (Rosch, 1973) or by how accurately children can sort pictured objects into taxonomic categories (Mervis, 1980). (The latter finding is not strictly relevant to issues about concept cores.) Further, the typical members of a concept are likely to be named first when subjects are asked to produce all members of a category (Mervis, Catlin, and Rosch, 1976). And typical members are also more likely to serve as cognitive reference points than are atypical members (Rosch, 1975); for example, people are more likely to say "An ellipse is almost a circle" (where *circle*, the more typical form, occurs in the reference position of the sentence) than "A circle is almost an ellipse" (where *ellipse*, the less typical form, occurs in the reference position). This list of effects could be extended (see, for example, Rosch, 1974, 1975, 1978), but it is adequate for our purposes.

What does all this have to do with the classical view? Simply this: typicality effects reveal that not all members of a concept are equal, or to put it more positively, that concepts possess an internal structure that favors typical members over less typical ones. The representational assumptions of the classical view, however, suggest that all members of a concept are equal, since all members of concept X must have the defining features of X. At first glance, then, typicality effects seem incompatible with the classical view, a conclusion that has been drawn many times. A more thorough analysis is needed here, however — one that considers processes as well as representations.

A Classical-View Model for Simple Typicality Effects

Since we need to interpret categorization results in terms of process models, the real question for the classical view is this: Can a model based on this view (that is, one that incorporates its three representational assumptions) account for the typicality effects we have described? The answer is clearly yes, and we will describe such a model in this section. We caution the reader, however, that the model presented will run into problems when later confronted with other findings; our reason for describing the model here is to demonstrate how easy it is to come up with a classical-view model that can account for effects frequently claimed to be inconsistent with this view.

We call our proposal the *complexity model*. It assumes that concepts are represented just as the classical view says they are, and that in a categorization task these representations are processed by two sequentially ordered stages, the *access* and *comparison* stages. The stages operate as follows:

1 .   When given the target and probe concepts, the subject starts accessing the defining features of both concepts, with access order being random over trials.

2.   As soon as any defining features are available, the subject compares those of the target concept to those of the probe. The subject responds affirmatively ("Yes, it's a member") only when every feature of the target has matched a feature of the probe, but can respond negatively ("No, it's not a member") as soon as any feature of the target mismatches a probe feature. This stage is limited in capacity, and therefore the time needed to compare probe and target concepts increases with the number of features in either concept.

Only one more assumption is needed, and it is the critical one: Typical members of a concept have fewer features than atypical ones; that is, typicality is in inverse measure of complexity. Figure 4 illustrates this idea. In the figure, features are assigned to concepts in accordance with the classical view; for example, the defining features of bird are contained in the defining features of robin and

Animal	Bird	Robin	Chicken
F_1	F_1	F_1	F_1
	F_2	F_2	F_2
		F_3	F_4
			F_5

Figure 4.   *Concept representations in a complexity model*

chicken. In addition, chicken is assumed to contain more of its own defining features — those that distinguish it from other species of birds — than does robin. This is in keeping with our critical assumption.

These assumptions suffice to explain all simple typicality effects. Since atypical probes contain more features than typical ones, atypical probes will require longer comparison stages, and consequently they will be categorized more slowly. Furthermore, because atypical probes require more comparisons than typical ones, they are more likely to lead to an error (assuming each comparison has some fixed probability of being in error). The complexity model also provides a reasonable explanation of the other typicality effects reported by Rosch and Mervis. The fact that typical concepts are learned before atypical ones becomes just another example of simple concepts being mastered before complex ones (see Brown, 1973). And the fact that typical concepts serve as reference points may just indicate our preference for simple concepts as anchors. Then there is the question of how this model would interpret the typicality ratings themselves. The simplest possibility is that subjects rate the similarity of the probe to the target concept, with similarity (1) increasing with the number of features shared by probe and target and (2) decreasing with the number of probe features not present in the target (Tversky, 1977). Now, (1) is constant across all members of a target concept (each contains all the defining features of the target), but (2) must increase with the number of defining features in a probe; it follows that typical probes, which contain fewer of their own defining features, will be judged more similar to the target concept and hence rated more typical. The fact that typical items are more similar to their parent concepts also accounts for the one remaining

simple typicality effect — when given a concept and asked to produce its instances, a subject will name typical members first. The
concept is essentially a memory probe, and research on memory
retrieval indicates that items similar to the probe are retrieved first
(see Tulving, 1974).

Despite what we have just discussed, we have no faith in the
complexity model. For one thing, it is inconsistent with the finding
that it takes no longer to respond to atypical than to typical probes
when the probe is not a member of the target concept. For example,
it takes no longer to disconfirm "a chicken is a fish" than "a robin is
a fish," even though chicken supposedly has more features than
robin and consequently should require more comparison time (see
Smith, Shoben, and Rips, 1974). Another problem for the complexity model comes from studies in which subjects are asked to list
features of various members of a concept. Such studies have found
either no difference in the number of features listed for typical versus atypical members, or that more features are listed for typical
members (Ashcraft, 1978; Malt and Smith, 1981a). To the extent
that the listed features correspond to the true core features of the instances involved, these findings contradict the complexity model's
assumption that atypical members have more features than typical
ones. To reiterate, our point in presenting the complexity model
was merely to show that simple typicality effects can readily be accounted for by a model based on the classical view.[3]

DETERMINANTS OF TYPICALITY: FAMILY RESEMBLANCE
MEASURES

Experimental Results

In addition to research showing the effects of typicality on
various measures of performance, there have been some studies
that have tried to specify the determinants of typicality. The most
important of these is Rosch and Mervis's work on family
resemblance (1975). We first present their results and then take up
the question of whether these findings are incompatible with the
classical view, as has often been claimed.

Some of Rosch and Mervis's experiments used natural concepts.
The subjects were asked to list features of various subsets of a
superordinate concept, like those of furniture, where the subsets
varied in typicality (table is typical, lamp atypical). Rosch and
Mervis showed that the distribution of listed features could provide
a basis for typicality. Their analysis is illustrated in Table 4. Each
feature listed for a subset is weighted by the total number of subsets
that it is listed for; then, for each subset, the weights of all of its

TABLE 4   FAMILY RESEMBLANCE ANALYSIS

Article of furniture	Listed features				Family resemblance measure
Chair	$F_1(5)^a$	$F_2(4)$	$F_3(3)$	$F_4(2)$	14
Sofa	$F_1(5)$	$F_2(4)$	$F_3(3)$	$F_5(2)$	14
Cushion	$F_1(5)$	$F_2(4)$	$F_6(1)$	$F_7(2)$	12
Rug	$F_1(5)$	$F_3(3)$	$F_7(2)$	$F_8(1)$	11
Vase	$F_1(5)$	$F_5(2)$	$F_9(1)$	$F_{10}(1)$	9
Telephone	$F_2(4)$	$F_4(2)$	$F_{11}(1)$	$F_{12}(1)$	8

Source: After Rosch and Mervis (1975).

a. Numbers in parentheses indicate how often each feature occurs in set of instances.

features are summed, yielding a measure called *family resemblance*. In Rosch and Mervis's study, these family resemblance measures were very highly correlated with typicality ratings of the subsets. In short, an item is a typical subset or member or a concept if it contains features shared by many other members of that same concept.

To back up this conclusion, Rosch and Mervis performed experiments with artificial concepts. In these experiments, subjects learned to assign visually presented letter strings to categories, with six strings belonging to one category and six to another. Table 5 illustrates two of the categories used. Each string can be treated as an instance of a concept, each letter in a string as a feature. Since no information but the letters was available to subjects, we may assume that the cores of the concepts were restricted to the letters. (This kind of assumption — that the core is restricted to the obvious perceptual features — is standard in studies of artificial concepts.) Note that the strings were constructed so that no feature (letter) was common to all instances of a concept, that is, there were no salient defining features for the concept. Though all strings in Table 5 contain the same number of letters, they vary with respect to their family resemblance scores; for example, a high family resemblance string like PHMQB contains letters that were usually shared by other strings in its category, while a low family resemblance string like JXPHM contains letters less likely to be shared by other strings. The results showed that the higher the family resemblance score of a string, the sooner it could be learned as a concept instance, the more quickly it could be categorized once learned, and the more typical it was rated of its concept. Thus an experimental manipulation in the distribution of features — that is, in family resemblance — produced many of the simple typicality effects found

Categories and Concepts

TABLE 5   ARTIFICIAL CATEGORIES USED BY ROSCH AND MERVIS (1975)

Category	Letter string	Family resemblance measure
Category A	JXPHM	15
	XPHMQ	19
	PHMQB	21
	HMOBL	21
	MQBLF	19
	QBLFS	15
Category B	GVRTC	15
	VRTCS	19
	RTCSF	21
	TCSFL	21
	CSFLB	19
	SFLBQ	15

with natural concepts. This is solid evidence that the distribution of features is the cause of simple typicality effects. Rosch, Simpson, and Miller (1976) have replicated some of these important findings.

Implications for the Classical View

What exactly are the implications of these results for the classical view? From the results with natural concepts, one could make the following argument.

1. The typicality variations observed when people categorize members of a superordinate concept are highly correlated with variations in family resemblance scores of the members.
2. The variations in family resemblance scores are due to features that are not common to all members. (A common feature would simply add a constant to all family resemblance scores — see Tables 4 and 5 — and hence could not influence the correlation with typicality.)
3. Therefore, typicality variations cannot be explained by variations in the defining features of the superordinate concept.
4. Therefore, typicality variations must be accounted for in terms of nondefining features, but the classical view precludes the latter.

We have no quarrel with premises 1 and 2, nor with conclusion

3, but conclusion 4 is fallacious. This is illustrated by Table 6, which is the same as Table 4 save two exceptions: (1) one common feature, F_0, has been added to all members; this feature is assumed to be defining for the superordinate concept of furniture, and it adds a constant of 6 to the family resemblance scores of all members; and (2) all features listed for a member are assumed to be defining of that subset (for example, chair's defining features are F_0-F_4). This example is consistent with the first three steps of the argument just presented but is inconsistent with the critical conclusion that typicality variations *must* be accounted for in terms of nondefining features. For Table 6 shows that, at least in principle, typicality variations can be explained in terms of variations in the defining features of the members; that is, the defining features of the individual members vary in frequency, and this variation may be responsible for the concomitant variation in typicality.

We seem to have saved the classical view from family resemblance. There are problems, however, with our rescue mission. One stems from our assumption that the features listed for concept members are defining ones. Inspection of the features actually listed makes this unlikely. For example, many people list as features of chair "made of wood" and "has four legs." Clearly these features are not true of all chairs, and consequently they are not defining of chair. Other problems arise from our assumption that the superordinate concept, furniture, may be represented by a defining feature. If there is such a feature (or features), why did subjects not list it? (No feature was listed for all instances of furniture.) Perhaps the feature was too abstract for naive subjects to verbalize; perhaps it was too obvious for anyone to mention; but then again perhaps it just wasn't there. Furthermore, this assumption about a defining feature is clearly unnecessary to explain the data of interest. Rosch and Mervis found the same relation between typicality and family resemblance with their artificial concepts, and these concepts were constructed in such a way that they had no obvious defining feature.

The problems mentioned above hinge on whether listed features are valid indicators of the true features of concepts. Putting this issue aside, there are further problems when we try to construct a classical-view model for how the representations in Table 6 could be processed so as to yield a correlation between family resemblance scores and categorization time (the latter being known to correlate with typicality). The complexity model won't do. It holds that the critical factor is the number of features in a concept member, whereas the data show that the critical factor is the distribution of the member's features. Let us try to construct another model of the same sort, that is, one in which the features of the probe and

TABLE 6   HOW FAMILY RESEMBLANCE MEASURES CAN
BE CONSISTENT WITH DEFINING FEATURES

Article of furniture	Listed features					Family resemblance measure
Chair	$F_0(6)$[a]	$F_1(5)$	$F_2(4)$	$F_3(3)$	$F_4(2)$	20
Sofa	$F_0(6)$	$F_1(5)$	$F_2(4)$	$F_3(3)$	$F_5(2)$	20
Cushion	$F_0(6)$	$F_1(5)$	$F_2(4)$	$F_6(1)$	$F_7(2)$	18
Rug	$F_0(6)$	$F_1(5)$	$F_3(3)$	$F_7(2)$	$F_8(1)$	17
Vase	$F_0(6)$	$F_1(5)$	$F_5(2)$	$F_9(1)$	$F_{10}(1)$	15
Telephone	$F_0(6)$	$F_2(4)$	$F_4(2)$	$F_{11}(1)$	$F_{12}(1)$	14

a. Numbers in parentheses indicate how often each feature
occurs in set of instances.

target concepts are accessed and compared, with the comparison process starting as soon as any features are available and continuing until all the features of the target have been matched or at least one has been mismatched.

In this kind of model the distribution of members' features could affect either the access or comparison processes. Both possibilities have their problems. Consider first the possibility that the access process is affected. Since a positive categorization must be based on retrieval of F_0 from this probe (it is the only feature that matches the defining feature of the superordinate concept; see Table 6), we seek a model in which the access time for F_0 can be affected by the access times for the other features in the probe concept. Such a model is embodied in the following assumptions:

1.   Assume that the processing capacity for accessing features is limited.
2.   Assume further that the amount of capacity needed to access a particular feature decreases with the frequency of that feature in concept members. This means that the amount of capacity needed to access features that define typical members (like F_1 and F_2) will be less than that needed to access features that define atypical members (like F_{11} and F_{12}).
3.   Therefore, more capacity can be devoted to accessing F_0 when it occurs in a typical probe than in an typical one.
4.   Therefore, F_0 should be accessed faster in typical than in atypical members, which in turn implies that typical members should be categorized faster.

Though this model accounts for the typicality effects associated with Table 6, it has a serious problem. The model implies that the fewer features a concept member contains, the faster it will be categorized (the fewer the features, the more capacity can be devoted to accessing each one); but Malt and Smith (1981a) found that those concept members that had a minimal number of features (as determined by attribute listings) are categorized slowest of all.

A similar situation results if we try to construct a model in which the distribution of members' features affects the comparison process. Now we would assume that the capacity needed to compare a feature decreases with the frequency of the feature in concept members. Consequently, less capacity will be needed for comparing features that define typical members, which means that more comparison-capacity can be devoted to F_0 (the feature that defines the superordinate) when it occurs in typical members, which in turn implies that typical members should be categorized faster than atypical ones. Again, though, this model erroneously predicts that the fewer features a concept member contains, the faster it will be categorized.

What this shows is that some simple classical models cannot explain the relation between certain typicality effects and family resemblance scores. We can construct more complex classical models that will do the job, but the ones we have tried all require some ad hoc assumptions (like the one that the common feature, F_0, though it occurs very frequently, is so complex that it is processed slower than features that occur less frequently). In short, we feel that if the Rosch and Mervis results are to be explained by the classical view, ad hoc processing assumptions are needed, which reflects badly on the view.

To summarize all we have said about the Rosch and Mervis results, the critical result is that typicality variations are due to the distribution of features of concept members. This by itself is not, in principle, inconsistent with the classical view, as is demonstrated by our example in Table 6. But to make the result consistent with the view, we had to make some precarious assumptions about the relations between the listed features and the true features of the concepts. To account for the results in terms of a classical model, we would have to make even more precarious assumptions. Like other findings we have covered and will cover, the present results do not decimate the classical view, but they do provide reasons for lessening our belief in it.

Use of Nonnecessary Features

Though Rosch and Mervis's work (1975) centered on an explanation of typicality effects, we noted that one of its main implications for the classical view involved the possible use of nondefining features. The work we now wish to discuss offers a more direct approach to the issue of nondefining features: it specifically tries to show that people use nonnecessary features in categorization.

A good example of this work is a study carried out by Hampton (1979). One group of subjects listed features that characterized concepts like bird, fruit, tool, and so on. Next, they rated the extent to which subsets of these concepts had the features listed. For example, if subjects listed "flies" for bird, they might specify that robin has this feature while chicken does not. These ratings were then used to predict categorization times for another group of subjects. The more features that were shared by a concept and one of its members, the faster that member could be categorized; that is, the number of shared features between member and concept was a good measure of the typicality of that concept member. There are two critical points:

1. Some features listed for a concept were nonnecessary ones (for example, "flies" for bird).
2. These nonnecessary features were correlated with categorization performance.

It follows by a correlational syllogism that

3. Nonnecessary features are used in categorization.

While this argument is similar to the one ascribed to Rosch and Mervis (1975), it is stronger because it involves a direct assessment of the nonnecessary features of the concept.

The conclusion from the argument given above is difficult to reconcile with categorization models based on the classical view. It is clearly incompatible with the complexity model, which assumes that when one has to decide whether a probe names an instance of a target concept, only necessary features of the target concept are considered. Indeed, any classical-view model that restricts itself to necessary features (an obvious restriction) must be incompatible with the use of nonnecessary features in categorization.

How can the classical view get around this argument? The weak point in Hampton's experiment, of course, is the assumption that the listed features correspond exactly to the true defining features of a concept, a point noted in our earlier discussion of Rosch and Mervis. It seems most unlikely that just anyone off the street can readily list the features of a concept, particularly since such a list may be sensitive to contextual factors, and since sophisticated semanticists have been unable to compose lists of defining features after decades of study. Thus a proponent of the classical view might argue that the "features" listed for a particular concept are simply an epiphenomenon in the following sense:

1. Categorization is based on defining features that are relatively inaccessible, or at least difficult to report or introspect on.
2. These defining features, however, are correlated with other nonnecessary features that are relatively easy to report.
3. Consequently, the corrrelation between categorization and nonnecessary features is being mediated by defining features.

Though this rebuttal is legitimate, it is based on the assumption that unspecifiable defining features just happen to be correlated with specifiable undefining ones. The rebuttal thus capitalizes on its own ignorance of defining features — a rather dubious state of affairs, and one that makes us take the findings on nonnecessary features as a serious problem for the classical view.

There is another source of evidence for the use of nonnecessary features in categorization that does not require subjects to list features. This source is based on multidimensional scaling studies (for example, Rips, Shoben, and Smith, 1973; Caramazza, Hersch, and Torgerson, 1976; Shoben, 1976). Subjects are given pairs of concepts from a particular domain, like robin-sparrow and robin-hawk, where each pair contains two subsets of a generic concept (birds); they are also given pairs that include the concept and one subset (for example, robin-bird, hawk-bird). The task is to rate each pair for its similarity of meaning. These ratings then become input to a scaling program whose output is a geometric space. The points in the space represent the items involved, while the distance between any pair of points reflects the dissimilarity between the two items. Figure 5 illustrates such a space for the concept of bird and 12 of its subsets. The representation seems a reasonable one, since similar birds are close together (for example, hawk and eagle) while dissimilar ones fall far apart (robin and goose).

There are two critical points about this multidimensional space:

1. The horizontal dimension appears to reflect variations in size while the vertical one depicts predatory relations or ferocity, where neither of these dimensions specifies anything necessary about being a bird or being any particular subset of a bird.
2. The distance between bird and any of its subsets correlates highly with how long it takes to categorize that subset as a bird.

Again it follows by a correlational syllogism that

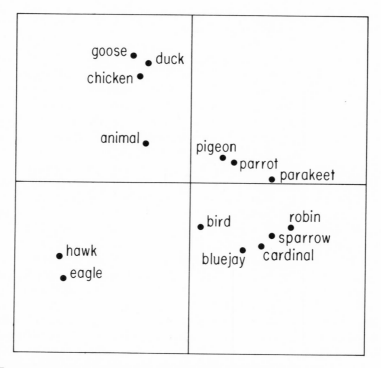

Figure 5 *Multidimensional space for bird and 12 of its subsets*

3. Nonnecessary properties are being used in categorization. (The properties here take the form of dimensions rather than features, but recall that any dimension can be represented by a set of nested features.)

Though one can raise arguments against taking these results at face value (see, for example, Clark and Clark, 1977, chap. 11; Tversky, 1977), the nature of such arguments differs from those raised against the feature-listing studies. In short, accepting that nonnecessary features are used in categorization is beginning to seem more parsimonious than accepting the arguments needed to salvage the classical view.

NESTED CONCEPTS

A final problem for the classical view stems from its third assumption: If concept X is a subset of concept Y, the defining features of Y are nested in those of X. Figure 6 shows the implica-

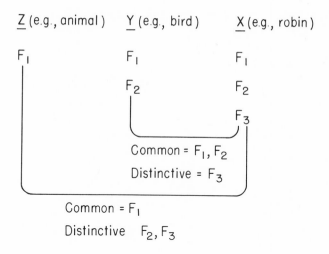

Figure 6 *Implications of the nesting assumption*

tions of this assumption for a nested triple of concepts X, Y, and Z, where X is a subset of Y and Y a subset of Z. As is clear from the figure, X and Y have more common features and fewer distinctive ones than X and Z, which implies that X should be judged more similar to Y than to Z (Tversky, 1977). Thus the third assumption of the classical view implies that a subset (for example, robin) should always be judged more similar to an immediate superordinate (for example, bird) than to a distant one (for example, animal). That this prediction has sometimes failed is a major problem for the classical view.

To judge the severity of this failing, we need to consider some specific results. One indirect way to measure the similarity between a subset and its superordinates is to give the subset to a group of subjects and ask them to produce its superordinates. The frequency with which a particular superordinate is produced is then a measure of its similarity to the subset. To illustrate, if the subset is rose, and 18 of 20 subjects produce flower as a superordinate, while only 10 produce plant, then rose is more similar to flower than to plant. This technique was used by Loftus and Sheff (1971), and their results showed that a subset was no more likely to produce its immediate superordinate than a distant one. Taken at face value, this finding is at odds with the classical view (see Smith, Shoben, and Rips, 1974).

As usual, there is good reason not to take the results at face value. The production frequency of a superordinate term probably depends not only on its similarity to the subset but on its general accessibility as well. Thus a better way to measure the similarity of a subset to its superordinates is by direct similarity ratings, that is, by having subjects give numerical ratings of the similarity of a subset to both its immediate and its distant superordinates. Numerous studies have used this technique (Rips, Shoben, and Smith, 1973; Smith, Shoben, and Rips, 1974; McCloskey, 1980; Roth and Shoben, 1980), and it was generally found that the majority of subsets are rated as more similar to their immediate than to their distant superordinates. There are some exceptions to this finding, however; some of them might be due to the use of unfamiliar superordinates such as alloy and mammal (McCloskey, 1980), but others cannot be explained away by familiarity. Thus chicken and duck are consistently rated as more similar to animal than to bird, and these seem to be clear-cut counterexamples of the classical view's prediction that a subset is more similar to its immediate than its distant superordinates. The bottom line is that although the classical view's prediction works in most cases, it does not work in all.

In addition to the similarity problem, the use of nested triples of concepts in categorization studies had led to another difficulty for the classical view. The problem is that classical-view models, like our complexity one, would predict that a probe concept should be categorized faster when the target concept is a distant superordinate than when it is an immediate one. For example, robin should be categorized faster as an animal than as a bird. But this prediction has often been disconfirmed. The reasoning behind the critical prediction is as follows. For a nested triple, the distant superordinate must contain fewer features than the immediate one—for example, animal has few features than bird—which is just the third assumption of the classical view at work again. And the fewer features there are in the target concept, the fewer must be compared in the comparison stage of our classical-view model, and the less time is needed to decide that the probe concept is indeed a member of the target. This prediction falls out of any classical-view model that assumes categorization is based on a limited-capacity comparison of probe and target features.

We will briefly summarize the experimental literature on this point. Early studies showed that categorizations were faster when the target was an immediate than a distant superordinate (Landauer and Freedman, 1968; Collins and Quillian, 1969; Meyer, 1970). This finding directly contradicts classical-view models of the sort described above. Later studies, however, found few consistent effects (Smith, Shoben, and Rips, 1974). And the most recent experiments show that in a majority of cases categorizations are faster with immediate than distant superordinates, though there are some exceptions (for example, Roth and Shoben, 1980). The exceptions turn out to be just those cases where the instance was rated as more similar to its distant than its immediate superordinate. For example, it takes longer to categorize chicken as a bird (an immediate superordinate) than as an animal (a distant superordinate).

We can summarize the foregoing discussion by two critical points:

1 . With respect to similarity judgments, the classical view predicts an advantage (higher similarity ratings) for immediate over distant superordinates; this prediction works for a majority of cases, but there are definite exceptions.
2 . With respect to categorization times, straightforward models based on the classical view predict an advantage (faster times) for distant over immediate superordinates; this prediction fails for a majority of cases, but works in a minority.

We can see no way to overcome point 1. It rests on the notion that similarity increases with common features and decreases with distinctive ones, and to maintain otherwise seems downright implausible. We can try to get around point 2, however, by going to a different kind of categorization model. To illustrate, we might have a model that computes the similarity between the probe and target concepts, and responds affirmatively ("the probe is a member of the target") as soon as the similarity score exceeds some threshold. This model predicts faster times for immediate than distant superordinates, which is consistent with the majority results, but it no longer handles the exceptions. In sum, the results with nested triples are difficult to reconcile with the classical view.

Summary

Table 7 summarizes the four sets of experimental findings just discussed. Again we need to ask, how badly do they damage the classical view? We argued at length that the first set of findings, simple typicality effects, do not really tarnish the classical view because they can be readily explained by the complexity model that is based on this view. The other three sets of results, however, pose serious problems for models based on the classical view.

The second set included Rosch and Mervis's family resemblance results (1975), which showed that typicality variations are cor-

TABLE 7   FOUR EXPERIMENTAL CRITICISMS OF THE CLASSICAL VIEW

1. Simple typicality effects — ratings, categorization times and errors, ease of learning, order of production, and cognitive reference points
2. Determinants of typicality — typicality and the distribution of features across concept members
3. Use of nonnecessary features
4. Nested concepts — similarity and categorization times

related with variations in the distribution of features across concept members. To accommodate these results to the classical view required many ad hoc assumptions; some were needed to explain the relation between listed and true features, while others arose in the effort to specify a classical-view model that could handle the critical results. All told, these results place a heavy burden on the classical view.

The third set of findings consisted of experimental demonstrations that people use nonnecessary features in making semantic categorizations. Taken at face value, these demonstrations constitute strong evidence against the classical view because any model based on the view would presumably be restricted to necessary and sufficient features. One could, however, challenge whether these experiments tapped the real features of concepts, but such challenges seem to invoke more tenuous assumptions.

Finally, we considered findings on nested concepts. The classical view clearly predicts that a subset should be judged more similar to its immediate than it distant superordinate. Although this is generally true, there are some counterexamples. Unless all counterexamples can be explained away by artifacts, they constitute solid evidence against the classical view. We also considered categorization results showing that times are generally faster for immediate than for distant superordinates, but there were some definite exceptions. The general result was inconsistent with most straightforward models based on the classical view. Though we could come up with another classical model that would handle the general result, the model would then be inconsistent with the exceptions.

Each of the last three sets of results offers some evidence against the classical view. In no single case is the evidence unimpeachable, but taken together the three sets of results start to mount a strong case. Furthermore, the three sets of results fit together like a glove. Certain nonnecessary features appear to be used in categorization, and the distribution of these features apparently leads to typicality effects as well as to cases where a subset is judged more similar to a distant than an immediate superordinate. In contrast, salvaging the classical view from the three critical sets of results involves a great deal of patchwork, where the patching needed in one spot is of no help in another.

When the three critical sets of results are combined with the general criticisms of the classical view discussed earlier, the case against the classical view of concepts starts to look very imposing.

Radical Attempts to Salvage the Classical View

So far we have attempted to defend the classical view by either challenging the basis of the evidence used against it, or by making minimal additions to the view (like the addition of the processing assumptions of the complexity model). As noted, however, these challenges and additions are too piecemeal, and they do not add up to a parsimonious proposal. It is time to consider some more sweeping and radical attempts to salvage the classical view.

In this section we consider three such attempts. The first is based on the assumption that categorization depends on interconcept links, not on the actual features of concepts. The next approach starts by dropping the third assumption of the classical view (the one dealing with the nesting of defining features) and explores the consequences of this move for the findings we have considered. Finally, the third approach takes off from our notion that every concept contains both a core and an identification procedure; while the core may conform to the classical view, the identification procedure need not, and the latter is assumed to be the source of the findings we have considered.

ACCESS LINKS BETWEEN CONCEPTS

Suppose that in addition to acquiring classical-view concepts, people also learn direct links between them that can be used to access one concept from another. This assumption has important implications for performance in a semantic categorization task, the task that has produced most of the experimental evidence against the classical view. Specifically, when asked whether one concept is a subset of another, people check the interconcept links and not the features of concepts. That is, performance in a semantic categorization task does not reflect the contents of concepts at all but rather the ease with which one can move from one concept to another. This idea is illustrated in Figure 7, where the interconcept links are represented by labeled paths. This kind of representation is borrowed from the current network models of knowledge representations (for example, Anderson and Bower, 1973; Collins and Loftus, 1975; Norman and Rumelhart, 1975; Anderson, 1976), but the

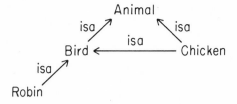

Figure 7   *Part of a network of interconcept links*

present proposal differs from most netword models in its claim that
the concepts being linked together conform to the classical view.
Indeed, the only existing network model that is close to the spirit of
Figure 7 is that proposed by Glass and Holyoak (1975), for they
also assumed that concepts have necessary and sufficient conditions. Some of the assumptions we make in the following analysis
are taken from Glass and Holyoak (1975), while others are borrowed from Collins and Loftus (1975).

There are two critical points about the links or paths in Figure 7.
First, the paths between adjacent levels vary in length, with longer
paths reflecting longer access times. This assumption is capable of
accounting for most simple typicality effects. When asked to judge
the typicality of a probe concept to a target one, subjects base their
judgments on the length of the path between the two concepts;
when categorizing the probe as a member of the target concept,
subjects traverse the probe-target path, where these paths are
shorter for typical probes (like the robin-bird path) than for
atypical probes (like the chicken-bird path); when subset relations
between concepts are being learned, relations characterized by
shorter paths are acquired earlier.

The second important point about the paths in Figure 7 is that
shortcuts are possible; that is, there are direct paths between concepts more than one level apart, and some of these may be shorter
than paths between adjacent levels. For example, there is a shortcut
between chicken and animal that is shorter and hence more accessible than the path between chicken and bird. This notion helps explain the data on nested concepts. Whenever a subset is judged
more similar to its distant than its immediate superordinate, this
can be attributed to the existence of a shortcut between the subset
and the distant superordinate that is shorter than the path between
the subset and the immediate superordinate. And since the shorter
path is more accessible, the subset will be categorized faster vis-à-
vis its distant than its immediate superordinate. Thus chicken will

be judged more similar to animal than to bird, and will also be categorized faster as animal than as bird. Conversely, whenever a subset is judged more similar to its immediate than its distant superordinate, there are no shortcuts (or if there are, they are relatively inaccessible); hence the subset will be categorized faster at the immediate superordinate level.

Despite its apparent successes, this access-path approach has serious drawbacks. First, although it accounts for some of the experimental findings that embarrassed the classical view, by no means does it account for all. In particular, it offers no explanation of why (1) typicality variations in natural concepts are correlated with variations in the distributions of listed features; (2) typicality variations in artificial concepts can be induced by variations in the distribution of features; and (3) various experiments have revealed evidence for the use of nonnecessary features in categorization. Second, the access-path approach does not even address some of the general empirical arguments raised against the classical view. There is nothing in the approach, for example, that comes to grips with the possible existence of disjunctive concepts, or the failure to specify the defining features of concepts. (Remember, the access-path approach assumes that there are defining features for concepts, even though they are not used in categorization tasks.) Third, in cases where the approach succeeds — as in explaining typicality effects — the access-path approach seems too unconstrained. Though there are some suggested empirical measures of the accessibility of one concept from another (roughly, the frequency with which one concept name leads to the other; see Glass and Holyoak, 1975), the approach still lacks criteria for specifying when paths are formed, what affects their lengths, and so on.

These drawbacks are serious, if not overwhelming. The move away from feature-based processes in categorization, and toward path-search processes, seems to have solved few problems. The next two attempts to salvage the classical view maintain a feature-based approach and seem a bit more promising.[4]

TRANSLATIONS BETWEEN FEATURES

Another radical modification of the classical view starts by dropping its third assumption — that the defining features of a concept are nested in those of its subsets. This assumption seems to be the cause of many shortcomings of the classical view: it is solely responsible for the prediction that a specific subset must always be judged more similar to its immediate than its distant superordinate, and it plays a major role in the prediction that there should be no unclear cases, since the nesting of a concept's defining features in

those of its subset is the basis of the classical view's supposed algorithm for determining subset membership. The nesting assumption may even be partly responsible for the failure of semanticists
to find defining features for many concepts, because the search may
have been overly constrained to features that meet the nesting criterion. Thus, dropping the nesting assumption seems a reasonable
starting point for a modification of the classical view.

Under this modification, classical-view concepts are still assumed
to be summary representations containing necessary and sufficient
features, but now at least some features of a particular concept do
not have to be identical to those in the concept's subsets. But in
such cases, how can one use features to determine if one concept is
a subset of another? The simplest answer is that there are rules or
relations for directly translating one feature into another. This idea
is illustrated in Figure 8. One defining feature of bird is "animate,"
and it is listed for robin but not for chicken. However, chicken includes the defining feature "egg-laying," where the latter implies
animate. Now one can establish that a target concept includes a
probe either by matching the target's features to those of the probe
(as in the bird-robin case in Figure 8) or by using the interfeature relations to translate one feature into another (the chicken-bird case).

These ideas can be used to account for most of the experimental
findings discussed earlier. To explain simple typicality effects, we
assume that the less typical a subset, the more features it contains
that require translation when it is compared to its parent concept.
In Figure 8, for example, the atypical chicken requires translation
of its egg-laying feature, while the more typical robin needs no
translation at all. Assuming a translation operation requires more
time and is more error-prone than a simple matching operation, we
would expect atypical instances to be categorized slower and less
accurately than typical ones. To account for Rosch and Mervis's
finding (1975) that typical subsets contain features that are fre-

Bird	Chicken	Robin
living	living	living
animate ←——— egg-laying ———→ animate		
feathered	feathered	feathered
——	——	——

Figure 8   *Direct translation between features*

quently listed for other subsets of the concept, we might assume that features listed for many subsets are more likely to be part of the concept's representation and hence require no translation. Again, typicality comes down to an inverse measure of the amount of translation needed in relating two concepts.

The data on nested concepts also fit nicely with this translation approach. When the features of a subset do not require any translation vis-à-vis the parent concept, we have a perfect nesting of the concept's features in those of the subset, and we expect the similarity predictions of the classical view to hold; when some features do require translation, we have less than perfect nesting, and exceptions to the similarity prediction are expected. Moreover, since atypical subsets are more likely to require translation, such subsets should constitute the bulk of the exceptions, which seems to be the case.

There is an interesting aspect to the above arguments. In all cases, the typical members of a concept are treated in roughly the way the classical view specifies (few or no translations are needed), whereas atypical members are treated differently (translations are frequently required). The direct-translation approach thus has the character of a rule-plus-exception approach, typical members being handled by the rule (the classical view) and atypical members being handled as exceptions. This approach has the desirable property that much of the machinery of the classical view is salvaged, the view now being limited to the more typical members.

The preceding discussion highlights some strong points of the translation approach. There is, however, one sore point for this approach when it comes to accounting for experimental findings. In explaining Rosch and Mervis's results (1975), we explicitly assumed that features listed of many subsets were often defining of the concept, and implicitly assumed that features listed for any subset were defining of it. Inspection of feature listings like those collected by Rosch and Mervis, however, provides little support for either assumption. Some frequently listed features are clearly non-necessary for parent concept or subset. This relates to a more general problem: the translation approach we have sketched has no natural way of dealing with the use of nonnecessary features in categorization, which is one of the major experimental findings.

Though the direct-translation approach can also be stretched to deal with some of the general empirical arguments raised against the classical view, most of what can be said is quite vague. We have already noted that it may be easier to specify defining features of concepts if we drop the nesting constraint. But this is merely a promissory note, particularly since the direct-translation approach still assumes a substantial degree of feature nesting between concepts and their typical members. The occurrence of unclear cases may be attributed to the need to translate between features. Perhaps there are subset relations, like "tomato-fruit," in which the needed translation relations are imperfect or unknown. Without some further specification of the actual interfeature relations, though, it is hard to evaluate this possibility. And finally, there is the question of what the direct translation approach has to say about disjunctive concepts. One possible answer might go as follows: Concepts are truly conjunctive, but they may appear disjunctive when we focus on their members and notice that the latter do not share many features; to illustrate with the concept of bird, we might focus on robin and chicken and note that one contains "animate," the other "egg-laying," and mistakenly conclude that bird is disjunctive. Although this answer is possible, we are hard pressed to put much credence in it.

Some of the problems just mentioned may be alleviated by a more extreme form of the translation approach.[5] So far we have assumed a direct translation between features, but translation can also operate indirectly in that two defining features (of two different concepts) might be connected by a third feature. To illustrate, a defining feature of fruit might be "seeds," while such a feature of orange might be "acidic." To translate between them, one could use the information that (1) seeded objects are often juicy and (2) acidic objects are often juicy. Hence both seeds and acidic lead to juicy, so juicy serves to translate between the two defining features. Note that this translation process is probabilistic, since the intermediate feature, juicy, is not true of all seeded objects. This kind of indirect translation is consistent with the use of nonnecessary features, for intermediate features may be nonnecessary yet used in the categorization process.

An indirect-translation process can also be elaborated to account for other experimental findings. Two examples should suffice. First, variations in the typicality of concept members might reflect either the necessity of translation or the ease with which the defining features of the members can be translated into the defining features of the concept. Second, the Rosch and Mervis correlations between typicality and the distribution of listed features (1975) might be explained by assuming that the listed features are those used in the translation process; for example, features used to translate many concept members may be more powerful or accessible than features used to translate few members.

The obvious problem with the indirect-translation approach is that it is extremely ad hoc. No constraints of any kind have been placed on the nature of intermediate features or on their relations to defining ones, and it is unclear what, if any, predictions follow from this approach. Nevertheless, indirect translation at least addresses a wide range of problems and may, if properly developed, have the potential to save the classical view. Such a rescue will come at a high price, however; for all explanations of empirical results will be in terms of intermediate features rather than defining ones. Indeed, the defining features, which are the heart of the classical view, seem to be doing no theoretical work at all, and it becomes unclear why one need posit them to explain categorization. To some extent, the same is true of the direct-translation approach, where most of the explanations hinged on relations between features rather than on the features per se. And as we will see, the identical problem arises in our third way of salvaging the classical view.

GREATER ACCESSIBILITY OF IDENTIFICATION PROCEDURES

Until now we have assumed the following about concept cores and identification procedures:

1. Though many concepts contain an identification procedure as well as a core, the core is more important psychologically because it must always be there and because it determines the contents of the identification procedure.
2. We must thus focus on empirical methods that are likely to involve the core rather than the identification procedure.
3. Therefore, we should concentrate on semantic categorization tasks rather than perceptual ones, since the semantic task requires a consideration of only the cores.

By challenging the third assumption, we generate our third attempt to salvage the classical view. Specifically, we now assume that the identification procedure is more accessible than the core; consequently, semantic categorization is often based on a comparison of the identification features of the target and probe concepts rather than on a comparison of the core's defining features. This new proposal also partly undermines assumption 1 above: if identification procedures are so widely used, it may be misleading to call the core "more important psychologically."

Given that semantic categorizations may be based on a comparison of identification procedures, most of the relevant experimental results fall into place. First, an immediate consequence is that many features used in categorization will be nonnecessary ones, since the features in identification procedures will often be nonnecessary. Second, simple typicality effects can now be explained in terms of similarity of identification features. The more similar are the identification features of a concept to the identification features of one of its members, the more typical that member is judged to be. Now a categorization model that computes the featural similarity between target and probe concepts will yield faster and more accurate decisions for typical members. Third, the Rosch and Mervis finding (1975) — that typical members contain features common to many other members — can be interpreted solely in terms of identification features. Identification features common to many members are likely to be included in the identification procedure of the concept itself, so again typicality comes down to a matter of similarity of identification features between a concept and its members. Finally, since a concept's identification features need not be perfectly nested in those of its subsets, the similarity prediction of the classical view is no longer expected to hold in all cases.

In addition to accounting for the above results, the assumption that semantic categorizations are based on identification features has another important experimental consequence: semantic categorizations should resemble perceptual ones, since both rely on the same identification features. Hence our earlier stricture against using results from perceptual categorization to evaluate views of concepts must be temporarily suspended, and we need to look briefly at some comparisons of semantic and perceptual categorization.

Though there are few research reports that afford a detailed comparison between semantic and perceptual categorization, what is available shows marked similarities between the two. If one asks subjects to rate a concept's members for typicality, the typicality ordering will be virtually identical for members presented as pictured instances and for members expressed as words (see Smith, Balzano, and Walker, 1978). Moreover, aside from the fact that pictures are responded to slightly faster than words, the effects of typicality are the same in perceptual and semantic categorization (see Guenther and Klatzky, 1977). Also, to the extent that comparable data are available, items that lead to faster categorizations with immediate than with distant superordinates do so regardless of whether the item is presented as a picture (that is, as a specific instance) or as a word (that is, as a subset; compare Smith, Shoben, and Rips, 1974, with Smith, Balzano, and Walker, 1978). And finally, the features listed for items presented as words substantially overlap the features listed for these same items presented as pictures (compare, for example, Hampton, 1979, with Rosch et al., 1976). Although some of these comparisons are tenuous because they involve contrasting results from different studies, they at least suggest that many of the same features are used in semantic and perceptual categorization. This bolsters our new assumption that identification procedures underlie semantic categorization.

The idea of accessible identification procedures can also offset one of the general empirical arguments raised against the classical view, namely, that some concepts are disjunctive. As mentioned earlier in this chapter, some concepts may appear disjunctive when we mistakenly focus on their identification features rather than on their core features. However, a reliance on identification features is of less help in warding off other general empirical arguments. Positing accessible identification features does not explain the prolonged failure to specify the defining features of the core; nor does it get rid of the problem of unclear cases: for example, if asked, "Is a tomato a fruit?" and given sufficient time to mull it over, one should be able to use the core features to resolve the matter.

Despite the two deficiencies just noted, the present approach gets rid of many of the classical view's empirical problems and correctly predicts a similarity between semantic and perceptual categorization. And it does not seem as unconstrained as the other attempts to salvage the classical view, since identification features would at least be restricted to properties that people actually use in deciding that a physical object is an instance of a concept. However, as was the case with the translation approach considered earlier, the present approach seems to save the classical view by shifting all the theoretical action away from the defining features of the core. Again we may raise the question, why bother to posit classical-view concept cores at all?

One possible answer that seems reasonable to us is that while the identification procedure may form the front line of categorization, the core is used as a backup procedure (this is similar to an argument made by Katz, 1977). That is, difficult categorizations, ones that cannot be done by the identification procedure, are eventually tackled by the classically defined core. This claim is seriously challenged, however, by the presence of unclear cases. Another possible answer is that while an identification procedure generally takes care of categorization, the core plays a major role when we do things with concepts other than categorizing. We may, for example, work mainly with classically defined cores when we combine simple concepts into complex ones (the conceptual-combination function of concepts), or when we draw inferences from existent propositional representations. We will not take up the pros and cons of this proposal since it would take us too far from the mainstream of this book. All we can conclude is that, when restricted to categorization phenomena, the proposal of accessible-identification procedures essentially salvages the classical view by ignoring it.

Summary

All three attempts to salvage the classical view have their problems. The first, or access-path approach, seems the most problematic. It fails to deal with most criticisms of the classical view — namely, the correlation between feature distributions and typicality, the use of nonnecessary features, the apparent presence of disjunctive concepts, and the inability to specify defining features. Moreover, the access-path approach runs up this rather impressive list of failings while imposing overly powerful and unconstrained assumptions.

The translation approach fares better. Direct translation seems to handle readily several experimental findings in a parsimonious fashion. However, it lacks convincing accounts of the general empirical problems of the classical view (for example, failure to specify defining features), and it cannot explain the use of nonnecessary features in categorization. The latter problem could be solved by positing indirect translation, with its notion of intermediate features, but at the cost of introducing many unconstrained assumptions.

The final approach, accessible identification procedures that determine semantic as well as perceptual categorizations, appears to have the most potential. However — and this is the critical point — all of its potential in handling categorization phenomena seems to be dependent on the nonnecessary (identification) features, and such nonnecessary features are the backbone of the probabilistic view. In short, the most promising attempt to salvage the classical view is promising because it moves toward the probabilistic view.

4 | The Probabilistic View: Featural Approach

I N DEALING WITH the classical view we restricted ourselves to featural descriptions of concepts, which helped us to state the view's assumptions with a bit of precision. Unfortunately, things are different with the probabilistic view. Some proponents of this view have used features to describe concepts, others have employed dimensions, and still others have rejected property descriptions altogether and favored holistic patterns instead (see Chapter 2 for a discussion of these issues). As a result, it is difficult to say much that is substantial about the probabilistic view in general. We can only come up with the following two assumptions: (1) the representation of a concept is a summary description of an entire class; and (2) the representation of a concept can *not* be restricted to a set of necessary and sufficient conditions; rather, it is some sort of measure of central tendency of the instances' properties or patterns. The first assumption is identical to the initial one of the classical view, so it cannot tell us anything about the differences between the views. The second assumption, which ideally should contain the essence of the view, is partly negative, partly vague. It can only be made more positive and more precise when one considers separately the featural, dimensional, and holistic approaches to the probabilistic view.

This is the tack we will take in studying the probabilistic view. In this chapter we take up the featural approach; we will consider how its representational assumptions avoid the difficulties faced by the classical view, how the process models it has generated can account for experimental results that plagued its classical predecessor, and what prices are being paid for these gains. The succeeding two chapters will provide the same kind of treatment for the dimensional approach and the holistic approach to the probabilistic view.

Assumptions of the Featural Approach

Summary Description

The first assumption of the featural approach is again that of a summary description for the concept. That is, the representation of a concept is assumed to be the result of an abstraction process; not necessarily realizable as an instance; and used whenever a decision must be made about membership in that concept.

Probabilistic Features

The second assumption of the featural approach is the critical one: The features that represent a concept are salient ones that have a substantial probability of occurring in instances of the concept. More precisely, if F_i is a feature and X_j a concept, F_i will be a feature of X_j to the extent that (1) F_i is salient (either perceptually or conceptually), and (2) the probability of F_i given X_j, $P(F_i / X_j)$, is high (for example, F_i tends to be true of an instance labeled as an X_j).

To clarify this assumption, it is helpful to work with the concrete example in Figure 9. Note first that the concepts illustrated contain some features that are not necessary ones. An example is "flies," which is listed for birds. Though some birds do not fly (chicken and penguin), flying is a very salient property that is true of most things called *birds*. This makes "flies" a reasonable addition to the list of concept criteria. By adding such nonnecessary features, we have departed from the major assumption of the classical view. We do, however, leave open the possibility that some features are necessary ones; for example, "feathered," a necessary feature, is associated with the concepts for all the birds in Figure 9.

Second, since features can vary in both their salience and their probability of occurring with a concept member, we explicitly indicate these variations in the representation. Each feature of a concept in Figure 9 is accompanied by a weight that reflects its combined salience and conditional probability. Thus, for the concept of bird, "feathered" and "winged" have high weights since they are salient and always occur with concept members, while "flies" and "sings" have lower weights because, though salient, they are less likely to occur with birds. This scheme ignores the distinction between necessity and probability mentioned earlier, since a weight reflects the probability that a feature is associated with a concept, not the necessity of that association.[1]

Third, each representation in Figure 9 presumably depicts the more *modal* features of a class. This will be true to the extent that learning a concept — that is, the abstraction process that results in the concept representation — takes the following form. After en-

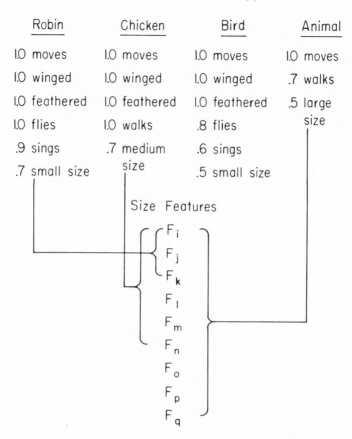

Figure 9   *Probabilistic featural representations*

countering the first instance of a concept, the learner has only its salient features — say, F_1, F_2, and F_3 — as a hypothesis about the contents of the concept. The second instance encountered may have three salient features, F_1, F_2, and F_4. Since F_1 and F_2 have now occurred with the concept twice while F_4 has occurred only once, the former two features are more likely to enter the concept representation. The third instance may contain F_3, F_5, and F_6. Now the frequency of F_3 occurring with a concept member has been raised, making it more likely to enter the concept representation. Hence F_1, F_2, and F_3 each have a frequency of 2 in our distribution of features, while all others have a frequency of 1. F_1, F_2, and F_3 are therefore the modal values of this distribution of experienced instances. And these three features are precisely the ones most likely to enter our summary representation of bird, since they have the higher probabilities of occurring with a concept member.[2]

In short, when learning progresses with an eye toward what features occur in a concept's instances, the features of a concept end up being the more modal features of that concept's instances, thereby making the representation a measure of central tendency of the instances' properties. Note that the idea of modal features is not the same as that of a modal instance, since the modal features of a class of instances may not be true of any particular instance. A representation of modal features will, however, be closer to some instances than others, and this is a critical aspect of probabilistic representations in general.

The three points discussed above cover the essentials of the present assumption — nonnecessary features that are modal ones, accompanied by weights that reflect the features' salience and conditional probability. There are two other points about the feature representations in Figure 9 that also deserve mention. One is that continuous properties, like size, are represented discretely. There are two mechanisms for doing this, and both are used in Figure 9. The first mechanism is to assign one of a small number of size features (for example, small, medium, and large) to each concept. This solution is too simple, however; it fails to represent the fact that people know a medium size is between a small and a large one, and that people often have fairly precise knowledge about the sizes of various entities. The second mechanism, illustrated in the bottom half of Figure 9, gets around these difficulties. It represents a continuous property like size by sets of nested features, as discussed earlier (see Chapter 2). Figure 9 contains both mechanisms because we are assuming that one feature of a concept offers a rough indication of its size (for example, small, medium, or large), and that this feature can be used to access more precise size information in the form of nested features. This goes along with our intuition that when we activate a concept we initially have only rough information about its supposedly continuous properties, but we can then access more detailed information if needed (see Banks, 1977).

The last point to be made concerns the perceptibility of features used in probabilistic representations. At the end of the chapter on the classical view we introduced findings suggesting that perceptual features are used in semantic tasks. Since various lines of evidence indicate that perceptual features are usually not necessary ones as required by the classical view, we appealed to the distinction between core and identification procedure, with the former supposedly containing defining features and the latter containing perceptual features. In moving to the probabilistic view, some of the reasons for keeping perceptual features out of the core are no longer relevant — true, some perceptual features are nonnecessary, but nonnecessary features are now permissible. For this reason many of the core features illustrated in Figure 9 are now perceptual. There are still reasons, though, why some core features must be functional ones even in probabilistic representations, like our earlier argument that the same object will sometimes be categorized as a kitchen table and other times as a work table. Thus the move to probabilistic representations does not completely eliminate functional or abstract features in the core, which means that we still sometimes need identification procedures. Fortunately, though, the empirical problems that plagued the classical view can now be explained just in terms of core features.

To derive these explanations, we need one more assumption — a general processing assumption that appears in some form or other in almost every specific model based on the probabilistic view. We will show how this assumption can be combined with the preceding representational assumptions to yield a general model of the current approach, and then consider how this model accounts for the findings that troubled the classical view.

GENERAL PROCESSING ASSUMPTION

The general assumption about categorization is as follows: An entity X is categorized as an instance or subset of concept Y if and only if X possesses some critical sum of the weighted features of Y. Figure 10 shows how the assumption might be implemented. Consider first the left-hand side of the figure, where a specific instance of an apple (for example, a picture of an apple) is compared to the concept of fruit. For the specific instance there is no need to represent its feature weights, since such weights are only meaningful when applied to a class. To determine that the instance is a member of the concept of fruit, one proceeds as follows: One first finds a feature match between the two representations (either directly if the concept's feature is perceptual, or via identification features if the concept's feature is abstract), next takes the weight of the matching feature and puts it in an accumulator or counter, and then repeats this process over other features until the counter reaches some criterion value. (One also needs a decision criterion for establishing that an instance is not a member of a concept, but this issue is best left until we consider specific models.)

The right-hand side of Figure 10 illustrates the case where a subset, such as the concept of apple, is compared to a concept like fruit. Now both representations have feature weights. The

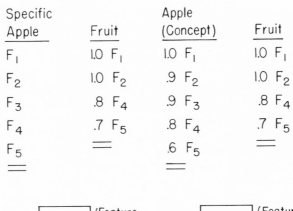

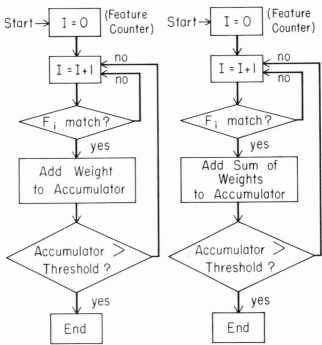

Figure 10 *Possible implementation of general processing assumption*

categorization process is the same as before, save one exception: on finding a feature match between two representations, one now combines the two relevant weights — say, by adding or multiplying them — and this combination then becomes input to the counter, where it is added to like computations.

We now have three assumptions of the featural approach to the probabilistic view — summary description, features that tend to occur with concept membership, and categorization determined by a weighted feature sum. These assumptions define what we will call the *general featural* model of the current approach. The model implies that people are sensitive to and make use of many more features than would be expected on the basis of the classical view; people are assumed to use features that are only generally true of a concept's instances in determining category membership. Although this approach gives up some of the crispness of the classical view, it does suggest an increased richness and skill in abstracting information about concepts. When a concept is being built, few if any useful features will be discarded because of the presence of an occasional outliner or exception (for example, penguin) to a generalization (all birds can fly).

Explanation of Problematic Findings

Our general featural model is sufficient to handle all the problems that embarrassed the classical view. To establish this, we will consider each problem in turn and see how it dissolves under the model. (We will omit mention of the so-called problem of functional features, since we argued earlier that this problem was more apparent than real.)

DISJUNCTIVE CONCEPTS

Recall that the classical view was incompatible with the existence of the disjunctive concepts. This is not the case with the probabilistic view:

1. According to the general featural model, category membership is based on a weighted sum of features.
2. Since the same weighted sum can be achieved by various combinations of features, it follows that various feature sets can be used to determine category membership.

This idea is diagrammed in Figure 11. Possible features are listed for two very different pieces of furniture, a specific chair and a specific rug, as well as for the concept of furniture. Both chair and rug match enough features of furniture to gain admission to this concept, but many of the matched features differ in the two cases. Hence there are two (at least) different sets of features for the concept of furniture; that is, furniture is in principle a disjunctive concept.

The above discussion unequivocally shows that the featural approach to the probabilistic view is consistent with disjunctive con-

Chair (specific)	Rug (specific)	Furniture	
F_1 (physical object)	F_1	1.0	F_1
F_2 (non-living)	F_2	1.0	F_2
F_3 (decorative)	F_3	.9	F_3
F_4 (rigid)	F_7 (covers floor)	.8	F_4
F_5 (has seat)	F_8 (can lie on it)	.5	F_5
F_6 (has legs)	——	.7	F_6
——		.4	F_7
		.6	F_8
		——	

Figure 11 *A disjunctive concept in the probabilistic view*

cepts. It might be a mistake, however, to make too much of this potential for disjunction. In the example we discussed, chair and rug matched different sets of features of furniture, but the two sets did have some features in common ("physical object," "used to decorate living spaces"). Had we chosen chair and couch as our specific instances, the features of furniture they would have matched would have been more similar. The point is that although there may be differences in the feature sets of a concept that its various instances match, these differences may not be very great. Indeed, we are hard pressed to come up with a single example in which two instances of a natural concept share no features at all — that is, a completely disjunctive concept. Another way to express this point is that there are degrees of disjunctiveness, ranging from a single feature difference in the sets used by various instances in matching a concept, to sets that have no features in common. While the featural approach to the probabilistic view is compatible with any degree of disjunctiveness, this degree may be quite small for natural concepts.

UNCLEAR CASES

Recall that the classical view contained an algorithm for determining concept membership — X is a subset of Y if Y's defining features are nested in those of X — and that this seemed inconsistent with the existence of unclear cases. Though the classical view could be brought into line with unclear cases by the addition of some assumptions, the general featural model of the probabilistic view seems to provide a more straightforward account of these cases. Specifically, an unclear case arises whenever the potential instance: (1) accumulates a weighted feature sum that is near but does not exceed the criterion value of a target concept, and/or (2) accumulates comparable feature sums for more than one concept. Both (1) and (2) seem to play a role in many unclear cases. For example, "tomato" may be an unclear case of "fruit" because tomato matches a comparable number of features of fruit and vegetable, where the weighted feature sums may be less than the criterion values for both target concepts.

FAILURE TO SPECIFY DEFINING FEATURES

The single most important failure of the classical view is its lack of progress in specifying necessary and sufficient features for natural concepts. This criticism completely dissolves in the probabilistic view, because this view does not require sets of defining features.

SIMPLE TYPICALITY EFFECTS

We argued earlier that simple typicality effects—for example, typical members being categorized faster than atypical ones—provide no damaging evidence against the classical view. The point we now wish to establish is that many of these effects can be so readily derived from the general featural model that they can be considered as evidence for the probabilistic view.

The only assumption we need to introduce is that the judged typicality of a concept member directly reflects the number of features it shares with its parent concept (Smith, Shoben, and Rips, 1974), or, better yet, with the weighted sum of these shared features. To illustrate, the concept of bird might contain some necessary features (for example, feathered and winged) and some nonnecessary ones (for example, flies and sings); while both robin and chicken would of course contain the necessary features, only robin would contain the nonnecessary ones, and this is why people rate robin as the more typical bird (see Figure 9). In addition to explaining the typicality ratings, this line of reasoning handles the categorization results. Since typical members match many features of a target concept, the weighted sum they need to attain the criterion value should be reached relatively quickly, and there should be little chance of "noise" in the feature-matching process resulting in an incorrect categorization. Hence typical members should be categorized faster and more accurately than atypical ones. Typicality effects in categorization thus fall neatly out of our general featural model.

It requires a little more work to derive some of the other simple typicality effects. Consider the finding that children learn typical members before atypical ones. This phenomenon may result from the fact that parents *teach* typical members before atypical ones (see Anglin, 1977, for some support for this idea); and parents may start with typical members because their features capture so many of the concept's features. Then there is the finding that when concept members are being listed, typical items are given before atypical ones. A simple explanation is that the concept is used as a probe to retrieve its members, and the more similar a member is to the retrieval probe, the sooner it is retrieved. Finally, consider the finding that typical members are more likely to serve as cognitive reference points than are atypical members. Perhaps all this finding reflects is that we prefer to use general concepts as reference points; since typical members are more similar to their general concepts than are atypical ones, typical members are also more preferred as reference points.

Determinants of Typicality

The same principles that were used to explain simple typicality effects can also explain Rosch and Mervis's finding (1975) that an item is a typical member of a concept to the extent that it contains features shared by many other members. Features shared by many members are the more modal features of a class, and hence likely to be in the representation of the class or concept itself. Thus the Rosch and Mervis findings are readily interpreted in terms of the above assumption that a member of a concept is judged typical to the extent that it shares many features with the concept itself.[3]

Use of Nonnecessary Features

While the use of nonnecessary features was problematic for any classical-view model, such features are built directly into probabilistic representations; so of course they will be used during categorization.

Nested Concepts

Recall that the major findings with nested concepts involved both similarity ratings and categorization times. Let us start by discussing similarity ratings.

For a nested triple — like robin, bird, and animal — the specific concept was usually judged more similar to its immediate superordinate than to its distant one, but there were some exceptions. The classical view was consistent with the usual cases but inconsistent with the exceptions. The general featural model is compatible with both kinds of cases, as Figure 12 shows. The critical aspects of the figure are the four nonnecessary features: (1) flies and (2) sings, which appear only with robin and bird, and (3) walks and (4) found on farms, which appear only with chicken and animal. The comparison of robin, bird, and animal offers an example of the usual case, since robin is judged more similar to its immediate superordinate (bird) than to its distant one (animal). In contrast, chicken, bird, and animal illustrate an exception, since chicken is judged more similar to its distant superordinate (animal) than to its immediate one (bird). These similarity ratings are in line with the representations in Figure 12. Robin and bird have more common features (and fewer distinctive ones) than do robin and animal, while chicken and animal have more common features (and fewer distinctive ones) than do chicken and bird. This similarity computation, however, ignores the feature weights. If we include them, by adding or multiplying the weights of matching features, the example still yields the correct predictions for similarity ratings.

Now let us consider the findings on categorization times. We saw that for a nested triple, the specific concept was usually categorized faster as an instance of its immediate than its distant superordinate; but there were some exceptions, which usually turned out to be the same triples that were exceptions in the similarity analysis. To see how the general featural model can accommodate

Robin	Chicken	Bird	Animal
1.0 moves	1.0 moves	1.0 moves	1.0 moves
1.0 winged	1.0 winged	1.0 winged	.7 walks
1.0 feathered	1.0 feathered	1.0 feathered	.6 found on farms
1.0 flies	1.0 walks	.8 flies	——
.9 sings	.7 found on farms	.6 sings	
——	——	——	

Figure 12 *Probabilistic representations that can explain similarity ratings for nested triples*

the usual and exceptional cases, we need only look at Figure 12 again. Since robin shares more features with bird than animal, the weighted sum will reach criterion sooner when robin is categorized as a bird; since chicken shares more features with animal than bird, the weighted sum will reach criterion sooner when chicken is categorized as an animal.

The preceding analysis shows that the probabilistic view is consistent with all data on nested concepts, but it may be that this flexibility is being bought at the price of ad hoc assumptions about nonnecessary features and their weights. A glance at Figure 12 suggests that this is at least partly the case; for "found on farms" is a suspicious feature for the concept of animals, and if its weight is reduced appreciably, the similarity computation no longer correctly predicts that chicken should be judged more similar to animal than to bird. We clearly need to specify more constraints on features and their weights. In defense of our analysis, however, we should mention two things. First, the analysis illustrated in Figure 12 does have some constaints. The same immediate and distant superordinates are used in the usual case and the exception; therefore any features attributed to the superordinates in order to derive a prediction for, say, the usual case will constrain the analysis of the exception. Second, we are not committed to a specific feature like "found on farms." All we need in order to derive the correct predictions is the existence of some moderately weighted feature that is in the representations of chicken and animal but not in those of robin and bird. "Found on farms" is an example of such a feature, but is may not be the correct one.

Summary

It is instructive to point out which of the above explanations follow directly from the three assumptions of the general featural model and which depend on additional assumptions. Table 8 shows which assumptions are used to explain various phenomena. The leftmost column lists the seven classes of phenomena of interest, and the corresponding rows give the assumptions invoked to explain those phenomena. Two points about the table are worth emphasizing. First, when the three assumptions of the general featural model are combined with the notion that typicality reflects feature overlap, the resulting package accounts for a host of findings. Second, all the other assumptions appear only once or twice in the table (that is, help to explain only one or two phenomena) and hence are suspiciously ad hoc. In some cases, however, this suspicion turns out to be unwarranted. For example, the assumption concerning weighted sums hovering about the threshold count,

TABLE 8   SUMMARY OF ASSUMPTIONS USED TO EXPLAIN PHENOMENA

Phenomena	Three assumptions of general featural model[a]	Typicality reflects featural overlap	Feature sum near threshold counts	Teach typical members first	Retrieval order based on similarity	Preferring general concepts as reference points	Specific assumptions about nonnecessary features
1. Disjunctive concepts	X[b]						
2. Unclear cases	X		X				
3. Failure to specify defining features	X						
4. Simple typicality effects							
Ratings	X	X					
Categorization	X	X					
Learning	X	X		X			
Production order	X	X			X		
Reference points	X	X				X	
5. Determinants of typicality: family resemblance measures (Rosch and Mervis)	X	X					
6. Use of nonnecessary features							
7. Nested concepts	X	X					X

a. Summary description, probabilistic features, and categorization determined by weighted feature sum.
b. An X indicates that the assumption in that column is needed to explain the phenomenon in that row.

which is used to explain unclear cases, is applicable to any decision about probabilistic information. Since categorization involves this kind of decision in the eyes of the probabilistic view, the assumption is a motivated one. A similar story holds for the assumption that a probe first retrieves items similar to itself, which is used to explain why typical instances are produced before atypical ones. Again the assumption is a motivated one — it is used in memory research to explain a variety of retrieval phenomena. In other cases, suspicion of ad hoc assumptions may be well founded; the obvious examples are the specific assumptions about nonnecessary features and their weights that were used to account for the findings with nested triples. Thus Table 8 gives us some idea of what is really explained by a general model based on the probabilistic view, and what is only consistent with this view under certain specific assumptions.

Finally, it is worth emphasizing that the general featural model does all its work with discrete features. This is important because it has often been claimed that the fact that there are "degrees" of concept membership — as manifested in unclear cases and typicality variations — implies that concepts are represented in terms of continuous dimensions. This claim is simply incorrect. The general featural model handles both unclear cases and typicality effects in terms of variations in discrete features. As we emphasized in Chapter 2, the distinctions between discrete features and continuous dimensions can be quite complex, and little can be gained by facile claims that some effect is consistent with one kind of property but not the other. We will try to say some nonfacile things about this issue later, after we have considered the dimensional approach.

Specific Models Based on the Featural Approach

Though the general featural model is useful for understanding many categorization phenomena, it is too general or too unconstrained in a number of respects. For example, it has little specific to say about how one determines that two concepts share any features, and nothing at all to say about how one decides that one concept is not an instance or subset of another. For these reasons, we need to consider some specific models based on the featural approach. Many of the specific models are essentially fleshed-out versions of the general featural model. In this class we would include the spreading activation model of Collins and Loftus (1975), the polythetic concept model of Hampton (1979), the property comparison model of McCloskey and Glucksberg (1979), and some of the models that have been discussed in research on artificial concepts (for example, Neumann, 1974; Hayes-Roth and Hayes-Roth,

1977). It will be sufficient to consider just one of these models in detail to see how the categorization process may be more precisely specified. For this purpose, we will use the spreading activation model, since it is perhaps the best known member of its class.

In addition to the models enumerated above, the work of Rosch and Mervis (1975) contains the beginnings of a cue validity model. This proposal can also be seen as a variant of our general featural model, but it contains enough new implications to merit some separate consideration. The only other featural model of consequence that is based on the probabilistic view is the feature comparison model of Smith, Shoben, and Rips (1974). This model, unlike other specific ones, cannot be thought of as an instantiation of our general featural model; it uses different sorts of processing mechanisms and, under some interpretations, places a greater emphasis on necessary features. Given these distinguishing traits, the feature comparison model also merits some separate discussion.

The Spreading Activation Model

Collins and Loftus (1975) were concerned with the kinds of evidence that one considers in deciding whether or not a test item is a member of a target concept. One major source of evidence includes the features of the test item and concept, and their treatment of how featural evidence is processed is remarkably close to that of our general model.[4]

Collins and Loftus's featural representations are clearly probabilistic. Concepts are represented as summary descriptions containing many nonnecessary features, with each feature being weighted by its importance in conferring concept membership, that is, by what Collins and Loftus call *criteriality*. However, instead of depicting a concept's features by a list as we have routinely done, Collins and Loftus use a network like that illustrated in Figure 13. Every concept that contains a particular feature is connected to it

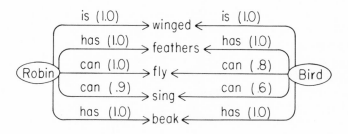

Figure 13 *Part of a network in the spreading activation model*

by a labeled link, with the criteriality of the feature depicted on the link. The label makes explicit what kinds of features we are dealing with; for example, "has" designates part features, "is" designates global characteristics, and "can" designates functions or habitual activities.

A critical question with this model is, how is the network processed to determine whether two concepts share features? Perhaps the most obvious possibility is to compare each labeled feature of one concept to all labeled features of the other to see if there is a match. This is a discrete search process of the sort found in many current processing models. It is not, however, the procedure that Collins and Loftus favor. They employ a *spreading activation* procedure, which is a continuous analog process rather than a discrete one. When a test item and concept are presented, activation from these sources begins to spread through the network, with the activation from each source being divided among all paths emanating from that source. If the two sources of activation intersect at some feature, the two paths leading to the intersection become available. Such paths are then evaluated to see if they have the same labels; if they do, then the two concepts share the relevant feature. To illustrate with Figure 13, when robin and bird are presented, activation from the two concepts will eventually intersect at the feature of feathers; since both paths leading to the intersection have the same label, "has," both robin and bird share the feature of feathers. There are also various outcomes of this process that can indicate that two concepts do not share a particular feature. Two concepts might intersect at a feature but have paths with different labels (for example, "has feathers" versus "wears feathers"); or two concepts might activate two different features that are known to be mutually exclusive (for example, big and small); or two concepts might fail to intersect at a particular feature in some fixed time period.

The activation process is such that potential matches and mismatches are continuously becoming available for evaluation. Once evaluated, the matches and mismatches are treated in the same fashion as in the general featural model. For each match, a positive amount of evidence is accumulated, the degree of positiveness increasing with the criteriality of the feature; for every mismatch, a negative amount of evidence is accumulated, with the degree again increasing with criteriality. This process is continued until either (1) the accumulated positive evidence exceeds some positive threshold, in which case one decides the test items belongs to the concept, or (2) the accumulated negative evidence exceeds a negative threshold, and one decides the test item does not belong to the concept.

The spreading activation model fleshes out the general featural model by specifying details about the match process and about how one decides that an item is not an instance or subset of a concept. The present model explains the empirical effects we have been concerned with in precisely the same manner as the general featural model. A few examples should suffice: since a concept contains weighted, nonnecessary features, the use of nonnecessary features is to be expected, as is the lack of progress in specifying defining features; because the positive threshold can be reached by various combinations of feature matches, the model is compatible with disjunctive concepts; and assuming that typical instances share more features with their concepts than do atypical instances, typical instances should accumulate positive evidence at a more rapid rate and consequently be categorized faster.

Though none of the above explanations hinges on the specific feature matching and evaluation assumptions of the spreading activation model, these assumptions about activation are needed to account for empirical effects other than those we have emphasized. In particular, these assumptions can be used to explain various priming effects. Two examples of such effects should suffice to show the range of results the spreading activation model can handle.

In a study by Rosch (1975), subjects were asked to decide whether two simultaneously presented words were physically identical or not. The words denoted concept instances that varied in typicality; for example, one physically identical pair might be "apple-apple" while another was "fig-fig." On some trials, prior to the presentation of a word pair, the name of the relevant concept (for example, "fruit") was presented as a prime. The critical finding was that relative to trials that did not contain a prime, the concept prime facilitated decisions only to word pairs naming typical instances (for example, "fruit" speeded decisions to "apple-apple" but not to "fig-fig."). The interpretation in terms of the spreading activation model is straightforward: When the prime is presented, it activates its associated concept. The activation spreads along all feature paths emanating from the concept, resulting in an activation of each member to the extent that the member shares features with the concept. Since typical members share more features with the concept than do atypical ones, the former will be primed more by the concept and facilitated more in the decision task. (Interestingly, Rosch also obtained the same results when pictures were used instead of words in the decision task, again attesting to the similarity of features used in semantic and perceptual tasks.)

For the second illustration of a priming effect, consider a paradigm used by Loftus and Cole (1974). Subjects were sequentially given two terms, one designating a concept and the other a feature (for example, vehicle and red). Their task was to produce a member of the concept that had that feature (for example, fire engine). Loftus and Cole found that the desired member was produced faster when the concept preceded the feature term than when the terms were presented in the reverse order. Thus the concept term (vehicle) seemed to prime the desired response (fire engine) more than the feature term (red) did. The spreading activation model accounts for this greater priming power of concept terms in the following way: Assuming there are fewer paths emanating from a concept than from a feature, the activation originating from the concept will be less subdivided than that originating from the feature, and consequently the path going from the concept to the desired response will be more activated than that going from the feature to the desired response.

We find it encouraging that the spreading activation model can accommodate these results; it suggests that the model may be useful in explaining other effects of context on concept usage. For priming effects *are* context effects—that is, the prime establishes a context that can facilitate the subsequent processing of the target concepts—and the kinds of explanations used above may be able to be generalized to richer context effects. Some support for this idea will be given later in this chapter.

Cue Validities

The starting point in discussing cue validities is an important finding of Rosch and Mervis (1975) that was not mentioned previously. In deciding whether or not an item is an instance or subset of a target concept, one considers not only the features the item shares with that concept but also the features the item shares with concepts that contrast with the target. We can illustrate with some of Rosch and Mervis's items. Suppose one has to decide whether a pictured item belongs to the concept of chair. Categorization will be more efficient if that instance shares few features with the concepts of sofa, stool, and cushion, where the last three are the contrast concepts of chair (these contrast concepts can be elicited by asking subjects, "If something is not a chair, what is it?").

Perhaps Rosch and Mervis's strongest evidence for this effect comes from their 1975 studies with artificial materials. In these studies two concepts were created, each consisting of six letter strings. The strings in a concept varied with respect to how many of their letters—that is, their features—also occurred in the strings belonging to the other concept. The greater the featural overlap with the contrast concept, the longer it took to categorize that string correctly, the more likely was the chance of categorizing it incorrectly, and the less typical it was rated of its appropriate concept. This is strong evidence that categorization of an instance depends on the instance's similarity to rival concepts.

As Rosch and Mervis note, these findings point to the need to consider something like the *cue validity* of a feature (an idea first introduced by Bourne and Restle in 1959). The cue validity of a particular feature, F_i, vis-à-vis a particular target concept, X_j, is such that it increases with the probability that F_i occurs with instances of X_j, and decreases with the probability that F_i occurs in instances of a concept that contrasts with X_j. To state this more formally (after Beach, 1964, and Reed, 1972):

$$\text{Cue validity of } F_i \text{ for } X_j \quad = P(X_j/F_i) \quad = \frac{P(F_i/X_j)}{P(F_i/X_j) + P(F_i/X_k)}$$

where X_k represents a concept that contrasts with X_j. (To keep things simple, we are assuming that X_j has only one contrast concept.) Thus the more probable it is that a feature comes from a contrast concept, the less evidence it supplies for the target concept.

Cue validities can be incorporated into the spreading activation model, or any other instantiation of the general featural model, in two different ways. One is that the cue validity of a feature, rather than just the conditional probability of the feature, can be used to determine feature weights. Now it is information about cue validities that is accumulated until a positive or negative threshold is reached. Alternatively, we can leave the feature weights untouched and let information about cue validities play a role in the process that evaluates paths. Now if two concepts have led to some feature, the process uses the cue validity of that feature to determine how much the counter should be incremented. Thus, although the use of contrast concepts is a significant finding, it requires only slight modifications of the previous model.

Perhaps the main reason this modification is slight is that most models of concept utilization have little to say about concept acquisition. And it is issues about learning that are most affected by the findings on contrast concepts. This is not the place to develop these issues, but some comment is in order. In the only mention we made of concept acquisition, we assumed that the learner keeps a rough record of which features are associated with the instances of a concept and eventually ends up with the more frequent features in the concept's representation. But if the cue validity of a feature is its critical aspect, the learner needs to track the extent to which a feature is more likely to go with a particular concept than with its contrasts. And from this point it seems a reasonable step to suggest that learners may often not focus on features of concept instances but rather on features of concept contrasts (Barrett, 1977). For example, a child acquiring the concept of dog needs to pay attention to those features that provide the sharpest contrast with other concepts in this domain, such as cat and cow. (This assumes that the child already has some notion of the domain.) In sum, if cue validities are what we learn about features, then acquisition must be based on accumulating knowledge about critical contrasts.

THE FEATURE COMPARISON MODEL

The feature comparison model of Smith, Shoben, and Rips (1974) offers a somewhat different approach to categorization from that provided by the general featural model and its various instantiations. While the feature comparison model incorporates the first two assumptions of the general feature model — a summary representation and weighted, nonnecessary features — it departs from the general model in its major assumption about processing.

Instead of relying on a weighted feature sum, Smith, Shoben, and Rips postulate that when a subject is given a test item and target concept, categorization is based on a two-stage process. In the first stage the subject ignores all weights and simply determines the number of feature matches between the test item and target concept. This can be accomplished, for example, by simultaneously comparing each feature of the target concept to every feature of the test item. If the number of matches exceeds a high criterion, the item very likely belongs to the concept and there is no need for second-stage processing. If the first stage yields a number of matches below some low criterion, the item is very likely not a member of the concept, and again there is no need for the second stage. However, when the first stage yields a number of matches between the two criteria, the second stage must be executed. In this stage one uses the feature weights; one selects only those features of the test item and concept with high weights, and determines whether each highly weighted feature of the concept matches such a feature of the item. If all such features match, the item is a member of the concept; otherwise, the item is not a member. The critical factor in categorization is again the number of features shared by test item and concept, but in this model the factor determines whether a second stage is needed. And the probability that a second stage is needed determines whether categorization is relatively rapid (mainly based on first-stage decisions) or relatively slow (mainly based on dual-stage decisions).

Since this model differs substantially from those considered earlier, it is worthwhile to illustrate how it accounts for the relevant empirical phenomena. As explicitly formulated, the model leaves open the question of whether the features used in the second stage are necessary ones or merely features whose weights exceed some threshold. As long as the second-stage features are not *both* necessary and sufficient, the model is consistent with the failure to specify defining features. It also assumes the use of nonnecessary features, which play a major role in determining the output of the first stage. And since the same number of feature matches can be reached by various combinations of first-stage features, the model is compatible with disjunctive concepts.

To account for typicality effects, Smith, Shoben, and Rips use an assumption identical to one invoked by the general featural model, namely, that the typicality of an item directly reflects the number of features it shares with its appropriate concept. This assumption immediately accounts for typicality ratings; it also accounts for Rosch and Mervis's finding (1975) that typical members of a concept contain features that are common to other members (since such common features are likely to be in the concept representation itself). Three other typicality findings—that typical members are learned earlier, produced earlier, and preferred as cognitive reference points— also arise because the features of typical members capture so many of the concept's features. (This is essentially the same account as that offered by the general featural model.) Other typicality effects are explained in terms of whether categorizations require only first-stage processing or both stages. Typical items are categorized faster than atypical ones because the number of feature matches in the first stage is higher for typical members, thereby making it less likely that such items will require second-stage processing. The findings on nested triples are handled in the same way. To illustrate, robin is categorized as a bird faster than as an animal because robin shares more features with bird than animal, thereby making it more likely that robin-bird categorizations can be accomplished in the first stage; chicken is categorized faster as an animal than as a bird because chicken shares more features with animal than bird, thereby making the chicken-animal categorization more likely to be accomplished in the first stage.

What about the other findings we turned up in our review of models—priming effects and the importance of contrast concepts? Though the feature comparison model was not formulated to account for these results, it requires little work to incorporate them. For example, Rosch's finding (1975) that a concept primes typical members more than atypical ones follows from the assumption that a concept shares more features with its typical members; and Rosch and Mervis's findings on contrast concepts (1975) may be handled by assuming that cue validities determine feature weights.

COMPARISON OF THE MODELS

On the one hand we have the general featural model and its instantiations like the spreading activation model; on the other we have the feature comparison model. Both seem to offer comparable accounts of the phenomena we have been concerned with. Are there any reasons for preferring one type of model over the other? In dealing with this question we will contrast the feature comparison model with the spreading activation one so that both models are at roughly the same level of detail.

General Considerations

In both models processing terminates earlier when more features (including nonnecessary ones) of a concept are matched by those of an instance or subset. In the spreading activation model, early termination comes about when the results of a single stage reach a threshold value; in the feature comparison model, early termination arises when the second stage need not be executed. Thus a choice between models depends partly on the merits of positing two processing stages rather than one. The notion of two stages seems justified to the extent that the hypothesized stages handle different kinds of information. If the features examined in the second stage of the feature comparison model are restricted to necessary ones (just necessary, not necessary *and* sufficient), then it makes sense to treat them differently from the features processed in the first stage, which include nonnecessary as well as necessary ones. (This is the usual interpretation of the feature comparison model, though it is not really stated in Smith, Shoben, and Rips's 1974 paper.)

Thus the merit of the two-stage assumption depends in part on the existence of necessary features for semantic concepts. While we have repeatedly noted how difficult it has been to come up with features that are *both* necessary and sufficient, coming up with just necessary ones might be a lot easier. Later in this chapter we will present some other arguments for the existence of necessary features; for now it suffices to point out that the possibility of necessary features provides a plausible rationale for the feature comparison model's assumption of two different processing stages.

Experimental Findings

At a less general level, we can try to judge the relative merits of the feature comparison and spreading activation models by looking at experiments that have tested predictions from either of the models. There has been no shortage of such experiments (for example, Reder and Anderson, 1974; Glass and Holyoak, 1975; Holyoak and Glass, 1975; Bock, 1976; Ashcraft, 1978; McCloskey and Glucksberg, 1978). To try to review them adequately, however, would bog us down in a quagmire of experimental details. Rather, we will briefly mention only one experiment that has the virtue of trying to get directly at the issue of whether categorization is best thought of as a single-stage or a dual-stage process.

McCloskey and Glucksberg (1978) attempted to test the two-stage assumption of the feature comparison model by means of the following logic: If typical items are categorized faster than atypical ones because the former are more likely to require only first-stage processing, then a categorization task that precludes first-stage decisions should also remove the advantage of typical items. To preclude first-stage decisions, McCloskey and Glucksberg used test items and target concepts that shared many features even when the item was not a member of the concept; for example, a test item might be "bird" and the target concept "robin." In this case, finding that test and target shared many features in the first stage would not reliably indicate that the test item belongs to the concept. Consequently most decisions, even for typical items, would have to be based on both processing stages. Yet the results showed that typical members were still categorized faster than atypical ones. While the experiment is by no means ironclad (for example, there is no way to guarantee that first-stage decisions were really prohibited; there are anomalies in the data on nonmembers), these results are a definite embarrassment to the feature comparison model. More results of this kind could create the data base needed to reject the two-stage assumption definitively in favor of a single-stage process.

Criticisms of the Featural Approach

Regardless of which featural model is used to instantiate the probabilistic view, there are three general shortcomings of this approach. First, just listing features does not go far enough in specifying the knowledge represented in a concept. People also know something about the relations between the features of a concept, and about the variability that is permissible on any feature. The featural approach needs some way of representing this additional information. Second, the featural approach has thus far failed to provide constraints on what features may be posited. We discussed the general issue of feature constraints earlier in the book (Chapter 2), but the work we have covered in this chapter raises new problems. Third, although there is ample evidence that context can

greatly affect concept usage, there has been little theoretical progress in dealing with context effects. The priming studies we discussed in connection with the spreading activation model are an exception to this, but they only begin to scratch the surface of context
effects.

REPRESENTING MORE KNOWLEDGE IN CONCEPTS

Relations between Features

To illustrate the issue of representing relations between features,
let us consider two possible features that might appear in the representation of bird: "sings" and "small." (For ease of exposition, we ignore the representation of detailed size information in the following
discussion.) The problem is that these two features are correlated
across instances of the concept — small birds are more likely to sing
than large ones — yet the models we have discussed do not represent
correlations between features. And there is good evidence — virtually all of which comes from studies of artificial concepts — that
people use such correlational information. Neumann (1974) was
among the first to show that subjects were sensitive to more than
just the frequency with which individual features occurred in instances of a concept; he demonstrated that categorizations were
more efficient for instances that contained correlated features.
Other studies with artificial concepts have supported this conclusion and provided evidence that correlations between more than
two features may matter as well (Hayes-Roth and Hayes-Roth,
1977; Medin and Schaffer, 1978). So the problem is a real one; the
question is how to solve it without throwing away all the
theoretical machinery in current featural models.[5]

We can think of two solutions. The first we call *conjunctive
features;* the idea is to include a pair of correlated features (or any
n-tuple whose correlation matters) as another feature, a conjunctive one, in the concept representation (see Neumann, 1974; Hayes-
Roth and Hayes-Roth, 1977). If, for example, "sings" and "small"
are correlated across various instances of bird, then "sings-and-
small" becomes a new feature of the bird concept. Though this
move will handle the categorization data, it is an unprincipled solution in several respects. For one thing, a conjunctive feature like
"sings-and-small" seems a gross violation of some of our constraints
on features, namely that features be general and that they not be
blatantly decomposable. Moreover, while the notion of conjunctive features may offer a solution to the problem of representing
correlations between features, it says nothing about representing
other kinds of relations between features and hence seems an ad

hoc solution. Let us expand on this point. In addition to correlation, two features might enter into an embedding relation. As an illustration, one feature of the concept for hawk would be "wings," and that feature itself has the feature "large." The latter feature is thus embedded in the former. We need a means for representing this kind of relation, and ideally we would like it to be the same means we use to represent correlations. Still another problem with conjunctive features is that such features can explode in number if there are many relations between features. If a concept has, say, 20 features that can all be pairwise related, we end up with more than 190 conjunctive features whose co-occurrence probabilities must be learned and utilized. Such a situation is possible, but it seems implausible.

The other solution, called *labeled relations*, derives from work in artificial intelligence. The idea is to represent relations between features by means of labels in a feature-concept network like that shown in Figure 14. The network is similar to the one used earlier to illustrate the spreading activation model (see Figure 13), but there are some changes. We now distinguish between the *types* and *tokens* of features. The type node for a particular feature like "sing" denotes singing in general, while a token node for "sing" denotes the singing of a particular subset of bird (see Figure 14). The rationale

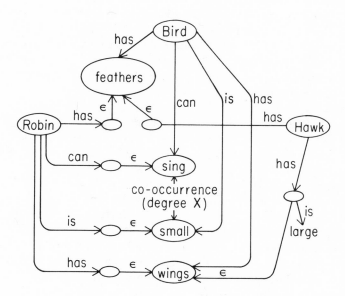

Figure 14 *Labeled relations between features (unfilled circles designate token nodes that are attached to their type nodes by ε links; criteriality weights are omitted for simplicity)*

for this distinction will soon be apparent. Another change is that rather than labeling only concept-feature links, we now label feature-feature links as well. The features "sing" and "small," for example, are connected by the labeled relation *co-occurrence* (with some indication of the degree of co-occurrence). Note that this relation is between the type nodes of these features (see Figure 14), since the relation is assumed to hold only across subsets of bird and not among the instances of a subset. In contrast, the features "wings" (of hawk) and "large" are connected by an *is* relation, and this relation involves a token node for wings because only the wings of a particular subset (hawk) are specified as large.

This labeled-relations solution takes care of some of the problems mentioned above (though not the explosion problem). There are no gross violations of our constraints on features, and the means used to depict correlations between features (that is, labels) can also be used to depict other relations between features. For these reasons, we favor the labeled-relations solution. This means that when it comes to complete descriptions of concepts, feature lists need to be replaced by feature networks.[6]

Feature Variability

People also seem to know how much variation is permissible for a feature. To illustrate, let us consider the concept of watermelon. Its size value could be represented by the two means discussed earlier: a rough indication equivalent to a label, for example, large (for a fruit), and precise information in the form of nested size features. But the precise information cannot be too precise, for people will accept as watermelons objects of varying sizes. And if asked directly, "What size is an average watermelon?" people seem to be most comfortable giving a range rather than a precise number. These observations suggest that we have not only rough and precise indicators of the size of objects, but also some notion of the range of variability of permissible values.

A study by Walker (1975) can be used to illustrate this point further. Walker asked her subjects to respond "true" or "false" to statements such as "A typical watermelon is 20 inches long." She systematically varied the size information (for example, replacing 20 in the preceding example with 16, 18, 22, or 24) and found that a subject would accept a range of size values as true characterizations of the object. This finding clearly suggests that the size feature is accompanied by some indication of permissible variability.

Recent developments in artificial intelligence provide some means for representing feature variability. The key idea amounts to distinguishing between a specification of a relatively abstract fea-

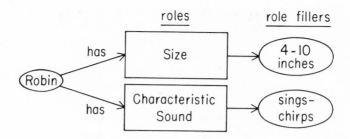

Figure 15 *Feature variability represented in a network (type-token distinction and criteriality weights omitted for simplicity)*

ture (for example, size) and a specification of the range of values that features can take (for example, 16–24 inches). One rendition of this idea is illustrated in Figure 15, which is based on Brachman's recent extension of network representations (1980). In the figure, "size" and "characteristic sound" specify abstract features, while "4–10 inches" and "sings-chirps" specify possible ranges of values for these features. The abstract features are called *roles* and the ranges are referred to as *role fillers*. (The same distinction also characterizes frame representations, where the abstract features are called *slots* and the ranges *slot fillers* — see, for example, Minsky, 1975; Charniak, 1977).[7]

LACK OF CONSTRAINTS

The featural approach to the probabilistic view is clearly a liberalization of the classical view. No longer must we be restricted to elusive defining features, since we can now latch on to any feature that tends to occur with the concept. There may be too much freedom here, however; the probabilistic view may be failing to capture important constraints that are operative in concept acquisition and use. Such constraints include our old friends, necessity and sufficiency, as well as other factors.

Necessary Features

We hinted at one example of a lack of constraints in our earlier discussion of how the present approach handles disjunctive concepts. Let us reiterate the two relevant points:

1. According to any featural model, disjunctive concepts arise because two different instances or subsets of a concept may match two different feature sets of that concept. For example, "furniture" is disjunctive because chair and table match two different feature sets of the concept.

2 . Though there are differences in the feature sets matched by
the instances or subsets, we conjectured that these differences are not great — that is, the degree of disjunctiveness
is generally small. For example, the feature sets of furniture matched by chair and table contain many common
features.

If one accepts these two points, then the problem for the present approach is that there is nothing in it that favors low degrees of
disjunctiveness over high ones. That is, the approach fails to
incorporate constraints that would limit the degree of disjunctiveness.

The solution to this problem, we think, is to require that some
features in a probabilistic representation be necessary but not sufficient. The concept of furniture, for example, may yield only small
degrees of disjunctiveness because a feature like "can be used in living spaces" might be necessary and hence appear in every instance.
Or consider the general concept of "person": here animacy seems to
be a necessary feature, since no one would say "yes" to "Is a manne-
quin a person?" even though mannequins must share many features
with persons. To give still another example, we suspect that very
few people would classify a particular object as a piece of clothing
if they had been told that the object had been manufactured for
some purpose *other* than to be worn by humans.

The examples given above — furniture, person, and clothing — are
all general, superordinate concepts. We chose such concepts to
make our point because they offer the most difficult cases. (Recall
that in studies where subjects list features for concepts, fewer common features are given for superordinates than for concepts at
more specific levels.) When it comes to specific concepts, like chair
and jacket, we think it will be even less problematic to come up
with some necessary-but-not-sufficient features.[8]

One last comment about necessary features: In discussing the
representation of feature variability, we introduced the notion of a
role feature, such as "size" or "characteristic sound" for various
subsets of bird. Some of these roles may qualify as necessary features. Consider size, for example; the property of "having a size"
seems to be necessary, or even essential, for any object. Another
example might be the feature "number of legs," which shows up in
some artificial-intelligence representations of animal concepts
(Fahlman, 1977); while a creature can be an elephant regardless of
the specific number of legs it has, the feature "number of legs" is
clearly always relevant to being an elephant, and perhaps "always
relevant" comes close to being "necessary."

Sufficient Features

It is also possible that many concepts have features that are sufficient for concept membership, but not necessary. We can illustrate with our old favorite, the concept of bird. Any object that (1) is animate, (2) is feathered, and (3) flies, may always be taken to be a bird. Features 1–3 thus form a sufficient set even though one of them — flies — is clearly nonnecessary.

So one restriction we can place on any posited nonnecessary feature is that it be sufficient, or part of a sufficient set. This constraint turns out to be readily expressible in the language of cue validities. Recall that the formula for the cue validity of a feature, F_i, vis-à-vis a target concept, X_j, is given by

$$\begin{matrix} \text{Cue validity} \\ \text{of } F_i \text{ for } X_j \end{matrix} \quad = \quad P(X_j/F_i) \quad = \quad \frac{P(F_i/X_j)}{P(F_i/X_j) + P(F_i/X_k)}$$

where $P(F_i/X_j)$ is the probability of F_i given the target concept, and $P(F_i/X_k)$ is the probability of F_i given the contrast concept. What we have been calling a sufficient feature is one that occurs only with the target concept. In the expression given above, this means that $P(F_i/X_k)$ is 0 and the cue validity of F_i for the target concept is 1.0. Thus restricting a nonnecessary feature to be sufficient amounts to restricting it to have maximal cue validity. Similarly, restricting a set of features to be sufficient means restricting their conjunction to have maximal cue validity (for example, $P(X_j/F_i \cdot F_{i'} \cdot F_{i''})$ must be 1.0).

Regardless of the terminology used to describe it, how realistic a constraint is sufficiency? How likely is it that a nonnecessary feature that has been posited as part of a concept will have a cue validity close to 1.0, either in isolation or as part of a small subset of features? Very likely, we think, if we liberalize the sufficiency constraint by applying it to only one contrast concept at a time. For example, for the concept "bird" the feature of wings does not seem sufficient vis-à-vis the contrast concepts of insects and mammals, since so many insects fly, but this feature is very close to sufficient vis-à-vis just mammals. Thus measuring the sufficiency of a feature against only one contrast concept at a time almost ensures that the constraint will be applicable to many features of concepts. Indeed, the problem with this constraint may be that too many nonnecessary features can meet it.

This suspicion receives some support from studies requiring subjects to list features. Table 9 provides a representative sample of features listed for 12 concepts, all of which are subsets of bird (from

TABLE 9   FEATURE LISTINGS FOR 12 CONCEPTS

Features	Blu[a]	Chi	Fal	Flm	Owl	Pen	Rob	San	Sea	Sta	Swa	Vul
Large	0	0	7	5	4	0	0	0	2	0	0	10
Gray/white	0	8	0	0	0	0	0	0	23	0	0	10
Eats fish	0	0	0	0	0	11	0	0	18	0	0	0
Large wings	0	0	5	2	0	0	0	0	9	0	0	9
Omen/symbol	0	0	0	0	0	0	0	0	0	0	0	0
Sea	0	0	0	12	0	0	0	15	27	0	0	0
Flies	12	0	7	0	0	0	9	5	9	6	7	2
Eggs	4	21	0	0	0	3	5	3	0	0	4	0
Beak	6	5	4	2	0	2	9	16	4	6	6	4
Large beak	0	0	12	9	4	4	0	4	3	0	1	13
Feathers	8	11	10	6	13	2	0	7	5	9	7	10
Black	0	0	6	0	0	0	0	0	0	0	0	20
Nocturnal	0	0	0	0	26	0	0	0	0	0	0	0
Caves	0	0	0	0	0	0	0	0	0	0	0	0
Ugly	0	0	0	0	0	0	0	0	0	0	0	15
Small	14	0	0	0	0	0	10	10	0	13	17	0
Eats insects	9	0	0	0	0	0	20	8	0	4	5	0
Predator	0	0	20	0	0	0	0	0	0	0	0	4

	Sings	Blue	In trees	Barnyard	Can't fly	Pack ground	Is food	Legs	Talons/claws	Sport/hunting	Flies fast	Eats small animals	Pink	Tropical	Long neck	Stands on one leg	Mimic/talk	Noisy	Says "who"	Big eyes
1	0	0	3	0	0	0	0	0	2	0	0	0	0	0	0	0	0	0	0	1
2	4	0	4	0	0	0	0	0	0	0	5	0	0	0	0	0	0	0	0	0
3	3	0	0	0	0	0	0	0	0	0	0	0	0	0	0	0	0	0	0	0
4	0	0	0	0	0	0	0	0	0	0	0	0	0	0	0	0	0	0	9	10
5	6	0	0	0	0	0	5	0	0	0	0	0	0	0	0	0	0	0	0	0
6	11	0	6	0	0	0	0	0	0	0	0	0	0	0	0	0	0	0	0	0
7	0	0	0	0	19	0	0	0	0	0	0	0	0	0	0	0	0	0	0	0
8	0	0	13	0	0	0	0	6	12	0	0	17	0	0	0	0	0	24	16	0
9	0	0	0	3	0	0	17	0	0	0	0	0	23	0	15	13	0	0	0	0
10	0	0	0	0	0	0	0	14	15	11	11	11	0	0	0	0	0	0	0	0
11	0	0	11	14	10	17	2	0	0	0	0	0	0	0	0	0	0	0	0	0
12	12	27	6	0	0	0	0	0	0	0	0	0	0	0	0	0	0	0	0	0

TABLE 9 (CONTINUED)

Features	Blu[a]	Chi	Fal	Flm	Owl	Pen	Rob	San	Sea	Sta	Swa	Vul
Wise	0	0	0	0	16	0	0	0	0	0	0	0
Cold region	0	0	0	0	0	27	0	0	0	0	0	0
Tuxedo	0	0	0	0	0	11	0	0	0	0	0	0
Waddles	0	0	0	0	0	18	0	0	0	0	0	0
Black/white	0	0	0	0	22	25	0	0	0	0	0	0
Swims	0	0	0	0	0	12	0	0	0	0	0	0
Social	0	0	0	0	0	0	0	0	0	0	0	0
Red breast	0	0	0	0	0	0	23	0	0	0	0	0
Spring/seas	0	0	0	0	0	0	16	0	0	0	0	0
Red/brown	0	0	0	0	0	0	16	0	0	0	0	0
Gray/brown	0	0	0	0	0	0	0	14	0	0	11	0
Beach	0	0	0	0	0	0	0	21	0	0	0	0
Scavenger	0	0	0	0	0	0	0	0	7	0	0	10
Eats dead	0	0	0	0	0	0	0	0	0	0	0	22
Circles overhead	0	0	0	0	0	0	0	0	0	0	0	13

Source: After Malt and Smith (1981b).

a. Blu = bluebird; Chi = chicken; Fal = falcon; Flm = flamingo; Pen =penguin; Rob = robin; San = sandpiper; Sea = seagull; Sta = starling; Swa = swallow; Vul = vulture.

Malt and Smith, 1981b). The column heads give the abbreviated names of the 12 concepts, the leftmost column specifies all the features, and each numerical entry reflects how often a particular feature was listed for a particular concept by 30 subjects. Any row that includes only one numerical entry indicates that the feature corresponding to that row was listed for only one concept. Such a feature is sufficient vis-à-vis any other concept in the table that can be assumed to contrast with the concept of interest. About half the features listed meet this criterion of sufficiency. Of course, if we had included more subsets of bird there would have been fewer features listed for only one concept, but a glance at some of the features listed (for example, "circles overhead," "stands on one leg") suggests that they would be unique even with a larger sample of birds.

Though the above argument about sufficiency is tenuous, because of the questionable validity of feature listings, it at least suggests the need to look at other constraints on nonnecessary features.

Other Constraints

The remaining ways to constrain nonnecessary features are largely empirical. The best way to proceed is to use several different empirical means to uncover nonnecessary features and hope that these divergent methods will converge on the same feature set for a given concept. The methods we have in mind are the standard ones: (1) the analytic use of intuitions that linguists have employed in their search for necessary features (for example, Fillmore, 1971; Katz, 1972); (2) feature listings like those discussed throughout this book; (3) multidimensional scaling techniques, such as those used by Henle (1969), Rips, Shoben, and Smith (1973), and Caramazza, Hersch, and Torgerson (1976) to uncover nonnecessary features of animal concepts; and (4) clustering techniques, particularly those of Sattath and Tversky (1977) and Shepard and Arabie (1979), which seem especially well suited for discovering features of partially nested concepts. One could argue that none of these methods has a great track record for uncovering features, but the convergent use of all methods might turn up more important results. Furthermore, when the conjunctive results of these techniques are combined with our liberalized sufficiency constraint, there is even more hope of coming up with nonnecessary features that offer non–ad hoc explanations of existent phenomena and that generate new predictions about natural concepts.

CONTEXT EFFECTS

The only context effects we have mentioned are the priming results discussed in conjunction with the spreading activation model.

But context effects are far more widespread than this, and featural models of the probabilistic view have had relatively little to say about them. Perhaps this is as it should be. After all, the models we have discussed deal only with the categorization function of concepts, while many context effects may arise when concepts are used for some other function, such as for the construction of propositional representations. Or to put it another way, the models of current interest deal with the representation and use of single concepts, not with procedures for combining concepts, yet the origin of many context effects may reside in combinatorial procedures (Smith, 1978).

While this defense of featural models from the onslaught of context effects clearly has merit, it seems too extreme even to our ears. Specifically, there may be some context effects that hinge only on the representation and use of single concepts, and thus that fall within the domain of this book. In what follows, we consider two such context effects. The first effect seems to reflect some temporary changes in the features of a concept; the second appears to result from the phenomenon of two different concepts underlying the same term, particularly superordinate terms.[9]

Temporary Changes in Features

When the same concept is used in slightly different sentential contexts, different features of it seem to become more accessible for the moment. This phenomenon is nicely illustrated by the following pair of sentences (taken from Barclay et al., 1974): "The man lifted the piano" and "The man tuned the piano." The sentence containing "lifted" seems to make the "heavy weight" feature of piano very accessible, whereas the "tuned" sentence does the same thing for the "produces music" feature of piano. And our intuition about what feature is most accessible in each context is bolstered by the experimental findings of Barclay and his colleagues. They presented statements like the above sentences and probed subjects' memories by cues such as "heavy" or "musical"; they found, for example, that "heavy" was a better cue than "musical" for the "lifted" sentence, while the ordering of cue effectiveness was reversed for the "tuned" sentence.

We know of no explicit attempt to account for these findings in a featural model, but it turns out to be a relatively easy task for the spreading activation model. When "The man lifted the piano" is presented, the concept of piano is activated along with its features "heavy weight" and "produces music." Another concept activated is that of "lifted," an action concept, and we assume that one of its features is weight. A feature having to do with weight is therefore activated by two concepts mentioned in the sentence, and all we need assume is that the more activation a feature receives, the more accessible it is. A similar analysis works for "The man tuned the piano." Here a feature concerned with music will have two sources of activation — one from the concept "piano," the other from the action concept "tuned" — and this feature will now be the most accessible.

This analysis of context effects is similar to one presented in Smith (1978), where it was pointed out that the analysis bogs down in many cases. We can illustrate with an example from Anderson and Ortony (1975): Compare the interpretation of the concept of container in "The container held the cola" versus that in "The container held the apples." In the "cola" sentence the concept of container seems to mean bottle, whereas in the "apples" sentence container appears to mean something like basket. If we apply our previous spreading activation analysis to the "cola" sentence we can start to see some of the problems. When "container" is presented there will be activation of the feature "can hold liquid," while the presentation of "cola" will activate features like "liquid" and "comes in a bottle," with the last two features being related. Somehow cola's feature of "comes in a bottle" is temporarily transferred to container. The details of this transfer mechanism, however, are obscure. Things are even stickier with the "apples" sentence. While one feature of container might be "can hold solid objects," it seems totally implausible to attribute to apple a feature like "comes in a basket"; so we do not even have a feature of apples that can be temporarily transferred to container so as to give it the intended interpretation.

The point is that the spreading activation model can handle temporary changes in the accessibility of existent features of a concept but has difficulty coping with a temporary transfer of features from one concept to the other. Since something like feature transfer seems to underlie many context effects, this difficulty is a serious one.

Two Different Concepts for the Same Term

Let us consider the term "animal." In some sentential contexts, such as "This planet has many animals," the concept denoted by animal seems to have its intended general meaning of any living, animate creature. In other contexts, such as "This zoo has many animals," animal is more likely to denote a much more restricted concept, roughly equivalent to mammals. The same kind of ambiguity is true of the term "plant." In a context like "This planet has many plants," the activated concept captures all kinds of vegetation; but in a context like "This apartment has many plants," the activated concept is far more restricted, roughly to house plants.

In short, certain terms designating superordinate object concepts seem to be ambiguous, denoting both a general class and a specific subset of that class, and which concept gets activated depends on the context. If this characterization of the phenomenon is correct, our featural model will have to posit two concepts for, say, animal, as well as specifying a process by which context can selectively pick out one of these concepts. Such a process may be hard to come by. How, for example, would a spreading activation process trigger the general concept of animal given the word "planet," but the specific concept of animal given "zoo"? No doubt the process would make use of connections between zoo and the specific concept of animal (either totally feature-based connections or direct access links between concepts), but it is not clear how to come up with an account that is not ad hoc.

It is not even clear that our ambiguity characterization of the phenomenon is correct. The reason for our suspicion is that something like the phenomenon of interest seems to occur with almost all superordinate terms and with some terms at a more specific level. For example, "vehicle," a superordinate term intended to cover various means of transportation, can take on a more restricted meaning (for example, motorized vehicles) in the right context ("We need a vehicle to get to Boston"). And bird, a less inclusive term than animal, can also be given a more restricted meaning in certain contexts, for example, "We need a bird for the holiday meal." These observations suggest that true ambiguity may not be involved here; rather, context may again do its magical work by temporarily changing the features of concepts, sometimes causing an increase in accessibility and sometimes causing a transfer. If so, we are back to the first type of context effect.

We can do little more than spell out these alternatives and difficulties. Accounting for context effects is clearly a major task, and it is not certain how much success we can expect when our theoretical machinery is restricted to that developed for handling "simple" categorization.

A Note on Transformations of Features

We have assumed throughout that the representation of a concept consists entirely of a description in terms of properties. However, it has sometimes been argued that property descriptions are only half the story of concept representations; the other half is a set of transformations that specify which alterations of the property description can count as instances of the concept. Since this idea has often been developed in relation to descriptions consisting of nonnecessary features (see Pick, 1965; Franks and Bransford, 1971; Lasky and Kallio, 1978), this section seems the appropriate place to comment on the role of transformations. As we will see, though, some aspects of the transformation idea do not completely fit with our general assumptions about probabilistic representations.

An experiment by Franks and Bransford (1971) illustrates the notion of transformations. The subjects' task was first to learn to sort instances into artificial concepts and then to categorize novel instances into those concepts. Sample instances from one of the concepts are given in Figure 16. We will refer to the topmost instance as the *Base*. It consists of two *major constituents*: (1) a small triangle superimposed on a large square and (2) a small diamond superimposed on a large circle. Each major constituent itself includes two *minor constituents*; for example, the first major constituent includes as minor constituents (1) a small triangle and (2) a large square. All the other instances in Figure 16 were generated by systematically transforming the Base's major or minor constituents: the second instance was generated by permuting the order of the Base's major constituents; the third instance was constructed by taking the Base's first major constituent and reversing the roles of its minor constituents; the fourth instance was generated by deleting the square from the Base's first major constituent; and the fifth instance was constructed by replacing one of the Base's minor constituents, the small triangle, with a new form. Thus each of the last four instances differs from the Base by one transformation — permutation, role reversal, deletion, or replacement. The remaining instances in Figure 16 differ from the Base by two transformations. The sixth instance, for example, was generated by first permuting the order of the major constituents in the Base, and then reversing the roles of the minor constituents of one of the majors.

The upshot is that the instances of a concept vary with respect to their transformational distance from the Base — for example, 0 transformations (the Base itself), 1 transformation (the second through fifth instances in Figure 16), or 2 transformations (the sixth and seventh instances in Figure 16). And the critical finding of the Franks and Bransford study was that the less the transformational distance between a novel instance and the Base, the more likely subjects were to categorize that instance correctly. This finding suggests that subjects were actually applying these transformations during categorization.

How exactly would the concept used in the Franks and Bransford study be represented? Figure 17 supplies an answer. The top half

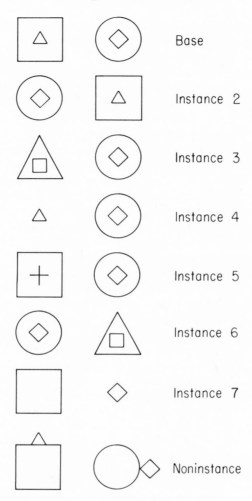

Figure 16   *A transformational concept (after Franks and Bransford, 1971)*

contains a description of the Base in terms of a network of features, and the bottom half lists the permissible transformations. Any pattern that can be generated by applying a sequence of these transformations to the Base is an instance of the concept. With such a representation, the most natural process model for a categorization task would go as follows: To determine whether or not a test item belongs to a target concept, one accesses the representation of the concept and determines whether or not the test item can be generated by applying the concept's transformations to the concept's Base.

Given this specific example, we can see which aspects of the representation are compatible with our general assumptions about the probabilistic view and which are not. First, let us discuss the compatible ones. There are no necessary features in the representation in Figure 17, because the deletion or replacement transformation, even when restricted to a single application, can remove any feature from the Base yet still yield an instance of the concept. More generally, a concept containing a transformation that can work directly on any feature of the Base will have no necessary features. What about concepts with transformations that operate only on relations between features, such as permutation or role reversal? Such concepts can have necessary features but not sufficient ones. For if the transformations operate on relations between features, the relations themselves must be among the criteria for concept membership, and this means that features per se cannot offer sufficient conditions. This idea is illustrated by the noninstance in Figure 16; it contains all the features used to describe the Base (a small triangle, a large square, and so on), but it is not an instance because the relations between its features cannot be generated by applying the permissible transformations to the Base. Thus concepts with transformations lack either necessary features or sufficient ones.

Now let us consider those aspects of a transformationally represented concept that are incompatible, or at least less compatible,

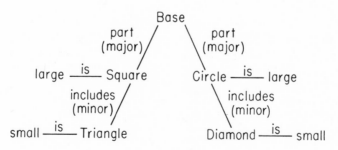

Transformations
(each can be applied only once)

Permute order of major constituents
Reverse role of minor constituents within a major
Delete any minor constituent
Replace any minor constituent with plus sign

Figure 17 *Transformational representation of the concept used in Franks and Bransford study (1971)*

with our general assumptions about probabilistic representations. First there is the Base description itself: while it can be a summary over instances, it can also be a specific instance, as it was in the Franks and Bransford study. This of course is unlike our usual probabilistic representations, which must be summary representations. (Note though, that even when the Base corresponds to a specific instance, the entire representation — Base plus transformations — meets our criteria for a summary representation: it is the result of an abstraction process, it does not correspond to a specific instance, and it is always used to determine concept membership).

Next let us consider the transformations. It is they that do most of the theoretical work, not feature matching or feature activation processes as in other probabilistic models we considered. Thus, under the present scheme, an instance is typical to the extent that it differs from its appropriate Base by few transformations, and typical instances are categorized faster because few time-consuming transformations are needed to establish concept membership. Accounts of many of the other phenomena we have been concerned with (for example, disjunctive concepts, similarity ratings for nested triples) would likewise invoke the transformations one way or another. Including transformations in concept representations thus causes some major changes in the featural approach to the probabilistic view. (It would cause equally major changes in any of the other approaches or views we have considered or will consider.) And some of these changes raise new problems; in particular, in addition to the usual problems of constraining features, we now have to worry about constraining transformations.

We have even fewer ideas about the set of possible transformations for natural concepts than we do about the set of possible features for such concepts. With the exception of Pittenger and Shaw's work (1975) on the categorization of faces, there have been strikingly few attempts to specify the transformations relevant to any natural concept. Given that the notion of transformations carries with it a lot of sticky problems, why bother to go beyond the usual featural approach and posit transformations at all? Or to put it another way, is there any evidence that compels us to opt for a transformational model over a strictly featural one, even in a limited domain? For natural object concepts we lack such evidence. The closest we can come to it is the proposal of Nelson (1974) that object concepts are best defined in terms of their function — for example, the concept of a ball is defined by the facts that it rolls in a certain fashion and traces out a certain trajectory when thrown. These changes of state can be construed as transformations of the features of a ball. But it is not clear that such a construal would be in keeping with the spirit of Nelson's proposals (that is, the concept core might contain the function of an object but not the specific transformations needed to execute this function); nor is it even clear that Nelson's arguments for the primacy of function are all that compelling (see, for example, Gentner, 1978). Thus we are left without a firm rationale for positing transformations as a critical part of natural concepts. Future work, however, could easily alter this conclusion.

5 | The Probabilistic View: Dimensional Approach

O
UR TREATMENT OF the dimensional approach will par-
allel that of the featural approach. Many issues in the two
approaches are the same, and there are some striking
similarities in how the approaches account for problematic findings. We will also discuss the important differences between the
two approaches.

Representational Assumptions

As usual, the first assumption is that the representation of a concept is a summary description that applies to all of its instances.
The second assumption has two parts: (1) any dimension used to
represent a concept must be a salient one, some of whose values
have a substantial probability of occurring in instances of the concept; and (2) the value of a dimension represented in a concept is
the (subjective) average of the values of the concept's subsets or instances on this dimension.[1]

The first important point about the second assumption is that it
says more than the comparable assumption in the featural approach. Part 1 is the dimensional equivalent of the featural assumption (which posited that the features representing a concept are
salient ones that tend to occur in instances of the concept), while
part 2 tells us something more. Knowing only that a dimension is
represented in a concept does not tell us what particular value of
that dimension is represented, so part 2 is needed to specify the unknown value. (Note that this kind of information was not needed in
the featural approach because once we know a feature is included
in a representation, we immediately know its "value" — namely the
feature itself.)

It is of interest to compare other aspects of the present assump-

Robin	Chicken	Bird
1.0 animacy – animate	1.0 animacy – animate	1.0 animacy – animate
.7 size – s_R	.7 size – s_C	.5 size – s_B
.4 ferocity – f_R	.4 ferocity – f_C	.5 ferocity – f_B

Figure 18 *Probabilistic dimensional representations. Lowercase letters (for example, s, f) designate specific values on a dimension*

tion to those of its featural counterpart. Figure 18 presents dimensional representations of some of the same animal concepts that were used to illustrate the featural approach. Just as the featural approach includes nonnecessary features for concepts, so the current approach contains some nonnecessary dimensions. One example is the dimension of size, another the dimension of ferocity. Each is represented in the concept of bird, along with a particular value that is the subjective average of the size or ferocity values of its instances and subsets. Again, we have departed from the critical assumption of the classical view that only necessary conditions are represented. Again, though, we leave open the possibility that some dimension values are necessary ones; for example, the value of animate on the two-valued dimension of animacy is associated with all subsets of bird.

In the featural approach we used weights to indicate the contribution of each feature to concept membership. We can also use weights in the dimensional approach, as shown in Figure 18. Each weight indicates the importance of variations in the associated dimension for concept membership. For example, for the concept of robin, a higher weight for the size dimension than for the ferocity dimension means that one is less likely to classify a specific item as a robin if it has an inappropriate size value than an inappropriate ferocity value.

The most obvious way in which the dimensional approach departs from the featural one is in its treatment of continuous dimensions, such as size. In the present approach each physically continuous dimension is represented as a psychologically continuous one; consequently, the difference between two concepts, or between a concept and a specific instance, is a matter of continuous degrees. And because each dimension is continuous, a concept learner may combine the values of various instances or subsets by taking their mean on each dimension. The upshot is that each concept depicts the *average* or *mean* dimension values of a class, in contrast to the featural approach, where each concept depicts the *modal* features of its class. This difference between a mean property and a modal one has a major psychological implication. If a concept contains average properties, it may be maximally similar to an instance whose properties are totally novel but happen to match the average values for that class; in contrast, an instance with totally novel properties will be maximally dissimilar to a concept that contains modal properties, since every feature of the instance will mismatch those of the concept. Thus the dimensional and featural approaches to the probabilistic view are in diametric opposition on a critical point. It should now be clear why the two approaches must be kept distinct, even though both approaches assume that a concept is a measure of central tendency (mean or mode).

The two assumptions discussed above are sufficient to describe a dimensional representation. However, many researchers employing the dimensional approach have invoked a third, and very powerful, assumption about representations. Roughly, it is as follows: Concepts having the same relevant dimensions can be

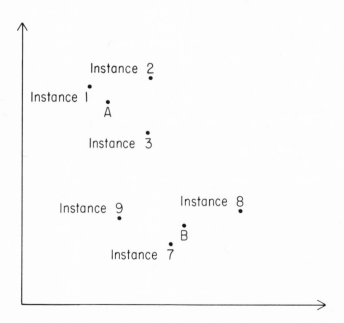

Figure 19 *A multidimensional metric space*

represented as points in a multidimensional *metric space*. Figure 19 should help to illustrate this assumption. It is assumed that the two dimensions in Figure 19 are the only relevant ones for concepts A and B, and that these dimensions are also relevant to the instances of A and B. Given this, it seems reasonable to depict each concept or instance by a single point in a multidimensional space. The space is constructed by an orthogonal arrangement of the two dimensions, and the point corresponding to an item is defined by the values it takes on the two dimensions. What does this buy us? Thus far, little more than a pictorial way of showing the dimension values that represent various items. Such a multidimensional description, however, can be given great power by assuming that the space is metric.

Ordinary physical space is one example of a metric space. More precisely, for a space to be metric means that (1) the distance between any point and itself is identical for all points (this aspect is called *minimality*); (2) the distance measured from point 1 to point 2 is identical to that measured from point 2 to point 1 (*symmetry*); and (3) given points 1, 2, and 3, the distance between any pair of them, for example, $d(1, 2)$, must be less than the sum of the other two pairwise distances, for example, $d(1, 3) + d(2, 3)$ (*triangular inequality*). It follows, then, if a space like that in Figure 19 is assumed to be metric, the relation between any pair of concepts or instances can be interpreted solely in terms of the distance between the corresponding pair of points. Models of categorization can now be based on distance computations rather than on probability computations, a major change from featural models.

We therefore have two kinds of dimensional representations, those that assume metric spaces and those that do not. The metric representations are of greater interest to us for two reasons. First, most researchers who have taken the dimensional approach to concept representations have used metric spaces; and second, the difference between processes operating on featural versus dimensional representations is far greater when we consider metric representations. In view of this, our treatment of categorization models will first briefly consider models that do not assume metric representations and then deal in depth with models that do make this assumption.

Models Based on the Dimensional Approach

Models without the Metric Assumption

While we know of no major models based on the dimensional approach that do not assume metric representations, it is easy enough to construct one. Its representations would look like those illustrated in Figure 18: for every concept, there would be a list of its relevant dimensions, the weights associated with them, and the average value for each dimension. To implement a processing model here, we might first assume that when one compares corresponding dimension values of a target concept and test item (for example, the average size values of bird and robin), one determines if the difference between the values is within some tolerable limit. If it is, the values are said to match; if not, the values mismatch. Given this, the critical processing assumption for categorization is virtually identical to that used in the general featural model, namely: An entity X is categorized as an instance or subset of concept Y if and only if the weights of the dimensions of Y matched by X exceed some critical sum. To illustrate, if n of bird's dimension values are close enough to robin's corresponding values to count as matches, and if the summed weights of these n dimensions exceed some threshold, then robin is categorized as a subset of bird.

What we have done is to assume that dimensional comparisons can be treated like feature comparisons — match versus no match — which allows us to use a categorization process like that used with features. In essence, we have "featurized" dimensional representations. It should come as no surprise that the model just described would handle all relevant empirical phenomena in precisely the same way as the general featural model.

We can remain more faithful to the spirit of dimensional representations in constructing a model of categorization. Instead of each comparison of dimension values yielding a match or mismatch, we may assume that each comparison yields a number that reflects the actual difference in values. Then the inverse of this number (we use the inverse so that a comparison of values yields a higher number for like than unlike values) could be multiplied by the weight associated with the dimension. The product would then be used as input to a counter, which accumulates similar computations until either a positive or a negative threshold is reached indicating the test item is or is not a member of the target concept. This model is also very similar to the general featural model: again, weighted degrees-of-matches are being cumulated over property comparisons, and again the model would handle the major empirical phenomena in the same manner as the general featural model.

Thus as long as the computations performed on dimensional representations are made on a component-by-component basis, the resulting models look similar to those developed for feature representations. For dimensional models that truly differ from their featural counterparts, we need to consider metric representations.

MODELS WITH THE METRIC ASSUMPTION

The Simple Distance Model

Figure 20 illustrates a metric, multidimensional space. It is essentially the same as Figure 19 (except for a few wrinkles), and again the relation between any pair of concepts or instances is given by the distance between the corresponding pair of points. To construct a categorization model, we can couple this representation with the following assumption: An entity X is categorized as an instance or subset of concept Y if and only if the metric distance between X and Y is less than some threshold distance. We will refer to the present proposal as the *simple distance* model. It has been discussed (though not favored) by Reed (1972) and Palmer (1978), explicitly used by Rosch, Simpson, and Miller (1976), and sometimes implicitly used in studies of natural concepts (Rips, Shoben, and Smith, 1973) and of artificial concepts (Hyman and Frost, 1975).

Figure 20 illustrates some consequences of the assumption given above. The threshold distance for membership in either concept is *r*—any item less than *r* units from A is an instance of A, while any item less than *r* units from B is an instance of B. Items 1–3 are therefore instances of A; items 7–9 are instances of B; and items 4–6, as we shall see, are unclear cases. Note that the categorization process

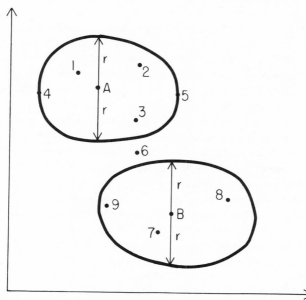

Figure 20 *How a multidimensional metric representation can be used in a categorization model*

does not need explicitly to consider the dimension values of each concept and instance; these values are implicit in the location of the instance or concept in the space. All that must be explicitly considered are the points designating the test item and target concept, and the metric distance between them. It is for this reason that proponents of metric representations sometimes hold that concepts are processed as units; that is, the points corresponding to concepts are not decomposed into their component properties during categorization.

The simple distance model has one more assumption: The closer item X is to concept Y, the faster and more accurately X will be categorized as a member of Y. For example, in Figure 20 item 1 is closer to A than is item 2, so 1 will be categorized as an instance of A more efficiently. This assumption gives the model a way of treating instances of a concept differentially, which is a hallmark of probabilistic models.

Explanation of Problematic Findings

Like the featural models discussed in the previous section, the simple distance model accounts for most of the basic phenomena that troubled the classical view. (The present model bogs down only on the results of Rosch and Mervis, 1975, as discussed below.)

Disjunctive concepts. Since two members of a concept can have different dimension values yet both be within the critical distance of the concept, it follows that different values can be used to determine membership in the same concept. In Figure 20, for example, items 2 and 3 share no dimension values but are exactly the same distance from A, and both are instances of this concept.

Unclear cases. An unclear case might arise whenever the potential instance is right at the threshold distance for a concept, or is at an equal distance from more than one concept, or both. A glance at Figure 20 shows that items 4 and 5 are unclear cases of concept A because each falls roughly *r* units away from this concept. Item 6 is an unclear case because it is equidistant from A and B without being within the threshold distance for either.

Failure to specify defining conditions. The representations of the present approach require only values that are correlated with concept membership, not defining conditions.

Simple typicality effects. The critical assumption needed here is similar to that used in the featural approach: the typicality of an instance reflects how close its dimension values are to the average values of its class, where the latter constitute the concept representation. This assumption provides a basis for typicality ratings. Furthermore, concept members whose values are close to the average will be close to the concept representation in a multidimensional space, and thus will be classified faster and more accurately than members further away from the concept. There is some direct support for these assumptions in the multidimensional scaling results reported by Rips, Shoben, and Smith (1973) and Rosch and Mervis (1975). In these solutions, general concepts (for example, birds, fruits, tools) tended to fall in the center of the space of instances, lending credence to the assumption that concepts represent an average over their members. Also, typical members were usually closer to their respective concepts than were atypical members. Other simple typicality effects would require the same assumptions as used in the featural approach—for example, typical items are named before atypical ones when concept members are being listed, because typical items are more similar to the concept.

Determinants of typicality. We run into a snag when it comes to accounting for Rosch and Mervis's finding (1975) that for both natural and artificial concepts, an item is a typical member of a concept to the extent that it contains properties shared by many other members. The problem for the simple distance model, and for any model based on the dimensional approach, is that most of Rosch and Mervis's properties look like features, not dimension values. To illustrate, some of the properties listed for the concept of chair include the following: legs, seat, back, arms, and holds people.[2] Each of these properties seems like something that an entity either has or does not have—like a feature—and not like one of several possible values along a dimension. The problem is even more severe with Rosch and Mervis's artificial concepts, where each instance is a letter string and a property is the presence of a particular letter in the string. This kind of property seems to capture perfectly the notion of a feature and to be at odds with the construct of a dimension value.

Use of nonnecessary conditions. Nonnecessary dimension values are built into a concept's representation.

Nested concepts. Recall that for nested triples the specific concept (for example, robin) was usually judged more similar to its immediate superordinate (bird) than to its distant one (animal); but there were some exceptions—for instance, chicken was judged more similar to animal than to bird. Figure 21 provides a multidimensional representation that is consistent with these findings: robin is less distant from bird than from animal, while chicken is more distant from bird than from animal. Since categorization processes operate on these distances, with categorization time increasing with the distance between concept and superordinate, the representation in Figure 21 is also consistent with the fact that

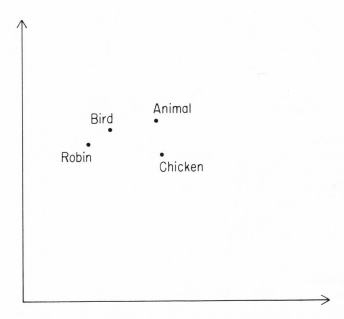

Figure 21 *Representation that can explain similarity ratings for nested triples*

categorization times show the same pattern of results as similarity ratings. It is worth pointing out that since the distance in Figure 21 themselves rest on the similarity of dimension values, the present account of nested triples reduces to assumptions that robin's values are closer to those of bird than animal, while the reverse holds for chicken's values. When the matter is stated this way, it is obvious that the present dimensional account parallels the earlier featural one.

The Comparative Distance Model

A problem with the simple distance model is that it does not consider the influence of contrasting concepts (Rosch and Mervis, 1975). Just as we had to alter featural models to include contrast information, we must now amend our dimensional model: we need to assume that categorization considers not only the distance between the test item and target concept, but also the distance between the test item and concepts that contrast with the target. Thus the two categorization assumptions of the simple distance model are replaced by the following: (1) an entity X is categorized as an instance or subset of concept Y if and only if the metric distance between X and Y is less than that between X and any concept that contrasts with Y, and (2) the greater the difference in distance between X and Y on the one hand, and X and any contrast of Y on the other, the faster and more accurately X will be categorized as a member of Y.

These new assumptions can again be illustrated by Figure 20 (see p. 107). A and B are now assumed to be contrasting concepts. Consider item 1 in the figure : it will be classified as an instance of concept A because the absolute distance between 1 and A, $|\text{item } 1 - A|$, is less than that between 1 and B, $|\text{item } 1 - B|$. That is, the difference between the distances, $\{|\text{item } 1 - B| - |\text{item } 1 - A|\}$, is positive and therefore favors concept A. Item 2 will also be categorized as an instance of A, since the difference between the distances, $\{|\text{item } 2 - B| - |\text{item } 2 - A|\}$, again favors A. But item 2 will not be categorized as quickly as item 1, since the difference between the relevant distances is greater when 1 is the instance, that is, $\{|\text{item } 1 - B| - |\text{item } 1 - A|\} > \{|\text{item } 2 - B| - |\text{item } 2 - A|\}$. So far the ordering of categorization times is the same as when computed the simple distance of an instance from its appropriate concept. But a comparison of items 2 and 3 shows how the new assumptions can lead to a change in the predicted ordering. While items 2 and 3 are equally distant from A, item 3 is somewhat closer to B, and consequently 3 will take longer to classify as an instance of A. In terms of the actual differences between distances, $\{|\text{item } 2 - B| - |\text{item } 2 - A|\} > \{|\text{item } 3 - B| - |\text{item } 3 - A|\}$.

Because it relies on a difference between distances, we refer to this model as the *comparative distance* model. It would account for the seven empirical phenomena reviewed earlier in the same fashion as its simple distance predecessor, except that simple distances are replaced by differences between distances. The comparative distance model has been considered by Palmer (1978) and others, and championed by Reed (1972). Reed compared the model to a host of other featural and dimensional models and found that it provided a good account of the acquisition of artificial concepts. The concepts were schematic faces that had been created by variations in a few continuous dimensions (for example, height of nose and eyes). An obvious implication is that a dimensional model works well when the conceptual domain is truly dimensionalized. Later, when we contrast the dimensional and featural approaches, we will have cause to question this implication.

Summary of Metric Models

Despite fundamental differences between metric-dimensional and featural representations of concepts — continuous dimensions versus discrete features, average values versus modal features, distance versus probabilistic computations — there are many similarities between the models based on these two approaches. Both types of models do the following:

1 .   Explain the use of nonnecessary properties, and the difficulty of specifying defining ones, by using representations that require only nonnecessary properties (this, of course, follows from their being based on the probabilistic view).
2.   Allow for degrees of disjunctiveness by permitting different combinations of properties to yield the same threshold quantity, this quantity being expressed as a weighted feature sum in featural models and as a distance (or difference between distances) in metric-dimensional models.
3.   Construe unclear cases to be items that do not quite reach the threshold quantity, or that are equally close to the thresholds of more than one concept.
4 .   Explain many simple typicality effects by assuming that the typicality of a member reflects how similar its properties are to those of its parent concept.
5 .   Account for data on nested triples by assuming that the properties of most concepts are more similar to those of their immediate than their distant superordinates, but that there are exceptions where these similarity relations reverse.
6 .   Explain the use of contrast concepts by considering the relation between a test item and its contrast concepts, either implicitly (cue validities as feature weights) or explicitly (computing differences between distances).

Given this list of similar assumptions, it is not surprising that dimensional models account for many of the phenomena that featural models handled.

Criticisms of the Dimensional Approach

The dimensional approach also resembles the featural one with regard to its shortcomings. Once more there are problems in (1) representing all the knowledge in concepts, particularly relations between properties, (2) constraining possible properties, and (3) explaining context effects. All these problems arise whether or not one makes the metric assumption. However, when one does make this assumption, a fourth problem occurs — namely, difficulties in reconciling aspects of metric spaces and distances with known aspects of concepts and categorization.

REPRESENTING MORE KNOWLEDGE IN CONCEPTS

Earlier we illustrated the problem of representing more knowledge in concepts by noting that the features "small" and "sings" tend to be correlated across instances of the concept bird. The same problem remains when "small" and "sings" are interpreted as dimension values. However, the two solutions proposed for representing interfeature relations—conjunctive features and labeled relations—cannot be generalized wholesale to the dimensional approach. It would make little sense, for instance, to posit a conjunctive dimension that would represent combined values of size and singing ability. How could one order the intermediate values along such a dimension? Where, for example, would "small-but-doesn't-sing" fall in relation to "large-and-sings"?

Difficulties also arise when we try to apply the idea of labeled relations to dimensional representations. If the representation is nonmetric, we could posit a labeled relation between pairs of dimensions—for example, size and singing ability would be connected by the label *correlation*. But then we are no longer construing dimensions to be orthogonal factors. If the representation is assumed to be metric, we run into the difficulty that all computations are based on interpoint distances, and we are not at all sure of the best way to express something like a correlation solely in terms of distance.[3]

A more promising approach to representing correlations is suggested by a paper of Krumhansl (1978). In her work, the psychological distance between two points depends not only on the metric distance between them, but also on the density of points in the region of the two critical ones. If two dimensions have correlated values, the points in the two-dimensional space may form certain clusters or dense regions—for example, for birds, many points in the region defined by "small" and "sings" and many points in the region corresponding to "large" and "doesn't sing." Consequently, the psychological distance between items that possess correlated values will differ from that between items with uncorrelated values, since density is greater in the former than the latter case. In this way, correlations between values could be represented directly in the dimensional approach. It is hard to tell how good a solution this is, however, since the idea of density affecting distance is still quite novel.

The dimensional approach seems to manage better when it comes to representing people's knowledge about the variability in permissible dimension values. The obvious move is to represent each concept by a distribution of possible values on each relevant dimension. Since each distribution would be a probability density function, some values in it could be far more likely than others. This kind of move would have implications for categorization models. For nonmetric models, we might posit that one would still compare dimension values during categorization, but now the value for each dimension would be a sample from the relevant distribution. For metric models, the final representation of a concept might consist of a distribution over the points in a space, and the categorization process would sample one point from each concept distribution and compute the relevant distance. Although this proposal seems viable, it greatly increases the complexity of a metric representation. This is particularly unfortunate because a major virtue of current metric representations is their use of simple visual displays to make relations between concepts transparent.

Lack of Constraints

There is little new to be said here about the issue of constraints. All the issues involved in specifying constraints in the featural approach are equally relevant to the dimensional approach. Thus the dimensional approach permits any degree of disjunctiveness for a concept, even though most natural concepts seem to have low degrees. Again, this suggests the need to specify some necessary dimension values for concepts (or at least some necessary range of values along particular dimensions). Similarly, the dimensional approach requires further constraints on what nonnecessary dimension values can contribute to concept representations. And once more we may want to restrict such values by imposing a sufficiency criterion, or by using methodological techniques like multidimensional scaling.

Context Effects

In regard to context effects, the situation here again resembles that with the featural approach. Little has been done in the analysis of context effects, but we can identify some possible starting points. For nonmetric models, where the categorizer compares concepts on a component-by-component basis, some context effects may again be attributed to a momentary increase in the accessibility of a component. Let us consider a previous example: In the sentence, "The man lifted the piano," the dimension of weight is activated by both "lifted" and "piano"; consequently this dimension, and the relatively extreme value both concepts take on it, becomes more accessible. For metric models, where the categorizer considers only distances, a different procedure is needed. Here we might expect that one concept activates another to the extent that the two are close together in space. It is as if the processor has to travel through a space, so a concept that is in the vicinity of previously processed ones can be handled quickly and efficiently (Hutchinson and Lockhead, 1977). This spatial metaphor nicely captures the general fact that the immediate context influences present processing of a concept; but it is not at all clear how to handle specific context effects like that illustrated by the "piano" sentence.

DISADVANTAGES OF THE USE OF METRIC SPACES

In introducing the idea that concepts can be represented in a metric space, we noted that we were going beyond the assumption that concepts are represented by the average values of their members. The metric assumption implies that any concept can be represented by a single point and that the dissimilarity between any pair of points is given by the metric distance between them. It is time to assess the potential liabilities of these added assumptions.

Problems with Metric Distances

Recall that to posit that a space is metric is to make the following assumptions about distances: (1) minimality, that is, the distance between any point and itself is identical for all points; (2) symmetry, that is, the distance measured from point 1 to point 2 is identical to that measured from 2 to 1; and (3) triangular inequality, which says that the distance between points 1 and 3 must be less than the sum of the distances between points 1 and 2 and points 2 and 3. The problem is that none of these assumptions may be psychologically valid.

The most elegant challenge to the metric assumptions comes from Tversky (1977), who provides some empirical evidence against each assumption. For instance, minimality is challenged by the well-known finding that the probability of judging two identical objects as "same" rather than "different" is not constant for all objects in a domain. If the objects are geometric objects, for example, the probability of a correct "same" judgment decreases with the complexity of the objects (see Nickerson, 1972, for a review). This suggests that the distance between any point and itself increases with the dimensionality of the point. The symmetry assumption is challenged by the many asymmetries that Tversky has turned up in his experimental studies. When asked to rate the similarity between pairs of countries, for example, subjects consistently rate North Korea as being more similar to Red China than Red China is to North Korea. The triangular inequality also has many counterexamples. To take another example from Tversky's 1977 paper, Jamaica is similar to Cuba (presumably because of geographical proximity); Cuba is similar to Russia (presumably because of political affinity); but Jamaica and Russia are not similar at all (that is, the distance between Jamaica and Russia is greater than the sum of the distances between (1) Jamaica and Cuba and (2) Cuba and Russia).

Tversky's criticisms are not the last word on the matter. Krumhansl (1978) has argued that the problems Tversky attributes to metric representations may really reflect the processes that operate on these representations; hence, metric representations may still be very robust. Though many of Krumhansl's arguments are ingenious, there is little independent support for them, and it seems academic to rehash them here. At the very least, Tversky's criticisms should at least make one uncomfortable about metric distances as the basis of categorization.

Can All Concepts be Treated as Single Points?

Given a metric-space representation, it is common to assume that the similarity between two concepts can be captured by the simple, euclidean distance between their corresponding points, which in turn suggests that each concept is processed as a unitary whole.[4] While we know of little evidence relevant to this suggestion for the kinds of semantic concepts we have considered, there is extensive work on the question of whether visual and auditory concepts can be treated as wholes. This evidence clearly indicates that many perceptual concepts are not processed in a unitary manner.

Much of this work has been done by Shepard (Shepard, Hoveland, and Jenkins, 1961; Shepard and Chang, 1963; Shepard, 1964 and by Garner (Garner and Felfoldy, 1970; Garner, 1974, chaps. 5 and 6; Garner, 1976). Their work converges in showing that there are two kinds of perceptual concepts: *integral* ones (like our concept of the color red), which are treated as unitary wholes in tasks requiring discrimination or selective attention; and *separable* ones (like concepts of geometric figures varying in form and size), which are processed in terms of their component properties in discrimination and selective-attention tasks. To make this more concrete, consider an experiment in which subjects are given patterns and are instructed to attend to one dimension and to ignore the others. If the patterns are geometric forms varying in size and shape, and subjects are instructed to attend to size, then variations in shape will have no effect on their response (Garner, 1976). Thus selective processing of dimensions has occurred. But if the patterns are color patches varying in hue and saturation, and subjects are instructed to attend to hue, variations in saturation will affect performance (Garner, 1976). In this situation there is no selective processing of dimensions. Indeed, subjects do not seem to be processing dimensions at all, but rather whole patterns.

Thus integral (perceptual) concepts are consistent with the assumption of unitary processing, but separable concepts are not. And the critical point for us is that, with the use of criteria like whether or not selective attention is possible, most perceptual concepts that have been studied turn out to be separable. Even concepts that intuitively seem to be integral, like schematic faces, turn out to be separable when their processing characteristics are investigated (Bradshaw, 1976). The implication is that if semantic concepts are like perceptual ones, then few of them may turn out to be integral.

One other line of research on unitary processing is worth mentioning. Markman has studied the acquisition of two kinds of concepts (Markman, 1979; Markman and Siebert, 1976): *classes*, which are the kind of concept we have been concerned with (for example, trees and furniture), and *collections* (for example, family and forest). The critical differences between the two are as follows: (1) while classes deal with membership relations, collections deal with part-whole relations (for example, father and mother are parts of a family); and (2) while classes do not require any specific relation between their members, collections do (for example, the father and mother of a family bear a very specific relation to one another). Markman has contrasted these two types of concepts in various developmental tasks and shown that children aged about 4 to 6 years treat class concepts in a less unitary fashion than collection concepts. For example, children have more trouble determining the number of items in a set when that set is presented as a class concept (determining the number of trees in a picture labeled "trees") than when that set is presented as a collection concept (determining the number of trees when that same picture is labeled "forest"). The implication is that the concepts of interest to us, class concepts, are not treated as wholes by young children. Therefore, at least for this population, metric representations of class concepts seem inappropriate (a conclusion that is independently supported by Smith and Kemler, 1978).

Can Concepts and Their Members Be Represented in the Same Space?

In both the simple distance and comparative distance models, categorization depends on computing the distance between a concept and one of its members. This presupposes that a concept and its members can be represented in the same space without violating any important assumption of metric spaces. The evidence for this presupposition is the simple fact that several researchers had scaled concepts and their members in the same space and found that the results were consistent with experimental findings on categorization; for example, the distance between an instance and its concept was positively correlated with the time needed to categorize the instance (Rips, Shoben, and Smith, 1973; Rosch and Mervis, 1975; Caramazza, Hersch, and Torgerson, 1976; Shoben, 1976). But there is newer evidence that bears more directly on the presupposition of interest, and it indicates that a concept and its members often cannot be represented in the same space.

This evidence comes from Tversky and Smith (forthcoming) and involves reanalyses of some of the scaling studies mentioned above (Rips, Shoben, and Smith, 1973, and Rosch and Mervis, 1975). In these studies, subjects first rated the similarity of a concept's subsets to one another, as well as the similarity of each subset to the concept itself. To use fruits as an example, subjects rated the similarity of apple to peach, to plum, to cherry, and to the general concept of fruit. Then these similarity ratings were used as input to a scaling program whose output was a multidimensional, metric representation of the concept of fruit and its subsets. Tversky and Smith's reanalysis focused on the similarity ratings themselves. They found that for most subsets, the item rated most similar to the subset was the general concept itself. For 17 of the 20 subsets of fruit used, the concept of fruit was the most similar to the subset; or to put it in more spatial terms, fruit was the closest neighbor to 17 of 20 subsets.

The problem raised by this result is that it is analytically impossible for one item in a metric space to be a closest neighbor to so many other items as long as the space is of relatively low dimensionality. Thus, in a two-dimensional space, the maximum number of subsets to which a concept term can serve as closest neighbor is five. One needs a minimum of an eight-dimensional space to accommodate the concept of fruit being the closest neighbor to 17 of its subsets. And once fruit is positioned in such a space so that it is the closest neighbor to the appropriate 17 subsets, there is no guarantee that the distances between the 17 subsets will adequately capture the similarity ratings for pairs of subsets. Hence the fact that semantic-concept terms serve as closest neighbors to so many of their subsets challenges the viability of low-dimensional metric representations, and most proponents of metric representations argue that they are useful for elucidating conceptual structures mainly when they are low-dimensional (see Shepard, 1974).

One more point needs to be made here. Given that the Tversky and Smith results (forthcoming) argue against using the same metric space to represent concepts and their members, what kind of representation would be consistent with the results? According to Tversky and Smith, it would be a representation in which the concept contains fewer properties than its members, and in which most of the properties of the concept are nested within those of the members. With such a representation, the concept would contain few properties that are distinctive vis-à-vis most members, and consequently it would be highly similar to most members (Tversky, 1977). This proposal has two important implications. First, it essentially says that concepts must be more abstract than all of their instances or subsets. This may seem obvious to some, but as we will see later, it is at odds with the basic tenet of the exemplar view. And second, the proposal holds that there must be a substantial degree of nesting of a concept's properties among its members' properties. In our treatment of the classical view, we provided evidence against a complete nesting of properties (features). Thus our best guess is that nesting is substantial — which is consistent with the Tversky and Smith results as well as with *most* concepts being judged more similar to their immediate than their distant superordinates — but less than perfect — which is consistent with some concepts being judged more similar to their distant than their immediate superordinates.

Summary

It is clear that the assumption of a metric space comes at a cost. First, Tversky (1977) has raised serious doubts about whether some concepts can be represented in metric spaces without violating the three basic assumptions of metric distances. Second, there is no direct evidence that semantic concepts can be treated as unitary wholes, as presupposed by many who take the dimensional approach, and we know from the work of Garner (1976) and Shepard (1964) that few perceptual concepts are processed in a unitary fashion. And third, the notion that concepts and their members can be represented in the same metric space is challenged by Tversky and Smith's finding that a concept term serves as the closest neighbor to a multitude of its subsets.

Of course, none of these problems amounts to a definitive case against metric representations. Tversky's points regarding violations of the metric assumptions have been challenged by Krumhansl (1978); the Garner-Shepard finding that unitary concepts are rare has been obtained only with perceptual concepts; and the Tversky-Smith result has direct implications only for low-dimensional metric spaces. Still, the three problems we have discussed start to shift the burden of proof onto those who favor metric representations for semantic concepts. And to the extent that such representations are problematic, so too is the notion that a concept may be specified by an average plus an indication of how distant its various instances can be. This notion, which is quite popular in the current literature, relies on metric distance and hence is somewhat suspect.

Dimensions versus Features

Having covered both the featural and dimensional approaches of the probabilistic view, we can close this chapter with some comments on the relative merits of the two. Before making any evaluative comments, though, a ground rule is in order. While we noted earlier in the book that either the featural or the dimensional approach can be extended to represent any property, we still think it a meaningful question to ask whether a property is more naturally represented as a feature or as a dimension value. To illustrate, although the property "feathered" could be represented as one value on a binary dimension (the other value being "not feathered"), this representation seems unnatural because it lacks dimensional aspects like continuity or betweenness. Consequently, to the extent that one can justify "feathered" as a property in concepts, we count this as evidence for the featural approach.

NATURAL CONCEPTS

Given the biggest stumbling block in the study of natural concepts has been the specification of properties (be they defining or otherwise), there is a limit to what this work can tell us about the issue of featural versus dimensional representations. Still, there are some trends in this work that seem relevant.

The Case for Features

Perhaps the best evidence for the prevalence of features comes from the analytic tradition of language study that systematically uses intuitions to specify the properties of object concepts. Such attempts have considered both natural objects, like animals and plants, and man-made ones, like tools and furniture, and have more often turned up discrete features than continuous dimensions. This is true regardless of whether the attempt has been made in linguistics (Katz and Fodor, 1963; Katz, 1972; Lyons, 1977), psycholinguistics (Clark, 1973; Clark and Clark, 1977), artificial intelligence (Winograd, 1972; Bobrow and Winograd, 1977), or the intersection of these fields Norman and Rumelhart, 1975; Miller and Johnson-Laird, 1976). For natural objects, these analyses consistently hit upon features like living, animate, human, male, female, adult, and so on, while for man-made objects, the analyses turn up features like inanimate, rigid, having a flat surface, made of wood, and so forth. Though one can question how successful these featural approaches have been, one could hardly argue that no progress at all has been made. And for every reasonable feature proposed in this work — like animate or male — it behooves an advocate of the dimensional approach to justify why a dimension should be posited instead. The problem with this line of evidence, though, is that there is little proof that the features posited are actually used in categorization.

As for experimental techniques for discovering properties of object concepts, some are of little use in answering the feature versus dimension question. Multidimensional scaling is geared to find dimensions; clustering techniques are oriented to discover features. At least one technique, however, seems less biased in this respect, namely, the attribute-listing procedure used by Rosch and Mervis (1975). With this technique the listed attributes overwhelmingly turn out to be features, (see, for example, the listings in Rosch et al., 1976). And for these features, we do have at least correlational evidence that they are used in categorization — for example, Rosch and Mervis's finding that the distribution of these features over concept members is correlated with the times needed to categorize the members. But once again, we hasten to point out that the features in question must be taken with a grain of salt because they may not be unbiased estimates of underlying properties.

The Case for Dimensions

There are three sets of findings that favor dimensional properties for object concepts. The first comes from recent experiments on comparative judgments. In these studies, subjects are given the names of object concepts, such as dog and bear, and have to indicate which object is the larger one. The results show that people can reliably make fine discriminations about the size of objects, implying that they have access to detailed, dimensionalized knowledge about these concepts (see Banks, 1977, and Holyoak, 1978, for recent reviews). Though these results indicate the use of dimensional representations, it is not clear that such dimensions are used in categorization. To our knowledge, subjects in the experiments just described are explicitly asked questions about the magnitude of objects, not about the natural categorization of objects. It is therefore possible that the dimensional property that subjects seem to be using is not part of the concept, or at least of its core, but is rather some ancillary information.

So we must seek experiments that demonstrate the use of dimensional properties in categorization. This brings us to the second set of relevant studies: those that use multidimensional scaling analyses to uncover dimensional properties of concepts and that show these properties are used in categorizing the concepts' members. We illustrated some of these findings in Chapter 3 when we presented the basic evidence for the use of nonnecessary properties in categorization (for example, Rips, Shoben, and Smith, 1973; Caramazza, Hersch, and Torgerson, 1976; Shoben, 1976). To reiterate some of the main points from our earlier discussion: (1) Multidimensional scaling solutions of animal terms consistently turn up two dimensions, size and ferocity, which subsets of animal concepts vary on; (2) the values of these dimensions for the parent concepts—bird, mammal, and animal—appear to be the average of their subsets values; and (3) the time needed to categorize a subset decreases with its distance from its parent concept in the multidimensional space; for example, subsets are categorized faster when their size and ferocity values are close to those of their appropriate concept. Taken at face value, these results strongly suggest that some properties of object concepts are represented dimensionally. The obvious problem is that the results rest on metric representations, and we have seen the difficulties involved in using such representations. But while there is reason to be suspicious, we do not think the results can be dismissed. The dimensions uncovered in this work, like the size and ferocity of animals, seem intuitively correct. Furthermore, these same two dimensions occur in solutions that scale only subsets—for example, only the subsets of the bird concept and not bird itself (see Henle, 1969; Hutchinson and Lockhead, 1977)—and hence these solutions at least escape the criticism that concepts and their members may not be representable in the same space.

If we accept that some properties of a concept are represented dimensionally, the next question is how many properties have this character. Our guess is, not many. The multidimensional solutions for birds, for example, never seem to reveal a dimension of flying ability, or of characteristic habitats, possibly because such properties are represented as discrete features and are unlikely to show up in multidimensional solutions. Indeed, properties that are represented as features may not even be considered by subjects in experiments that provide the data for multidimensional scaling. In such experiments, subjects typically have to rate the similarity of many possible pairs of subsets of the same concept, and this requirement may induce subjects to focus on just those properties that vary continuously among subsets, that is, on dimensions.

Given the above, it is of interest to seek evidence for the use of dimensions in categorization other than multidimensional scaling findings. This leads us to the third set of relevant results, best exemplified by a well-known experiment of Labov's (1973) in which he presented pictures of containerlike objects and asked his subjects to label them. As the ratio of the diameter to the height of the container varied, so did the probability that subjects would label the container a cup (as opposed to, for example, a bowl). Inspection of the data suggests that subjects were able to distinguish reliably several different diameter-to-height ratios, indicating that this property was being treated as a dimension.

Note that Labov's data are based on perceptual categorization, while the other lines of evidence we have considered are from semantic tasks. Thus to assess the full implications of Labov's results, we again have to consider the relation between perceptual and semantic categorization. When we first raised this issue (Chapter 2), we argued that perceptual and semantic tasks should be kept distinct because perceptual categorization must be based on the properties given by the identification procedure of a concept while semantic categorization can rest on the core of a concept. If we hold tight to this distinction, Labov's data would be interpreted as follows: identification procedures include dimensional properties, but nothing has been shown about concept cores and semantic categorization. Near the end of our treatment of the classical view (Chapter 3), however, we found cause to question this distinction. There we suggested that identification procedures may be used in semantic categorization, and we provided some empirical data in support of this idea. We thus blurred the distinction between abstract information in concept cores and perceptual information in identification procedures, and thereafter generally ignored the distinction in our treatment of the probabilistic view. From this perspective, Labov's results have implications for semantic as well as perceptual categorization.

In summary, each of the three lines of evidence we have reviewed has its limitations, but the last two — multidimensional scaling analysis and perceptual categorization — provide some support for dimensional properties. However, there is nothing to suggest that most properties of a concept are of this form. It seems, then, that we will need both features and dimensions to characterize natural concepts.

Artificial Concepts

In this discussion we will be concerned with experiments using artificial concepts that clearly have a probabilistic structure, that is, concepts that have no salient defining properties and that often have no necessary or sufficient ones either. We can divide these experiments into two types: (1) those that use variations in discrete features to generate the concepts' instances, like the Rosch and Mervis experiments (1975) where a concept consists of a set of letter strings and each property of a string is the presence of a particular letter; and (2) those that use variations in continuous dimensions to generate the concepts' instances, like Reed's experiments (1972) where a concept consists of a set of faces and each property of a face is the value of a dimension such as nose length. If the type 1 experiments showed that subjects used features while the type 2 experiments showed that they used dimensions, all we could get out of these studies would be what was put into them; nothing of consequence would have been learned. In fact, while the type 1 experiments do show strong evidence for the use of features (for example, Neumann, 1974; Rosch and Mervis, 1975; Rosch, Simpson, and Miller, 1976; Hayes-Roth and Hayes-Roth, 1977; Medin and Schaffer, 1978, experiments 1 and 2), the type 2 experiments sometimes indicate that the dimensional variations are being treated as featural ones (Goldman and Homa, 1977; Neumann, 1977; Smith and Balzano, 1977). Hence it is the type 2 experiments that we need to consider further.

In considering experiments with dimensional variations, we will restrict ourselves to those with *subjectively quantitative* dimensions and ignore studies with *subjectively qualitative* ones. A subjectively quantitative dimension, like length, is such that each successive value is perceived as an addition to the previous one; for example, a length of 5 inches differs from one of 4 inches in that the former is perceived as equal to the latter plus some additional amount. A subjectively qualitative dimension, like color, does not have such psychological additivity. Rather, each successive value is perceived as a substitute for the previous one; for example, a value of orange substitutes for a value of red. With instances generated from a qualitative dimension, there is no reason to expect subjects to average the values into a mean value for a concept, since averaging presupposes additivity. People exposed to red and blue items usually do not respond as if they have seen purple ones (Hirschfeld, Bart, and Hirschfeld, 1975). So a fair test of the use of dimensional representations requires that we look only at experiments in which the items have been generated from subjectively quantitative dimensions. Two kinds of items that meet this constraint are schematic faces and dot patterns, and there has been a great deal of research with both kinds of materials.

Schematic Faces

In an important set of experiments, Reed (1972) had subjects learn to sort schematic faces into two classes or concepts. The faces varied with respect to dimensions like the height of the eyes and nose. Reed compared a variety of featural and dimensional models in their ability to account for certain aspects of the learning data. For our purposes, one of his major contrasts was between a cue validity featural model (similar to the cue validity version of our general featural model discussed in the previous chapter) and what we have called the comparative distance model of the dimensional approach. Both models did a reasonable job of accounting for the accuracy with which faces were categorized, though the dimensional one seemed to fare a bit better. Reed ended up favoring the dimensional model primarily because it was more compatible with subjects' reports of their learning strategies and because of a specific contrast between the subjects' accuracy in classifying the average face and that in categorizing a suitable control face. The details of these two additional tests need not concern us, since Medin and Schaffer (1978) have shown that both are methodologically flawed. Thus the safest conclusion to be drawn from the Reed study is that a featural model of the cue-validity sort and a dimensional model that includes comparative distances can both account for the general aspects of learning concepts of schematic faces, though there may be a slight advantage to the dimensional model.

Subsequent research with schematic faces, however, has favored a featural model. Smith and Balzano (1977) focused on the times needed to categorize learned faces, and their results favored a featural cue validity model over the dimensional comparative distance model. These results challenge Reed's conclusion, but they hardly constitute overpowering evidence for the featural approach. Stronger evidence for this approach is given by a study of Goldman and Homa (1977). In this experiment, after learning two classes of schematic faces, subjects were given two novel test faces for each class and asked which was more representative of the concept. One test face contained values that were averages over the instances; the other contained model values of the instances, where the properties are essentially treated as features. Subjects clearly preferred the modal face to the average one. Thus even in a situation where instances are generated by exclusively quantitative dimensions, there is evidence for properties being represented as features. This finding does constitute a challenge to the dimensional approach.

Dot Patterns

In a seminal study, Posner and Keele (1968) introduced the use of dot patterns as a class of materials for studying concept acquisition. Figure 22 presents some sample patterns from two artificial concepts labeled A and B. The pattern at the upper left of Figure 22 is called the *prototype* of concept A. Instances of this concept are generated by distorting the dots in the prototype in accordance

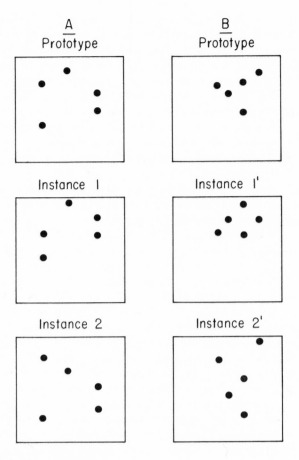

Figure 22 *Sample dot patterns*

with some statistical rule. For example, instances 1 and 2 were generated by a rule that says that each dot in prototype A has a 0.5
probability of moving up one cell in the grid and a 0.5 probability
of moving down one cell. Instances 1' and 2' were generated by applying the same rule to prototype B. Notice that one can interpret
each dot in the prototype as a dimension whose values are the
possible locations of that dot after the statistical rule is applied;
given this, when all the dimensional values of instances 1 and 2 are
averaged, the result is prototype A. Under this interpretation, distorted dot patterns become instances generated by variations in
quantitative dimensions (an interpretation that is implicit or explicit in several studies using these patterns, for example, Peterson
et al., 1973; Hyman and Frost, 1975).

Experiments using these patterns all follow the same general procedure. Subjects are given instances of two or more concepts, but not the prototypes themselves, and they learn to put all instances of the same prototype in the same category. To illustrate with the patterns in Figure 22, subjects would learn to make one response to instances 1 and 2, and another to instances 1' and 2'. After training, there are test trials in which subjects have to categorize the learned instances as well as new instances of the concepts (other distortions of the prototypes), and the prototypes themselves. The basic hypothesis is that learning to categorize the instances involves constructing representations of the prototypes, that is, forming a representation made up of the average values of all relevant dimensions. Two pieces of evidence support this hypothesis. First, on test trials given soon after training, subjects categorize the prototype patterns they have never seen before virtually as quickly and accurately as they do the learned instances (Posner and Keele, 1968; Peterson et al., 1973; Homa and Vosburgh, 1976). Second, when the delay between training and test is on the order of days, there is more forgetting of the originally learned instances than of the prototypes (Posner and Keele, 1970; Homa and Vosburgh, 1976). (See Hintzman and Ludlam, 1980, however, for an interpretation of these delay effects based on the exemplar view.)

Do these results really provide solid evidence for dimensionally represented concepts? There is reason to be skeptical. It seems implausible that subjects could ever abstract a prototype from its instances by averaging the corresponding dot locations of the instances; for how would a subject know which are the corresponding dots that have to be averaged? The dilemma is illustrated in Figure 23. The figure shows which dots of prototype A go with which transformed dots in instances 1 and 2. Since subjects are only given the instances, how would they know, for example, to average the two b dots in the instances, rather than the d dot in instance 1 and the b dot in the instance 2? It seems that the only way to tell which dots to average is to know the prototype in advance. But it is only the experimenter who knows this, not the subjects. Thus if one wants to claim that the instances are perceived dimensionally, the dimensions must be something other than specific dot locations. Without the experimenter having precise knowledge about what the relevant dimensions are, there is no real reason for using artificial concepts rather than natural ones.[5]

It is even possible that some of the critical properties of these dot patterns are features rather than dimension values. This possibility is suggested by the work of Barresi, Robbins, and Shain (1975), who showed that distortions yielding instances with distinctive features—features that reliably discriminate between instances of

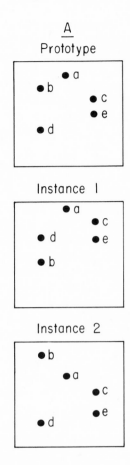

Figure 23 *Prototype and two instances showing difficulty of finding corresponding dots in the instances*

different concepts — led to better classification learning than distortions that did not result in distinctive features. Dot patterns, then, may be a mixture of features and dimension values. And for all we know, they may sometimes be treated as holistic patterns, a possibility we will consider in the next chapter.

In short, many of the studies that have used continuous dimensions to generate artificial concepts have failed to make a convincing case that these dimensions are actually used in categorization. This is not to say it cannot be done. With dot patterns, for example, our intuitions are that some of the critical properties are represented dimensionally in terms of the density of dots in particular regions. In any of the studies mentioned above, if one were to average all instances of a prototype with respect to the density of dots in each quadrant of the pattern, one might recover a reasonable facsimile to the prototype. If so, this would account for the experimental results showing better performance with a prototype and would provide support for some properties of dot patterns being represented dimensionally.

Summary

Let us briefly review the main arguments on the issue of features versus dimensions. For natural concepts, the best argument in support of features is that analytic specifications of concepts (for example, Katz, 1972; Miller and Johnson-Laird, 1976) as well as attribute listings (for example, Rosch and Mervis, 1975) consistently turn up properties that look like features. The best arguments for dimensional properties in natural concepts come from multidimensional scaling solutions and studies of perceptual categorization (Labov, 1973), though even in these studies it seems that only a few properties are represented dimensionally. For artificial concepts, experiments that use variations in features to generate the items generally show that subjects incorporate these features in their concept representations (for example, Rosch and Mervis, 1975). Experiments that use variations in dimensions have not fared as well; studies with schematic faces and dot patterns have failed to provide solid evidence that the dimensions varied by the experimenter are used by the subjects. Thus, considering both natural and artificial concepts, there is plenty of evidence for features, and some for dimensions.

The obvious way to put all the results together is to assume that while numerous properties of a concept are represented featurally, some are represented dimensionally. Although this conclusion may appear innocuous, it has implications for what kinds of processes can be used to compare concept representations. Roughly, the process that compares features should be compatible, if not virtually identical, with that which compares dimensions. Thus, if features are to be compared on a component-by-component basis, so must dimensions. And we can imagine a property-comparator that would yield matches or mismatches for featural properties and degrees of difference for dimensional properties. What will not work is a process that compares concepts by computing metric distances between them, for such a process seems incompatible with featural properties of the representation. Interestingly, then, our attempt to put features and dimensions together in a representation supplies another reason for being wary of metric representation of concepts.

6 | The Probabilistic View: Holistic Approach

W E TURN NOW to the case where a probabilistic concept is represented by a single holistic property. Though there may be numerous ways to instantiate this notion, we will use just one, namely a template, which roughly offers a point-for-point isomorphism with the object being represented. We focus on a template because it is the only clear-cut case of a holistic property that has received some systematic development.[1]

Some Background on Templates

We first need to make explicit what we mean by a template. Figure 24 shows the contrast between a template representation of the concept of a cup and featural and dimensional representations of this concept. Only the template has the same form — that is, looks like — the object it represents. A feature such as "has a handle" does not *look* like a handle; nor does a point in a multidimensional space bear any resemblance to a cup. But the fact that templates look like what they represent means they can only be used to represent concepts of concrete objects. It makes little sense, for example, to talk of a template for "justice" or "truth." Hence the isomorphic aspect of templates restricts the approach to a limited set of concepts.

In addition to their isomorphic quality, it is typically assumed that templates are unanalyzable. No part of a template can be singled out and interpreted alone; the cup template in Figure 24 in no way singles out the part corresponding to the handle as having any special status. And since there are no separable components of a template, there is no need to spell out the relations between components. In some sense, though, these relations are implicit in the template; our cup template, for example, implicitly shows us the relation between the handle and the rest of the cup. It is for this

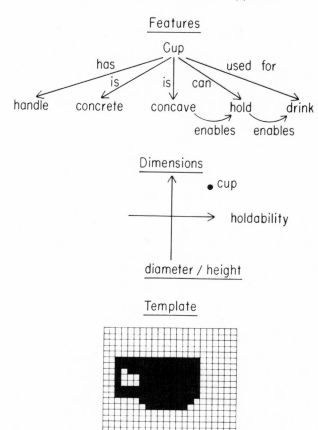

Figure 24   *Three kinds of representations of a cup*

reason that templates are often said to be relational gestalts. In sum, templates differ from featural and dimensional representations in that only a template is (1) isomorphic to the object it represents, (2) unanalyzable, and (3) inherently relational.[2]

Another issue concerns the kind of process that is inevitably coupled with template representations, namely, template matching. The general idea of this process is that one establishes whether or not a particular object belongs to a class by determining whether or not the object provides an overall or holistic match to the template representing the class. An object is a cup, for example, if and only if it matches our cup template. As many have noted (for example, Neisser, 1967; Lindsay and Norman, 1977), this process has the serious drawback that various transformations of an object can block a match between the object and its appropriate template. Thus a mismatch between a particular, input cup and our cup template can result if the input is substantially smaller or larger than our template, or if the input is hanging by its handle rather than being in its usual orientation. The standard solution to this problem is to propose the use of preprocessing mechanisms that standardize the size and orientation of input objects. As we will see later, though, there are other basic problems with template-matching processes.

Concept Representations and Categorization Processes

The following discussion should not be taken as the standard template theory of concept representations. As far as we know, no such theory exists. What follows instead is our rendition of how template notions might be used to represent concepts of concrete objects.

Summary Representation

Recall that we use three criteria as guides to whether a representation is truly a summary. A template representation of a concept clearly meets two of them, namely, that it is the result of an abstraction process and that it is applicable to all relevant test items. The cup template illustrated in Figure 24, for example, is presumably induced from experience with specific instances and is accessed whenever there is a question about membership in the cup concept. However, a template representation may not always meet our third criterion, which is that a summary representation need not correspond to a particular instance. One version of a template representation that we consider will fail on this criterion (that is, the "summary" will always correspond to a specific instance), though another will succeed. So a template representation is a summary to some degree.

Probabilistic Templates

Determining Concept Templates from Instances

It is common practice to construe a template as a matrix of cells, with each cell defined by its position and color (see Palmer, 1978). The position is given by the horizontal and vertical coordinates of a cell, while the color is either black or white (corresponding to filled or unfilled). This sets the stage for a critical question: What is the relation between the color of a particular cell in a concept representation and the colors of the corresponding cells in the concepts' instances? (This presupposes that instances are also represented in templates.) Perhaps the simplest answer, as shown in Figure 25, is that the color of a concept cell is the value that occurs most frequently in the corresponding cells of the instances.

The three templates at the top of Figure 25 represent specific instances of the letter *B* (we use letters rather than objects for the sake of simplicity); the template at the bottom depicts the concept of *B*. Each cell in the concept template takes the color value most frequently occurring in the corresponding cells of the instances; for example, the concept cell defined by the first row and second column has a value of black since two of the three corresponding cells in the instances are black. This leads us to our second assumption: The color value of each cell of a template representing a concept is the most frequent or probable value found in the corresponding cells of its instances. Note that such a concept representation is not different in kind from a representation of an instance (this is what we meant when we mentioned earlier that one version of template representations would fail to meet one of our criteria for a summary representation).[3]

The preceding assumption implies that the color of a concept cell need not be identical to the color of a corresponding cell in a particular instance. This means that the template for a concept need not perfectly match every, or even any, instance. These aspects of template representations are in keeping with other approaches to the probabilistic view in that concept representations do not require necessary conditions, that is, they do not require cells that

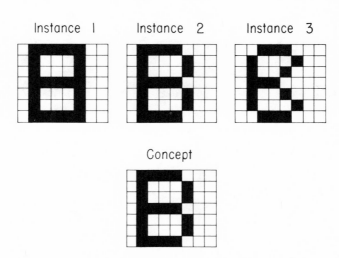

Figure 25 *How a concept template can be constructed from instances by picking the most frequent color value*

have a particular color value. Rather, such representations offer only probabilistic guides to concept membership.

There is, however, a serious problem with our proposed procedure for determining a concept template from its instances. Though trying to describe a holistic representation, our procedure requires computations that seem well defined only on a cell-by-cell basis. There is no obvious way to select the most frequent color in a particular cell of instances without extracting that cell. We are led to the uncomfortable suggestion that although templates may ultimately function as holistic representations, their construction involves the extraction of components.

Another way of constructing a concept template from instances gets around this problem. Assume that rather than being either black or white, a cell in a concept template can take any shade of brightness, with black and white being the endpoints of a continum. Then the color of a particular cell in a concept template may be determined by averaging the colors of the corresponding cells in the instances, as shown in Figure 26. In contrast to the previous solution, a concept template now differs in kind from an instance template in that only the former can contain cells with intermediate color values. More importantly, even though our averaging mechanism results in cell-by-cell changes, the cells of instances do not

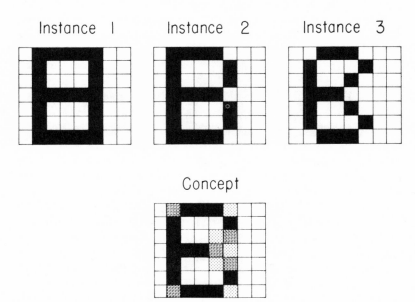

Figure 26   *How a concept template can be constructed from instances by averaging*

have to be extracted in constructing the concept template. Rather, we can construe the averaging mechanism to operate by super-imposing instance templates on top of one another, with the averaging of brightness being done by some analog process. Averaging, then, seems closer to the spirit of holistic representations than our more-frequent-value proposal.

Applications to Experiments on Dot Patterns

It is useful to apply our two proposals about the construction of concept templates to the studies involving dot patterns that we described in the previous chapter. Recall that in these experiments subjects were given distortions, or instances, of a prototype (the supposed concept), and learned something about the prototype itself even though it had never been presented. According to the proposals just considered, each pattern presented would be construed as a k-celled template. And subjects would presumably construct a template for the prototype or concept either by determining the more frequent color values in the instances' cells or by averaging the colors of the instances. In either case, the more instances there were that had black in a given cell, the more likely it would be that the concept's template would have this value in its corresponding cell. So the concept template would at least roughly resemble the prototype that generated the instances.

This account has an immediate advantage over the dimensional explanation considered earlier: there is no longer any mystery about how subjects come to combine the correct things to recover the prototype, for the things to be combined do not require prior knowledge of the prototype itself. But exactly how good a facsimile of the prototype will result from our proposed processes? The answer depends on at least three factors: (1) the number of instances presented, (2) the average distortion of instances from the prototype, and (3) the assumed fineness of the matrices of cells that define the instance and concept templates. As the number of instances entering into construction of the concept template increases and as the average distortion of these instances decreases, the concept template should approximate the prototype with increasing accuracy. Numerous studies with dot patterns support this hypothesis (for example, Homa et al., 1973; Peterson et al., 1973). And as long as the matrices defining the instances and concept are not too fine (that is, do not have too much resolution), there should be enough instances having the same color in a cell to construct a concept template that looks like the prototype. Thus, if a given cell in the concept template corresponds to some broad region of the instance templates, there would be a good chance of constructing a concept template that closely resembles the prototype. (The issue of fineness corresponds closely with the issue of distortion level of instances: there must be some minimum level of correspondence among instances for a meaningful concept template to be formed.)

Our proposals about constructing concept templates thus seem consistent with the finding that subjects abstract something like a prototype in studies of dot patterns. This is not a trivial observation. The processes we proposed for recovering the prototype from its instances give no explicit consideration to the statistical rules actually used to generate the instances from the prototype (such rules are defined with respect to the prototype's dots, while our processes are defined with respect to the instances' color values). The issue of fineness, though, suggests that in forming a concept template, we are limited in the precision with which we can represent the details of instances. As a consequence, the concept essentially encodes information about the density of dots in regions of the instances, which is in keeping with our earlier suggestion that density-per-region may be the operative dimension in dot patterns.[4]

A Template-matching Model

For purposes of sketching a categorization model, we will assume that a concept template is constructed by picking the most frequent values. Given that the templates for both concept and test instance can be described in terms of only black or white cells, the following processing assumption is a natural one: An entity X is categorized as an instance or subset of concept Y if and only if the templates for X and Y match to some criterion degree. Since matching is itself defined in terms of whether corresponding cells have like colors, the assumption can be rewritten as follows: An entity X is categorized as an instance or subset of concept Y if and only if a criterial number of X's cells match those of Y.[5]

This matching process is illustrated in Figure 27. In the figure, a test letter is to be classified as either a *J* or a *T*. To compute the degree of match between the instance and a concept, one superimposes the two matrices and counts the number of matches. In this example there are 11 matches with the *J* concept and 8 matches with the *T* concept, so the test instance would be more likely to be categorized as a *J*.

As many have pointed out, this matching process amounts to computing a correlation coefficient between concept and test-item templates (see Roberts, 1960). Though the correlation is computed over the templates' cells, the process can be executed holistically. To illustrate, consider the following metaphor (adapted from Crowder, forthcoming): Imagine a concept template as a

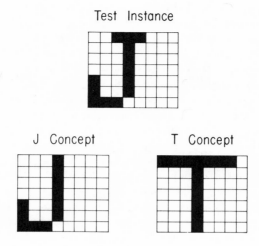

Figure 27 *Template matching*

transparent photographic negative of a simple outline figure like a letter. The template for a test instance would be a positive transparency. To match the two templates, the two transparencies would be held up together against a light source, and a measure would be made of the light that passes through. To the extent that the positive and negative match, the result would be a uniform gray; to the extent that they mismatch, the result would be non-uniform, with certain regions being darker or lighter than others. The resulting degree of light uniformity thus provides a holistic measure of the correlation over cells, and it can be used as the criterion for class membership.

EXPLANATIONS OF PROBLEMATIC FINDINGS

Since the holistic approach has not been extensively developed, there is little reason to provide a detailed description of how it accounts for the phenomena that troubled the classical view. Instead, a few examples should suffice.

We have already noted that there are no necessary cells or defining conditions in a concept template, so the present approach is consistent with the general failure to specify defining conditions. Furthermore, since the color values of cells in a concept template are nonnecessary yet are used in template matching, our template-matching model is consistent with the use of nonnecessary properties in categorization. Categorization itself is a matter of finding a critical number of matching cells in instance template and concept template. Since two instances of the same concept can reach a criterion value by matching two different sets of cells in the concept template, our template-matching model can accommodate disjunctive concepts. Finally, in the present approach the typicality of an instance would be measured by the number of its cells that match corresponding cells in the concept template. The more matches there are, the greater would be the output by the holistic comparison process, and presumably the less time needed to reach a decision.

Criticisms of the Holistic Approach

The present approach is easy to criticize. Part of its vulnerability may be a result of the fact that the template approach has not been systematically developed; but part seems endemic to the nature of template representations and to the matching processes that operate on them.

Consider first the matching process. Even if one posits preprocessing mechanisms that allow adjustments for size and orientation, template matching is still too rigid a system to serve as a robust categorization device. This point is illustrated by the test instance and concept templates shown in Figure 28. Most people would classify the test item as an *E*, yet its overlap with the *E* concept yields no more matches than its overlap with the *C* concept. The problem is that the middle horizontal segment of the test item

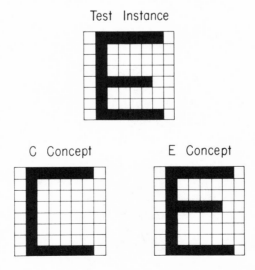

Figure 28 *Test instance and two concepts illustrating a basic problem with template matching*

and the *E* template do not line up and hence produce no matches.

Computer scientists working on pattern recognition have overcome this limitation by introducing a richer conception of the matching process. The key idea is that rather than matching individual cells, the process might encode matches between pairs of cells. For the instance and concept templates shown in Figure 29, for instance, an overlap score based on individual cells would fail to yield matches on 13 of the 14 black cells of the test item. Consider, however, relationships among pairs of cells. In the top two rows of each matrix, horizontally adjacent cells tend to have the same value while vertically adjacent cells tend to have different values. In the rest of the matrix, any pair of cells in the same column has the same value. Near the middle two columns of the matrix, horizontally adjacent cells tend to have different values. On this level of description, then, the concept and test item have a very substantial number of matches. In short, template matching based on 2-tuples of cells overcomes many of the problems associated with considering each cell independently (see Bledsoe and Browning, 1959), and this idea may be generalized to *n*-tuples larger than 2.

Though the method described above may be a help to pattern recognition by computer, it is of dubious value in developing a psychological theory of concepts and categorization. For one thing, although a template-matching process using *n*-tuples solves some problems for templates, it requires a substantial amount of com-

Test Instance

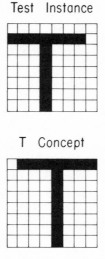

T Concept

Figure 29 *Template matching based on 2-tuples*

putational space. Given a template composed of 64 cells, there are 2,016 pairs of cells and roughly 2^{64} n-tuples potentially to be considered during the matching process. To keep from being overwhelmed by this huge array of possibilities, one would need an additional learning mechanism that would save those n-tuples that had a history of classifying items appropriately and that would discard less diagnostic n-tuples (Uhr, 1966; Holland and Reitman, 1978). A second problem with proposing n-tuples is more conceptual: the proposal seems to undermine the holistic nature of the matching process. If, for example, the match takes into consideration individual cells, pairs of cells, and triples of cells, then it is unclear how the process can be interpreted holistically even at a metaphorical level. The photographic transparency metaphor offered earlier makes no sense in this case, for it seems that the pairs and triples must be extracted from the relevant templates. This is clearly true if a learning mechanism is added, so that only certain pairs and triples are considered. And it is not just the matching process whose holism is being compromised here; our very notion of a template is being undermined, since a template is supposed to be unanalyzable yet we are now talking about selecting out *certain* n-tuples. If one must talk such talk, it seems preferable to refer to the n-tuples as "features" and to acknowledge that we are back to the featural approach to concepts.

Perhaps the single biggest problem with the template approach, however, lies in the notion of a template itself. The heart of this notion is that the representation is isomorphic to the class of entities it represents. As we noted at the outset, this restricts the template approach to concepts of concrete objects; and it is even unlikely that many classes of concrete objects can be represented isomorphically. For one thing, intuition — as well as the results of Rosch and her colleagues (1976) — strongly suggests that superordinate concepts, like furniture and clothing, do not have enough perceptual characteristics to make isomorphic representations a reasonable possibility. For another, many aspects of concrete objects, including specific ones like chairs and robins, may be functional, like "can be sat on" or "can fly," and there is no place for such aspects in a representation intended to capture visual isomorphisms.

In short, the most one can expect from the template approach is that it work for a very limited set of concepts. Perhaps a more realistic possibility is that the core of a concept can be represented in terms of features/or dimensions (or both), and that for some concepts of concrete objects one can use the core information to generate a template for that class, with the template being used to identify presented objects.

A Note on the Relevance of Machine Pattern Recognition

Since this chapter has brought us closer to the study of pattern recognition by machine than has previous chapters, it is important to emphasize that our criticisms of templates and simple matching processes should not be taken as a general argument against the relevance of machine pattern recognition to concerns about concepts. Template matching is just one of many classification schemes employed in machine pattern recognition. Many of the other schemes involve elegant and powerful algorithms that deserve serious attention by psychologists interested in concepts (see in particular the schemes discussed in Rodwan and Hake, 1964; Dodwell, 1970; Fakunaga, 1972; Watanabe, 1972; Cacoullos, 1973; Chen, 1973; Winston, 1975; de Dombal and Gremy, 1976; and Reed, 1979). It would take us too far afield to consider all these schemes, but it seems worthwhile to comment briefly on at least one of them.

The technique of interest is a special case of discriminant analysis, namely, *linear discriminant functions.* If A is a pattern having n properties $[A = (a_1, a_2, \ldots a_n)]$, then

$$g(A) = w_1a_1 + w_2a_2 + \ldots + w_na_n + w_{n+1}$$

is a linear discriminant function where the w_1-w_n are property weights (and w_{n+1} is another constant, which we ignore in what follows). To illustrate, if A is a class of simple geometric figures, say rectangles, and if a_1 indicates height, a_2 indicates width, and both properties have weights of 10, then $g(A) = 10$ (height) $+ 10$ (width). This function assigns a value to every rectangle (for example, it assigns the value 30" to a 1" × 2" rectangle). Most important, if it assigns higher values to all instances on one class than to those of another, then the function provides an algorithm for categorization; that is, computing the function for a test item will tell you whether or not that item belongs in the target class. In such a case, the two classes are said to be *linearly separable.* (This can also be described in geometric terms: two classes are linearly separable if a linear discriminant function exists that provides a boundary between the two sets of instances, this boundary being a straight line if the instances are described in two-space, a plane if the instances are described in three-space, and so on.)

There is a close relationship between the equation shown above and the processing assumption of the general featural model presented in Chapter 4. The latter assumption — that categorization is based on some critical sum of weighted features — implies that there is a linear discriminant function separating a target concept from its contrast sets. In fact, all the probabilistic models we considered (and some of the exemplar models we will take up in the next chapter) require that concepts be linearly separable for flawless categorization to occur. That is, there must exist some additive combination of properties and weights that can be used to accept all concept members correctly and to reject all nonmembers. Thus the technique of linear discriminant analysis, a staple of machine pattern recognition, clearly has relevance to proposals about human concepts.

Given this, it is surprising that there have been almost no attempts to determine whether or not natural concepts are linearly separable. Informal observations suggest that some pairs of natural concepts may not be. For example, people judge whales to be more typical of the concept "fish" than sea lampreys are, even though then know that whales are not fish while sea lampreys are (McCloskey and Glucksberg, 1978). Taken at face value, this result suggests that people's concepts of fish and mammal are not linearly separable, in that at least one mammal instance (whale) is closer to the concept of fish than is a fish instance (sea lamprey). The only hard evidence on the issue of linear separability comes from experiments with artificial concepts. Medin and Schwanenflugel (forthcoming) used two categorization tasks that were similar in major respects, except that in one the concepts were linearly separable while in the other they were not. Four experiments were conducted that varied the number and nature of the items as well as the type of instructions; all studies failed to find any advantage for linearly separable concepts.

These few studies are hardly sufficient to argue that linear separability is not an important constraint on human concepts. That is not the point. Our aim in discussing linear separability is to illustrate the profitable interactions that might arise from the interface of work in machine pattern recognition and theories of concepts and categorization (see Reed, 1973).

7 | The Exemplar View

I N THIS CHAPTER we take up our third view of concepts, the exemplar view. Since this view is quite new and has not been extensively developed, we will not give separate treatments of featural, dimensional, and holistic approaches. Instead, we will sometimes rely on featural descriptions, other times on dimensional ones.

Rationale for the Exemplar View

As its name suggests, the exemplar view holds that concepts are represented by their exemplars (at least in part) rather than by an abstract summary. This idea conflicts not only with the previous views but also with common intuitions. To talk about concepts means for most people to talk about abstractions; but if concepts are represented by their exemplars, there appears to be no room for abstractions. So we first need some rationale for this seemingly bold move.

Aside from a few extreme cases, the move is nowhere as bold as it sounds because the term *exemplar* is often used ambiguously; it can refer either to a specific instance of a concept or to a subset of that concept. An exemplar of the concept clothing, for example, could be either "your favorite pair of faded blue jeans" or the subset of clothing that corresponds to blue jeans in general. In the latter case, the so-called "exemplar" is of course an abstraction. Hence, even the exemplar view permits abstractions.[1]

A second point is that some models based on the exemplar view do not exclude summary-type information (for example, the context model of Medin and Schaffer, 1978). Such models might, for example, represent the information that "all clothing is intended to be worn" (this is summary information), yet at the same time represent exemplars of clothing. The critical claim of such models, though, is that the exemplars usually play the dominant role in categorization, presumably because they are more accessible than the summary information.

These rationales for the exemplar view accentuate the negative—roughly speaking, the view is plausible because its representations are *not* really restricted to specific exemplars. Of course, there are also positive reasons for taking this view. A number of studies in different domains indicate that people frequently use exemplars when making decisions and categorizations. In the experiments of Kahneman and Tversky (1973), for example, it was found that when subjects try to estimate the relative frequencies of occurrence of particular classes of events, they tend to retrieve a few exemplars from the relevant classes and base their estimates on these exemplars. To illustrate, when asked if there are more four-letter words in English that (1) begin with k or (2) have k as their third letter, subjects consistently opt for the former alternative (which is incorrect); presumably they do so because they can rapidly generate more exemplars that begin with k. In studies of categorization, subjects sometimes decide that a test item is *not* an instance of a target category by retrieving a counterexample; for example, subjects base their negative decision to "All birds are eagles" on their rapid retrieval of the exemplar "robins" (Holyoak and Glass, 1975). And if people use exemplar retrieval to make negative decisions about category membership, they may also use exemplars as positive evidence of category membership (see Collins and Loftus, 1975; Holyoak and Glass, 1975).

The studies mentioned above merely scratch the surface of what is rapidly becoming a substantial body of evidence for the use of exemplars in categorical decisions (see, for example, Walker, 1975; Reber, 1976; Brooks, 1978; Medin and Schaffer, 1978; Kossan, 1978; Reber and Allen, 1978. This body of literature constitutes the best rationale for the exemplar view.

Concept Representations and Categorization Processes

The Critical Assumption

There is probably only one assumption that all proponents of the exemplar view would accept: The representation of a concept consists of separate descriptions of some of its exemplars (either instances or subsets). Figure 30 illustrates this assumption. In the figure the concept of bird is represented in terms of some of its exemplars. The exemplars themselves can be represented in different ways, partly depending on whether they are themselves subsets (like robin, bluejay, and sparrow) or instances (the pet canary

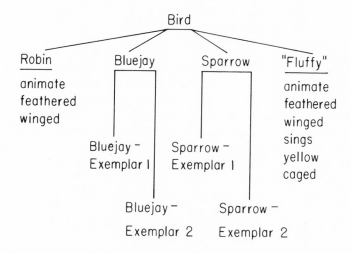

Figure 30 *An exemplar representation*

"Fluffy"). If the exemplar is a subset, its representation can consist either of other exemplars, or of a description of the relevant properties, or both (these possibilities are illustrated in Figure 30). On the other hand, if the exemplar is an instance, it must be represented by a property description. In short, the representation is explicitly disjunctive, and the properties of a concept are the sum of the exemplar's properties.

This assumption conflicts with that of a summary representation, and it is useful to pinpoint the extent of the conflict. Recall that we use three criteria for a summary representation: it is the result of an abstraction process, it need not correspond to a specific instance, and it is always applied when a question of category membership arises. To what extent is each of these criteria violated by the above assumption? We can best answer this by considering each criterion in turn.

The representation in Figure 30 shows a clear-cut lack of abstraction in two respects. First, it contains a specific instance, "Fluffy"; second, it contains subsets (for example, robin and bluejay) whose properties overlap enough to permit some amalgamation. Note, however, that the very fact that some exemplars are subsets means that some abstraction has taken place. Thus lack of abstraction is a matter of degree, and our safest conclusion is that exemplar-based representations show a substantially greater lack of abstraction than representations based on the classical or the probabilistic view. This aspect, as we shall see, is the only thing common to all present models based on the exemplar view; so it is the real meat of the critical assumption.

The representation in Figure 30 also seems at odds with our second criterion, for it contains a component corresponding to a specific instance. Again, the offender is our friend "Fluffy." But if we remove this instance, the representation still qualifies as an exemplar one. That is, some models based on the exemplar view (for example, Medin and Schaffer, 1978) permit representations with no specific instances. Thus, whether or not part of a representation corresponds to a instance is a point on which various exemplar models vary, not a criterion for being an exemplar model.

Finally, there is the summary-representation criterion that the same information is always accessed when category membership is being determined. This issue concerns categorization processes, so the sample representation in Figure 30 is neutral on this point. Once we consider categorization models based on the exemplar view, it turns out that some violate this criterion (for example, different test items would access different exemplars in the representation in Figure 30), while others are consistent with the criterion (for example, the entire representation in Figure 30 would always be accessed when there is a question of birdhood). Again, then, the criterion is really a choice point for various exemplar models.

The Proximity Model as an Extreme Case

We have seen that the critical assumption behind the present view is that the representation lacks abstraction and is "needlessly disjunctive." All exemplar models violate this criterion of a summary representation. Exemplar models differ among themselves, however, with respect to the other two criteria of summary representations; consequently some exemplar models depart from previous views more than others. To appreciate this, it is useful to consider briefly an extreme case of the exemplar view, the *proximity* model (see Reed, 1972). This model violates all three criteria of a summary representation.

In the proximity model, each concept is represented by all of its instances that have been encountered. When a novel test item is presented along with a target category, the test item automatically retrieves the item in memory that is most similar to it. The test item will be categorized as an instance of the target concept if and only if the retrieved item is a known instance of that concept. Thus: (1) the concept representation is lacking entirely in abstraction; (2) every exemplar in the representation is realizable as an instance; and (3) the information retrieved in making a decision about a particular concept varies with the test item presented.

Since the proximity model leaves no room at all for abstraction, it conflicts with the intuitions we mentioned earlier. There is another obvious problem with the model. Adults have experienced an enormous number of instances for most natural concepts, and it seems highly implausible that each instance would be a separate part of the representation; the memory load seems too great. For an exemplar model to be plausible, then, there must be some means of restricting the exemplars in the representation. The models that we now consider attempt to do this.

Models of Categorization

BEST-EXAMPLES MODEL

Assumptions

Though Rosch explicitly disavows a concern with models (1975, 1978), her work—and that of her collaborator, Mervis, (1980)—points to a particular kind of categorization model. In the following discussion, we will try to develop it.

In addition to the assumption of exemplar descriptions, the best-examples model assumes that the representation is restricted to exemplars that are typical of the concept — what Rosch often refers to as the *focal instances* (1975). More specifically:

(1) The exemplars represented are those that share some criterial number of properties with other exemplars of the concept; that is, the exemplars have some criterial family resemblance score. (Since family resemblance is highly correlated with typicality, this amounts to assuming that the exemplars represented meet some criterial level of typicality.)

This assumption raises some questions. First, why leave room for multiple typical exemplars rather than restricting the representation to the single best example? A good reason for not using such a restriction comes directly from data. Inspection of actual family resemblance scores indicates that usually a few instances share the highest score (Rosch and Mervis, 1975; Malt and Smith, 1981b). Similarly, inspection of virtually any set of typicality ratings (for example, Rips, Shoben, and Smith, 1973; Rosch, 1975) shows that two or more instances attain comparable maximal ratings. Another reason for permitting multiple best examples is that some superordinate concepts seem to demand them. It is hard to imagine that the concept of animal, for instance, has a single best example; at a minimum, it seems to require best examples of bird, mammal, and fish.

A second question about our best-examples assumption is, How does the learner determine the best exemplars? This question is difficult to answer; all we can do is to mention a few possibilities. At one extreme, the learner might first abstract a summary representation of the concept, then compare this summary to each exemplar, with the closest matches becoming the best exemplars, and finally discard the summary representation. Though this proposal removes any mystery from the determination of best examples, it seems wildly implausible. Why bother with determining best examples when you already have a summary representation? And why ever throw the latter away? A second possibility seems more in keeping with the exemplar view. The learner stores whatever exemplars are first encountered, periodically computes the equivalent of each one's family resemblance score, and maintains only those with high scores. The problem with this method is that it might attribute more computations to the learner than are actually necessary. Empirical data indicate that the initial exemplars encountered tend to have high family resemblance scores; for instance, Anglin's results (1977) indicate that parents tend to teach typical exemplars before atypical ones. This suggests a very simple solution to how best examples are learned—namely, they are taught. The simplicity is misleading, however; for now we need an account of how the teachers determine the best examples. No doubt they too were taught, but this instructional regress must stop somewhere. At some point in this account there must be a computational process like the ones described above.

In any event, given a concept representation that is restricted to the most typical exemplars, we can turn to some processing assumptions that will flesh out the model. These assumptions concern our paradigm case of categorization—an individual must decide whether or not a test item is a member of a target concept. One possible set of assumptions holds that:

(2a) All exemplars in the concept representation are retrieved and are available for comparison to the test item.

(2b) The test item is judged to be a concept member if and only if it provides a sufficient match to at least one exemplar.

If the matching process for each exemplar is like one of those considered in previous chapters—for example, exemplars and test item are described by features, and a sufficient match means accumulating a criterial sum of weighted features—then our exemplar-based model is a straightforward extension of models considered earlier. Since few new ideas would arise in fleshing out this proposal, we will adopt an alternative set of processing assumptions.

The alternative is taken from Medin and Schaffer's context model (1978). (Since this is the only exemplar model other than the best-examples model that we will consider, it simplifies matters to use the same set of processing assumptions.) The assumptions of interest are as follows:

(3a) An entity X is categorized as an instance or subset of concept Y if and only if X retrieves a criterial number of Y's exemplars before retrieving a criterial number of exemplars from any contrasting concept.

(3b) The probability that entity X retrieves any specific exemplar is a direct function of the similarity of X and that exemplar.

To illustrate, consider a case where a subject is given a pictured entity (the test item) and asked to decide whether or not it is a bird (the target concept). To keep things simple, let us assume for now that categorization is based on the first exemplar retrieved (the criterial number of exemplars is 1). The presentation of the picture retrieves an item from memory — an exemplar from some concept or other. Only if the retrieved item is a known bird exemplar would one categorize the pictured entity as a bird (this is assumption 3a). The probability that the retrieved item is in fact a bird exemplar increases with the property similarity of the probe to stored exemplars of bird (this is assumption 3b). Clearly, categorization will be accurate to the extent that a test instance is similar to stored exemplars of its appropriate concept and dissimilar to stored exemplars of a contrast concept.

The process described above amounts to an induction based on a single case. Increasing the criterial number of exemplars for categorization simply raises the number of cases the induction is based on. Suppose one would classify the pictured entity as a bird if and only if k bird exemplars are retrieved. Then the only change in the process would be that one might retrieve a sample of n items from memory $(n > k)$ and classify the pictured item as a bird if and only if one samples k bird exemplars before sampling k exemplars of another concept. Categorization will be accurate to the extent that a test instance is similar to several stored exemplars of the appropriate concept and dissimilar to stored exemplars of contrasting concepts; these same factors will also govern the speed of categorization, assuming that the sampling process takes time.

Note that processing assumptions 3a and 3b differ from the previous ones (2a and 2b) in that the present assumptions postulate that different information in the concept is accessed for different test items. This is one of the theoretical choice points we mentioned earlier.

One more issue remains: How is the similarity between a test instance and an exemplar determined? The answer depends, of course, on how we describe the properties of representations — as features, dimension values, or templates. In keeping with the spirit of Rosch's ideas (for example, Rosch and Mervis, 1975; Rosch et al., 1976), we will use feature descriptions and assume that the similarity between a test instance and an exemplar is a direct measure of shared features.

Explanations of Empirical Phenomena

In this section we will briefly describe how well the model of interest can account for the seven phenomena that troubled the classical view.

Disjunctive concepts. Each concept representation is explicitly disjunctive — an item belongs to a concept if it matches this exemplar, *or* that exemplar, and so on.

Unclear cases. An item can be an unclear case either because it fails to retrieve a criterion number of exemplars from the relevant concept, or because it is as likely to retrieve a criterion number of exemplars from one concept as from another.

Failure to specify defining features. There is no reason why the feature of one exemplar should be a feature of other exemplars; that is, the features need not be necessary ones. And since the concept is disjunctive, there is no need for sufficient features.

Simple typicality effects. There are two bases for typicality ratings. First, since the representation is restricted to typical exemplars, a typical test item is more likely to find an exact match in the concept. Second, for cases where a test item is not identical to a stored exemplar, the more typical the test item the greater is its featural similarity to the stored exemplars. Both factors should also play a role in categorization; for example, since typical instances are more similar to the stored exemplars of a concept, they should retrieve the criterial number of exemplars relatively quickly. And the same factors can be used to explain why typical items are named before atypical ones when concept members are being listed. That is, the exemplars comprising the concept representation function as retrieval cues, and the cues themselves should be named first, followed by instances most similar to them. As for why typical exemplars are learned earlier, we have already considered means by which this could come about; for example, the learner may use a kind of family-resemblance computation to decide which exemplars to maintain.

Determinants of typicality. The fact that typical instances share more features with other concept members is essentially presupposed by the present model.

Use of nonnecessary features.   As already noted, there is no requirement that the features of one exemplar be true of all other exemplars.

Nested concepts.   Figure 31 illustrates why some instances (for example, robin) are judged more similar to their immediate than their distant superordinates, while other instances (for example, chicken) manifest the reverse similarity relations. In this illustration robin is one of the represented exemplars for bird, but not for animal. This alone makes it likely that robin is rated more similar to bird than to animal. On the other hand, chicken is a represented exemplar of animal but not of bird, thereby making it likely that chicken is rated as being more similar to animal. In essence, the set of exemplars in a concept may shift with the level of concept.

CONTEXT MODEL

The context model of Medin and Schaffer (1978) differs from the preceding proposal in two critical respects. One concerns the learning of exemplar representations; the other deals with the computation of similarity in categorization processes. We will consider each issue in turn.

Nature of the representation

To understand the representational assumptions of the context model, we will begin with a simple case. Suppose that subjects in an experiment on artificial concepts have to learn to classify schematic faces into two categories, A and B; the distribution of facial properties for each category is presented abstractly at the top of Figure 32. Here the relevant properties will be treated as dimensions. They correspond to eye height (EH), eye separation (ES),

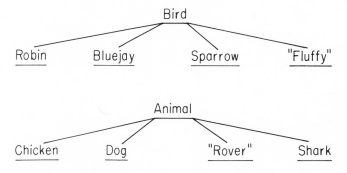

Figure 31   *Representations that can explain similarity ratings for nested triples*

nose length (NL), and mouth height (MH). Each dimension can take on one of two values, for example, a short or a long nose; these values are depicted by a binary notation in Figure 32. For example, a nose length of 0 indicates a short nose, a value of 1 signals a long nose. The structure of concepts A and B is presumably that of natural concepts — though A and B lack defining conditions, for each concept there are certain dimension values that tend to occur with it instances. The instances of A, for example, tend to have large noses, while those of B favor small noses.

How, according to the context model, is this information represented by the concept learner? The answer depends on

| Category A | | | | | Category B | | | | |
| Instances | Dimension Values | | | | Instances | Dimension Values | | | |
	EH	ES	NL	MH		EH	ES	NL	MH
1	1	1	1	0	1	1	1	0	0
2	1	0	1	0	2	0	1	1	0
3	1	0	1	1	3	0	0	0	1
4	1	1	0	1	4	0	0	0	0
5	0	1	1	1					

| Category A | | | | Category B | | | |
| Instances | Dimension Values | | | Instances | Dimension Values | | |
	EH	ES	NL		EH	ES	NL
1'	1	1	1	1'	1	1	0
2'	1	0	1	2'	0	1	1
3'	1	1	0	3'	0	0	0
4'	0	1	1				

Category A	Category B
$.8^a$ high eyes	$.75^a$ low eyes

a = weight associated with dimension value

Figure 32 *Representational assumptions of the context model*

the strategies employed. If our concept learner attends equally to all instances and their dimension values, her final representation should be isomorphic to what is depicted in the top part of Figure 32 — each exemplar would be represented by its set of values. However, if our concept learner selectively attends to some dimensions more than others — say she ignores mouth-height entirely — her representation should be isomorphic to the middle part of Figure 32. Here instances 2 and 3 of concept A have been collapsed into a single exemplar, and the same is true for instances 3 and 4 of concept B (remember, exemplars can be abstract). This strategy-based abstraction can be even more extensive. To take the extreme case, if our learner attends only to eye height, she will end up with concept representations like those at the bottom of Figure 32. Here there is no trace of exemplars; instead, the representations are like those in models based on the probabilistic view.

The notion of strategy-based abstraction gives the context model a means of restricting representations to a limited number of exemplars when natural concepts are at issue. (Recall that a plausible exemplar model needs such a restriction.) In particular, suppose that a learner when acquiring a natural concept primarily attends to properties that occur frequently among concept members; then the learner will end up with detailed representations of typical exemplars, which contain the focused properties, but with only incomplete or collapsed representations of atypical exemplars, which do not contain the focused properties. In this way the context model can derive the notion that typical exemplars dominate the representation, rather than assuming this notion outright as is done in the best-examples model. In addition, the context model can assume that in the usual artificial concept study, where there are very few items, each exemplar is fully represented (unless instructions encourage otherwise). Hence in artificial-concept studies, the context model's representations may differ substantially from those assumed by the best-examples model.

Similarity Computations in Categorization

The general assumptions about categorization processes in the present model are identical to those in the best-examples model (this is no accident, since we deliberately used the context model's assumptions in developing the best-examples proposal). To reiterate these assumptions:

(3a) An entity X is categorized as an instance or subset of the concept Y if and only if X retrieves a criterial number of Y's exemplars

before retrieving a criterial number of exemplars from any con-
strasting concept.

(3b)   The probability that entity X retrieves any specific exemplar is a direct function of the similarity of X and that exemplar.

There is, however, an important difference between the context
model and the previous one with regard to how these assumptions
are instantiated. The difference concerns how similarity, the heart
of assumption 3b, is computed.

Thus far, whenever we have detailed a similarity computation
we have used an *additive* combination. In featural models, the similarity between a test item and a concept representation (whether it
is summary or an exemplar) has been some additive combination of
the individual feature matches and mismatches. In dimensional
models, similarity between test item and concept representation has
been measured by an additive combination of differences on
component dimensions. This notion of additivity is rejected by the
context model. According to the present model, computing the similarity between test instances and exemplar involves *multiplying*
differences along component dimensions.

This process is illustrated in Figure 33. The top half repeats some
representations given in the previous figure. Associated with each
dimensional difference is a similarity parameter, α_i, with high
values indicating high similarity. Thus α_{NL} is a measure of the
similarity between a long and a short nose. Two factors can decrease the size of each parameter, that is, decrease the similarity
between the values of a dimension. One factor is the psychophysical difference between the two values of a dimension; the other is
the salience of the dimension, which is itself determined by the at-
tentional and strategy considerations that we discussed earlier.
Given a fixed set of parameters, one computes similarity between
test item and exemplar by multiplying the four parameters. As examples, the similarity between a test item and exemplar that have
different values on every dimension would be $\alpha_{EH} \cdot \alpha_{ES} \cdot \alpha_{NL} \cdot \alpha_{MH}$,
while the similarity between a test item and exemplar that have
identical values on all dimensions would be $1 \cdot 1 \cdot 1 \cdot 1 = 1$. Some
intermediate cases are shown in the middle part of Figure 33. The
bottom part of Figure 33 shows how these similarity computations
between test item and exemplar are cumulated over all relevant exemplars to derive a final categorization of the test item. The probability of assigning a test item to, say, concept A is equal to the sum
of the similarities of the test items to all stored exemplars of A,
divided by the sum of the similarities of the test item to all stored
exemplars of both A and B (this instantiates assumption 3b).

Sample representations

	Category A Dimension Values					Category B Dimension Values			
Instances	EH	ES	NL	MH	Instances	EH	ES	NL	MH
1	1	1	1	0	1	1	1	0	0
2	1	0	1	0	2	0	1	1	0
3	1	0	1	1	3	0	0	0	1
4	1	1	0	1	4	0	0	0	0
5	0	1	1	1					

Sample computations for Category A exemplars

$$S(A1,A1)^* = 1 \cdot 1 \cdot 1 \cdot 1 = 1.0 \qquad S(A2,A1) = 1 \cdot \alpha_{ES} \cdot 1 \cdot 1 = \alpha_{ES}$$

$$S(A1,A2) = 1 \cdot \alpha_{ES} \cdot 1 \cdot 1 = \alpha_{ES} \quad S(A2,A2) = 1 \cdot 1 \cdot 1 \cdot 1 = 1.0$$

$$S(A1,A3) = 1 \cdot \alpha_{ES} \cdot 1 \cdot \alpha_{MH} \quad S(A2,A3) = 1 \cdot 1 \cdot 1 \cdot \alpha_{MH}$$
$$= \alpha_{ES} \cdot \alpha_{MH} \qquad\qquad = \alpha_{MH}$$

$$S(A1,A4) = 1 \cdot 1 \cdot \alpha_{NL} \cdot \alpha_{MH} \quad S(A2,A4) = 1 \cdot \alpha_{ES} \cdot \alpha_{NL} \cdot \alpha_{MH}$$
$$= \alpha_{NL} \cdot \alpha_{MH} \qquad\qquad = \alpha_{ES} \cdot \alpha_{NL} \cdot \alpha_{MH}$$

$$S(A1,A5) = \alpha_{EH} \cdot 1 \cdot 1 \cdot \alpha_{MH} \quad S(A2,A5) = \alpha_{EH} \cdot \alpha_{ES} \cdot 1 \cdot \alpha_{MH}$$
$$= \alpha_{EH} \cdot \alpha_{MH} \qquad\qquad = \alpha_{EH} \cdot \alpha_{MH}$$

Final categorization

$$P(A1 \subset \text{Category A})^{**}$$

$$= \frac{1.0 + \alpha_{ES} + \alpha_{ES} \cdot \alpha_{MH} + \alpha_{NL} \cdot \alpha_{MH} + \alpha_{EH} \cdot \alpha_{MH}}{\sum_X S(A1, X)}$$

$$P(A2 \subset \text{Category A})$$

$$= \frac{\alpha_{ES} + 1.0 + \alpha_{MH} + \alpha_{ES} \cdot \alpha_{NL} \cdot \alpha_{MH} + \alpha_{EH} \cdot \alpha_{ES} \cdot \alpha_{MH}}{\sum_X S(A2, X)}$$

---

* $S(i,j)$ = Similarity between i and j
** $P(i \subset \text{Category A})$ = Probability that i is assigned to Category A

Figure 33 *How the context model computes similarity*

How much hinges on computing similarity by a multiplicative rule rather than by an additive one? Quite a bit, as the two cases illustrated in the middle part of Figure 33 demonstrate. Following the multiplicative rule, instance 2 should be easier to learn and categorize than instance 1. This essentially reflects the fact that instance 2 is highly similar (that is, differing on only one dimension) to two exemplars of category A (instances 1 and 3) but is not highly similar to any exemplar of concept B; instance 1, on the other hand, is highly similar to only one exemplar in A (instance 2) but to the first two exemplars in B. Had we computed similarity by an additive rule, this prediction would reverse. This can be seen by noting that instance 1 shares an average of more than two values with other exemplars of A, while instance 2 shares an average of exactly two values with other A exemplars. (Both instances share the same average number of values with B exemplars.) These contrasting predictions were tested in a number of artificial-concept experiments by Medin and Schaffer (1978), and the results uniformly supported the multiplicative rule: instance 2 was learned faster and categorized more efficiently than instance 1. In a follow-up study (Medin and Smith, 1981) we found that the superiority of instance 2 held across widely different instructions, including ones that implicitly suggested an additive rule to subjects.

Admittedly, this particular contrast between multiplicative and additive similarity computations is highly specific, and is probably only realizable with artificial materials. Still, it provides some basis for favoring the context model's way of instantiating the exemplar-based processing assumptions over that specified by the best-examples model. Other reasons for favoring the multiplicative rule will be given later in the chapter.

Explanations of Empirical Phenomena

There is no need to detail how the context model handles our standard list of phenomena, since these accounts are virtually identical to those given for the best-examples model. Again, the explicitly disjunctive nature of an exemplar-based representation immediately accounts for the existence of disjunctive concepts, the failure to specify defining properties, and the use of nonnecessary properties during categorization. And to the extent that the learning strategies posited by the context model eventuate in a representation dominated by typical exemplars, the model would explain typicality effects in the same manner as the best-examples model.

Criticisms of the Exemplar View

Having discussed some of the strengths of the exemplar view, we now consider its weaknesses. We will first take up those difficulties that the present view shares with the probabilistic one; that is, problems in (1) representing all the knowledge in concepts, (2) constraining possible properties, and (3) accounting for context effects. Then we will consider a fourth set of problems — those that are specific to the exemplar view's critical assumption that a concept is represented by a disjunction of exemplars.

REPRESENTING MORE KNOWLEDGE IN CONCEPTS

To return to our standard example, how can we represent the knowledge that the properties "small" and "sings" tend to be correlated across exemplars of the concept of bird? Note that the solutions we considered in conjunction with the probabilistic view, such as labeling relations between properties, are irrelevant here. For in the present view exemplars tend to be represented separately, so how can we represent something that pertains to all exemplars?

The most promising solution appears to be this: knowledge about a correlation between properties is *computed* from an exemplar-based representation when needed, rather than *prestored* in the representation. We can illustrate with the kind of representation used in the best-examples model. Suppose that the concept of bird is represented by two best examples, one corresponding to robin, the other to eagle. Then one can compute the negative correlation between size and singing ability by noting that the best example that is small (robin) also sings, while the best example that is large (eagle) does not. More generally, to the extent that each best example contains properties that characterize a particular cluster of instances (for example, many of a robin's properties also apply to bluejays and sparrows), then property differences between best examples reflect correlations among properties in the instances at large.

Another kind of additional knowledge that we have routinely been concerned with has to do with variability in properties associated with a concept. Some knowledge of this sort is implicit in any exemplar representation. The different exemplars represented must manifest some differences in their features or dimension values, and one can use these differences to compute estimates of property variability. The problem, though, is that these computations would probably yield smaller estimates of variability than those actually obtained in relevant experiments (Walker, 1975). This would clearly be the case for computations based on best-examples representations, since only a few highly typical exemplars are represented here, and typical exemplars show only limited variation in their properties (see Rosch and Mervis, 1975). The situation seems more promising for the context model: it is at least compatible with a concept representation containing multiple exemplars, some of which may be atypical, and its representations therefore permit a more realistic computation of property variability.

LACK OF CONSTRAINTS

There really are two problems involving constraints with the exemplar view: a lack of constraints on the properties associated with any exemplar, and a lack of constraints on the relations between exemplars included in the same representation. We will treat only the first problem here, saving the second for our discussion of problems specific to the exemplar view.

We start with the obvious. For exemplars corresponding to instances, there is no issue of specifying constraints in the form of necessary or sufficient properties, since we are dealing with individuals. So the following applies only to exemplars that correspond to subsets of a concept, for example, the exemplars "chair" and "table" of the concept "furniture." With regard to the latter kind of exemplar, the problem of unconstrained properties *vis-à-vis* an exemplar is identical to that problem *vis-à-vis* a summary representation. This is so because a subset-exemplar is a summary representation of that subset — there need be no difference between the representation of chair when it is included as one component of an exemplar representation of furniture and when it stands alone as a probabilistic representation. Hence, all our suggestions about how to constrain properties in probabilistic representations apply *mutatis mutandis* to exemplar representations. For the best-examples model, then, there may be a need to specify some necessary features, *or* some sufficient ones, for each exemplar represented in a concept; otherwise we are left with problems such as the exemplar permitting too great a degree of disjunctiveness.

The same, of course, holds for the context model, but here one can naturally incorporate necessary properties via similarity parameters and the multiplicative rule for computing similarity. Specifically, a dimension is a necessary one to the extent that its similarity parameter goes to zero when values on the dimension increasingly differ; and given a near-zero value on one parameter, the multiplication rule ensures that the product of all relevant parameters will also be close to zero. An illustration should be helpful: a creature 90 feet tall might possibly be classified as a human being, but one 9,000 feet tall would hardly be. In the former case, the parameter associated with the height difference between the creature and known human beings would be small but nonzero; in the latter case, the parameter for height difference might be effectively zero, and consequently the overall, multiplicative similarity between creature and human being would be effectively zero regardless of how many other properties they shared. In essence, we have specified a necessary range of values along the height dimension for human beings. To the extent that this is a useful means of capturing property constraints, we have another reason for favoring multiplicative over additive rules in computing similarity.

Context Effects

Thus far little has been done in analyzing context effects of the sort we described in conjunction with the probabilistic view. We will merely point out here what seems to us to be the most natural way for exemplar models to approach context effects.

The basic idea is that prior context raises the probability of retrieving some exemplars in a representation. To return to our standard example of "The man lifted the piano," the context preceding "piano" may increase the availability of exemplars of heavy pianos (that is, exemplars whose representations emphasize the property of weight), thereby making it likely that one of them will actually be retrieved when "piano" occurs. This effect of prior context is itself reducible to similarity considerations; for example, the context in the above sentence is more similar to some piano exemplars than to others. Retrievability is thus still governed by similarity to stored exemplars, and our proposal amounts to increasing the factors that enter into the similarity computation.

The above proposal seems workable to the extent that a representation contains numerous exemplars. If there are only a few exemplars, then many contexts will fail to activate a similar exemplar. To illustrate, consider the sentence "The holiday platter held a large bird," where the context seems to activate a meaning of bird akin to chicken or turkey. If the representation of bird is restricted to a few typical exemplars, like robin and eagle, there is no way the preceding context effect can be accounted for. Since the best-examples model is restricted in just this way, it will have difficulty accounting for many context effects through differential retrievability of exemplars. The context model is less committed to this kind of restriction, and thus may fare better.

Problems Specific to Exemplar Representations

We see two major problems that stem from the assumption that a concept is represented by a disjunction of exemplars. The first concerns the relation between the disjuncts; the second, the learning of summary information. Both can be stated succinctly.

According to the ideas presented thus far, the only relation between the exemplars in a given representation is that they all point to the same concept. But "exemplars that point to the same concept" can be a trait of totally unnatural concepts. For example, let FURDS be the "concept" represented by the exemplars of chair, table, robin, and eagle; again each exemplar points to the same "concept", but this collection of exemplars will not meet anyone's pretheoretical notion of a concept. The point is that the exemplar view has failed to specify principled constraints on the relation between exemplars that can be joined in a representation.

Since any added constraint must deal with the relation between concept exemplars, the constraint must be something that applies to all exemplars. For the concept of furniture, it might be that all the exemplars tend to be found in living spaces, or are likely to be used for some specific purpose. Positing such a constraint therefore amounts to positing something that *summarizes* all exemplars. In short, any added constraint forces a retreat from a pure exemplar representation toward the direction of a summary representation. The retreat, however, need not be total. The summary constraints may be far less accessible than the exemplars themselves (perhaps because the former are less concrete than the latter), and consequently categorization might be based mainly on exemplars. This proposal would leave the currently formulated exemplar models with plenty of explanatory power; it also seems compatible with Medin and Schaffer's statement of the context model (1978), which does not prohibit properties that apply to the entire concept. But whether our proposal is compatible with the spirit behind the best-examples model (that is, the work of Rosch and her colleagues) is at best debatable.

With regard to learning summary information, we are concerned with the situation where someone (say, an adult) tells a concept learner (say, a child) something like "All birds lay eggs." What, according to the exemplar view, is the learner to do with such information — list it separately with each stored bird exemplar and then throw away the summary information? This seems implausible. What seems more likely is that when one is given summary information, one holds onto it as such. Again, we have a rationale for introducing a bit of a summary representation into exemplar-based models.

CONCLUSIONS

With regard to those problems it shares with probabilistic approaches, the exemplar view offers some new ideas about potential solutions. Thus computing property correlations from exemplars that represent different clusters is an interesting alternative to prestoring the correlation, say, by means of a labeled relation. Similarly, accounting for context effects via differential retrieval of exemplars seems a viable alternative to the context-sensitive devices proposed for the probabilistic view. And the context model's multiplicative rule for computing similarity offers a particularly natural way of incorporating necessary properties into representations that can also contain nonnecessary ones. But the exemplar view has two unique problems — specifying relations between disjuncts and handling summary-level information — and the solution to these problems seems to require something of a summary representation. This suggests that it would be a useful move to try to integrate the two views. This suggestion among other issues, will be a concern of the next and final chapter.

8 | Summary and Implications

I N THIS FINAL CHAPTER we try to provide some additional perspective on the three views of concepts. We begin by summarizing the high points of the three views, with the probabilistic and exemplar views depicted as alternative means of solving the same set of problems. A contrast between these two views is the exclusive concern of the second section of this chapter. In the final section, we discuss some limits of the present work — in particular, the limits on what an analysis of object concepts and categorization can tell us about other kinds of concepts and other kinds of conceptual functions.

Summary of the Three Views

We began with the classical view, which holds that a concept is a summary description typically cast in features. The view further assumes that the features are defining ones (singly necessary and jointly sufficient), and that the defining features of a concept are nested within those of its subordinates. Though this view has long been successful in elucidating many classification phenomena — why people treat various objects as equivalent, how people can use some properties of an object to infer others, and so on — lately the view has run into numerous problems.

We first considered some very general problems, including (1) the existence of disjunctive concepts (which is prohibited by the view's assumption that features are defining); (2) the existence of unclear cases (which is difficult to reconcile with the view's assumption that a concept's defining features are nested within those of its subordinates); and (3) the general failure to specify defining features for most concepts. We then moved on to four problems that were more tied to experimental results: (1) the occurrence of simple typicality effects (for example, more typical members are categorized more efficiently); (2) the correlation between typicality and family resemblance; (3) the use of nonnecessary features in categorization; and (4) the finding that concepts are sometimes judged more similar to (and categorized faster as members of) their distant than their immediate superordinates.

At this point we had delineated the fundamental issue in this book: the seeming incompatibility of the classical view with the seven phenomena listed above. The rest of the book was concerned primarily with solving this problem. We began our problem-solving attempts by trying to alter the classical view radically, by positing either access links between concepts, translation processes between defining features of different concepts, or identification procedures that were more accessible than concept cores. Since none of these attempted solutions proved satisfactory, the stage was set for our consideration of alternative views.

The chief alternative was the probabilistic view, which could be described in terms of features, dimensions, or holistic properties. The featural approach again assumes that a concept is a summary description, but postulates that the features entering into the summary need only be probabilistically related to concept membership. To these representational assumptions, we added a general assumption about categorization, roughly that one matches features of test item and target concept until one accumulates a threshold amount of probabilistic evidence. We called this package the general featural model and demonstrated that it was compatible with the seven critical phenomena that plagued the classical view. We also considered more specific models based on this approach and showed that they too were consistent with the critical phenomena, as well as with other findings (for example, priming results and the effects of contrast concepts).

The dimensional approach to the probabilistic view parallels the featural one with respect to certain assumptions. Again a concept is a summary representation, where the components are dimension values that are probabilistically related to concept membership. There are a number of distinct aspects of the dimensional approach, the most important of which is the assumption that concepts having the same relevant dimensions can be represented as points in a multidimensional metric space. Armed with this metric assumption, we were led to consider categorization processes that hinged on a determination of whether a test item was within some threshold distance of a target concept. We considered two models that incorporated such metric-distance computations and showed that both were consistent with the critical phenomena that were problems for the classical view.

There are striking similarities in how the featural and dimensional approaches account for the critical phenomena. Thus both approaches: (1) explain the use of nonnecessary properties, and the difficulty of specifying defining ones, by requiring nonnecessary properties in representations; (2) allow for degrees of disjunctiveness by permitting different combinations of properties to yield the same threshold quantity (be it a feature sum or a distance); (3) construe unclear cases to be items that do not quite reach a concept's threshold, or that are equally close to the threshold of more than one concept; (4) explain most typicality effects by assuming that the typicality of a member reflects how similar its properties are to those of its parent concept; and (5) account for data on nested triples by assuming that the properties of most concepts are more similar to those of their immediate than their distant superordinates, though there are exceptions where these similarity relations reverse. These similarities suggest that it may be possible to combine the featural and dimensional approaches into a single position, which we can refer to as the *component* approach to the probabilistic view.

The success of the component approach was not shared by the holistic approach to the probabilistic view. Here we took the summary representation of a concept to be a template whose cell values are probabilistically related to concept membership, and we assumed that categorization is based on matching concept and test-item templates. Unlike its predecessor, the holistic approach seemed restricted to only certain object concepts. And even in this limited range, we showed that there were difficulties in ensuring that any viable matching process could operate in a holistic fashion.

The remaining alternative that we considered was the exemplar view, which argues that a concept is represented not by a summary representation but rather by separate descriptions of some of its exemplars. We considered two models based on this view. In both of these models, typical exemplars dominate concept representations, and a test item is categorized as a member of a target concept if and only if the former retrieves a criterial number of the latter's exemplars. Both models seem able to account for the seven phenomena that have continually been of interest, although the nature of these accounts is somewhat different from what we encountered with the probabilistic view. Thus the exemplar view: (1) explains the use of nonnecessary properties, and the difficulty of specifying defining ones, by placing no requirements on properties other than that they characterize at least one exemplar; (2) allows for disjunctiveness by explicitly building it into each representation; and (3) explains some typicality effects by assuming that the exemplars in a concept representation are likely to be typical.

The summary we have thus far provided is illustrated in Figure 34, which charts our progress from the classical view to the seven critical problems, and then to our various attempts to solve these problems. Two of these attempts—the radical alterations of the classical view and the holistic approach to the probabilistic view— led to such severe problems that they were deemed unsuccessful. Two other attempts—the featural and dimensional approaches— can for summary purposes be combined into the component approach to the probabilistic view. The component approach and the exemplar view thus offer two viable proposals about the nature of object concepts and their role in categorization. In the next section we will contrast these two proposals in detail.

Before turning to that contrast, though, we need to say something about the fact that even our two more successful proposals have their associated problems (see Figure 34).[1] Some of these problems are really phenomena that have not yet been satisfactorily explained by the probabilistic or exemplar views. We have tried throughout to provide some idea of what the needed explanations might look like, and we think it plausible that many of these explanations can be fleshed out. The remaining problems are perhaps more troubling. They all deal with a lack of constraints—

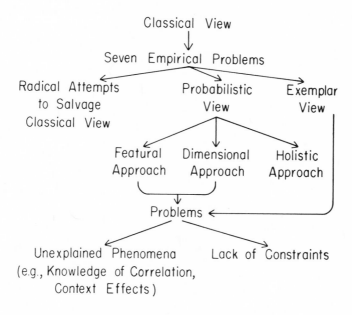

Figure 34 *Summary of the three views*

for example, too few constraints on the properties used in probabilistic representations, too few constraints on the relations between the exemplars of a concept in the exemplar view. These problems deprive models based on the probabilistic and exemplar views of any true explanatory power; with no constraints on possible features, for example, probabilistic models can explain virtually any result.

A lack of constraints means that the probabilistic and exemplar views are telling us little about what constitutes a concept or a categorization process. (In contrast, the classical view told us a lot—namely, that a concept must have necessary and sufficient properties.) Indeed, the closest that either of the more liberal views came to a constraint was the stipulation of probabilistic models that concepts be linearly separable (that is, that a weighted combination of properties accepts all members and rejects all nonmembers); but what little evidence there was did not support the importance of linear separability for human categorization. How, then, can we get some constraints on these views? One possibility is to move a step back in the direction of the classical view, and to posit constraints akin to necessity or sufficiency on the properties in probabilistic and exemplar representations. Another possible constraint on such properties is that they be correlated. Such a constraint would be consistent with the claim that categories are organized in such a way as to exploit correlations among properties (Rosch, 1978), thereby permitting predictions and inferences from partial information to be maximized—for example, that animate creature perched on the branch can probably fly. (One bit of evidence in support of the latter idea is the recent finding by Mervis, Medin, and Rosch, forthcoming, that two correlated attributes are perceptually more salient than would be predicted on the basis of the salience of the attributes considered separately.)

Comparison of the Probabilistic and Exemplar Views

Since the probabilistic and exemplar views are rivals of a sort, a detailed comparison of these two views seems worthwhile. In particular, we want to focus on three general questions: (1) what are the critical differences between these two views? (2) assuming that both views have some truth to them, and that some concepts are represented in probabilistic form and others in exemplar form, what factors determine which way a concept is represented? and (3) assuming that both views have some truth to them, what can be said about the possibility that the representation for a single concept is *mixed*, that is, partly probabilistic, partly exemplar?

DIFFERENCES BETWEEN THE VIEWS

Implicit versus Explicit Disjunction

Part of what we have to say here was foreshadowed in our discussion of the exemplar view. There were two major points in that discussion: (1) the critical assumption of the exemplar view is that the representation of a concept consists of separate descriptions of some of its exemplars; and (2) this assumption conflicts with one of our criteria for a summary representation, namely that the representation be as abstract as possible and not be "needlessly disjunctive." These points are relevant to our present concern. Specifically, since summary representations are assumed by the probabilistic but not by the exemplar view, the two views can be distinguished on the basis of abstractness. Roughly, exemplar representations are "needlessly disjunctive" when compared to probabilistic representations.

But this distinction is clearly too rough. A more precise way of capturing the difference in abstractness between the views is to note that the probabilistic view is *implicitly disjunctive*, while the exemplar view is *explicitly disjunctive*. This distinction is illustrated in Figure 35. The top half of the figure contains a probabilistic (featural) representation of a hypothetical concept along with the

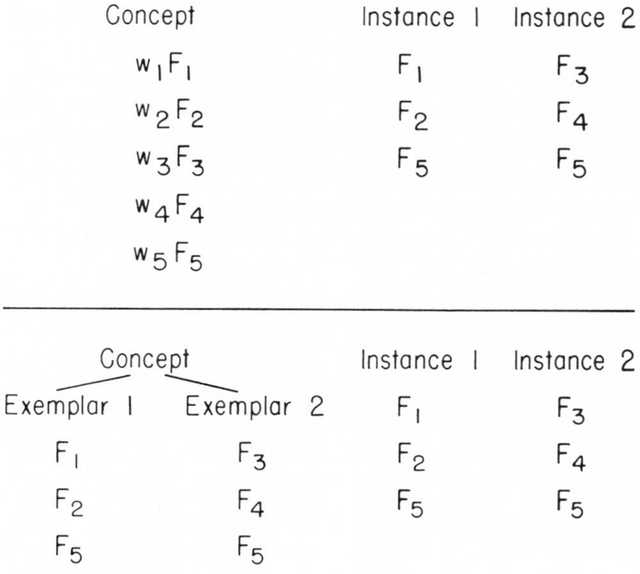

Concept	Instance 1	Instance 2
$w_1 F_1$	F_1	F_3
$w_2 F_2$	F_2	F_4
$w_3 F_3$	F_5	F_5
$w_4 F_4$		
$w_5 F_5$		

Concept		Instance 1	Instance 2
Exemplar 1	Exemplar 2	F_1	F_3
F_1	F_3	F_2	F_4
F_2	F_4	F_5	F_5
F_5	F_5		

Figure 35 *Implicit versus explicit disjunction (w_1 refers to feature weight)*

(featural) representations of two specific instances that would be categorized as members of this concept. The bottom half of the figure provides the equivalent for an exemplar (featural) representation of the same concept. Note that for both probabilistic and exemplar representations, different feature sets of the concept are used to match different instances — that is, F_1, and F_2, and F_5 match the first instance; F_3, F_4, and F_5 match the second. These different feature sets constitute different disjuncts of the concept. Though the disjuncts are identical in the top and bottom of Figure 35, they are represented very differently in the two cases. In the exemplar case, the disjuncts correspond to stored exemplars and hence are represented explicitly; in the probabilistic case, the disjuncts exist only during categorization and hence are represented only implicitly. This captures what we mean when we say that exemplar representations are explicitly disjunctive and probabilistic representations implicitly disjunctive.

We can recast this distinction in another terminology (one used by Smith, 1978), and say that the disjuncts of an exemplar theory are *prestored*, while those of a probabilistic theory are *computed.* This terminology makes apparent a major implication of our distinction: exemplar representations generally require more storage space than probabilistic ones. Note that the "inverse" of this — that exemplar representations require less processing — does not necessarily hold; since there can be numerous exemplars per concept, there can be numerous computations too, and consequently there can be as many or more processing requirements with an exemplar as with a probabilistic representation. It may be the case, however, that the computations required by an exemplar model are simpler than those required by a probabilistic one. For example, computations that consider feature weights may be unusually difficult, and such computations will be needed only in a probabilistic model.[2]

In sum, we hold that *the* critical difference between the probabilistic and exemplar views is that between implicit and explicit disjunction, and that this difference has implications for storage requirements and possibly for computations as well. As we will see, this difference also has implications for deciding when a concept is likely to be represented in probabilistic form, and when in exemplar form.

Correlated Differences

There are three other differences between the probabilistic and exemplar views that are correlated with the critical difference discussed above. Each deserves some brief discussion.

Partial retrieval. As noted earlier, some exemplar models depart from the criteria of a summary representation (and hence from the probabilistic view) by disavowing that the same representation is always retrieved in decisions about concept membership. In some exemplar models, different parts of the representation — different exemplars — are retrieved for different test items. Partial versus total retrieval is therefore another difference between exemplar and probabilistic models.

Partial retrieval seems to fit better with explicit than implicit disjunction, since explicit disjunction leads to a larger storage load. However, it may be useful to allow partial retrieval in probabilistic models, that is, to assume that only some properties of a summary representation are retrieved by a test item. Such a move may allow us to deal with the apparent instability of some concepts (for example, the extent to which an individual has different sets of properties in mind when accessing the supposedly same concept on different occasions). Another reason for favoring partial retrieval is that it might help probabilistic models explain certain context effects. To use our old chestnut, in the sentence "The man lifted the piano," "lifted" may emphasize the weight feature of piano by restricting retrieval to just that feature.

Representation realizable as an instance. We noted earlier that in some exemplar models — the proximity and best-examples models — all representations (that is, exemplars) are realizable as specific instances. Often this is not the case in probabilistic models. However, this difference does not constitute a critical distinction between the two views because some exemplar models — for example, the context model — do not assume that exemplars *must* correspond to specific instances.

All this sounds like old hat, and the more cynical might question whether anything really hinges on the assumption that a representation (or part of it) is realizable as an instance. We think something may indeed hinge on this, namely the notion of a *prototype*. We have generally avoided this term because it has been used in the literature to mean too many things. But we think there is one meaning of prototype that is central: a representation of a concept, or part of such a representation, that (1) reflects some measure of central tendency of the instances' properties or patterns; (2) consequently is more similar to some concept members than others; and (3) is itself realizable as an instance. We hold that this definition of a prototype captures most of the important intuitions behind common usage of the term. Given this definition, many probabilistic representations are clearly not prototypes since they need not correspond to specific instances. However, some probabilistic representations would meet this criterion, for example, some dimensional and template representations. Conversely, many exemplar representations would be prototypes, though some (for example, those in the context model) would not because they are not necessarily realizable as instances. Thus the notion of a prototype is not entailed by either of the views.

Probability of properties. A property in a probabilistic representation must have a substantial probability of occurring among the concept's instances. Though this criterion is vague, it clearly differs from the comparable criterion in the exemplar view, where a property can be part of a representation if it is characteristic of a single instance. To illustrate, if someone's exemplar representation of mammals included a "tiger" exemplar, then the property "striped" could be part of the representation yet have a very low probability of occurring among mammal instances.

The probability of a property applying to an instance therefore offers still another way of distinguishing the probabilistic and exemplar views. As was the case with the previous two distinctions, though, the present one can serve only as a rough guide. Though in principle an exemplar representation can contain properties that apply to just a few instances, in practice the properties of stored exemplars will apply to many instances as long as the exemplars are typical ones.

Factors That Determine the Type of Representation

Though we have often talked as if only one of the views under consideration can be correct, things are very unlikely to be that simple. One possible complication is that some concepts are represented as the probabilistic view says they are, while others are represented in accordance with the exemplar view. A more complex complication is that representation of even a single concept may be partly probabilistic, partly exemplar. In this section we take up the first possibility and try to specify what factors determine whether a concept is represented in probabilistic or exemplar form. Two kinds of factors will be considered: those dealing with the concept learner, and those dealing with the concept itself.

Learner Factors

Development. Since exemplar representations are relatively concrete, and since they may require only simple operations such as retrieval, they may be more prevalent than probabilistic representations at early developmental stages. All other things being equal, then, the preference for probabilistic over exemplar representations may increase with age. Kossan (1978) found some support for this developmental hypothesis. She had second and fifth graders learn a relatively complex artificial concept; the instructions that preceded learning emphasized either abstraction or memory of instances. The rationale (which was based on Brooks, 1978) was that performance should be better with the abstraction instructions if the concept was represented in probabilistic form, but better with the memorization instructions if the concept was represented in exemplar form. As predicted by the developmental hypothesis, fifth graders performed better with the abstraction instructions (indicating that they used probabilistic representations), while second graders did better with memorization instructions (indicating they used exemplar representations).

We do not want to make too much of this single experiment. For one thing, the artificial concepts used may differ in fundamental ways from natural ones. For another, the logic relating performance under different kinds of instructions to probabilistic and exemplar representation is somewhat tenuous. Still, the Kossan study is a suggestive one that deserves to be pursued.

Task orientation. In an interesting series of experiments, Brooks (1978) tried to show that the task orientation of the concept learner can determine whether a probabilistic or exemplar representation is formed. Task orientation in a concept-learning task was varied in a number of ways, but roughly, any manipulation that favored storage of information about individual instances seemed to increase the likelihood that the learner would construct an exemplar representation. Thus instructions that emphasized memorization, or the use of a concurrent task that required memorizing information about specific instances, led to performance that seemed more in line with exemplar than probabilistic representations.

At first blush, one may wonder about the ecological validity of the above manipulations. How often does a concept learner have to memorize a set of instances? However, some reflection suggests that concept learners often have to store detailed information about instances; to use Brook's example, a child needs to know not only that a particular creature is a dog, but also that this is the one that will let you pat him and the other is the one that will take your arm off.

Concept Factors

Distribution of properties. Perhaps the most obvious determinant of the form of a concept representation is the structure of the concept itself. All other things being equal, if the instances of a concept share numerous (nondefining) properties, that concept will likely be represented in probabilistic form; if the instances share few properties, that concept is likely to be in exemplar form.[3] To put it another way, the greater the intraclass similarity, the more likely it is that the representation will be in the form of a summary rather than in the form of exemplars.

This determinant of representational form is closely tied to the critical distinction between probabilistic and exemplar representations. To the extent that instances of a concept share few properties, each instance must be distinctly represented in the concept, and we end up with the explicit disjuncts that are the hallmark of the exemplar view.

Relation to basic level.   At various points we have mentioned the distinction of Rosch and her colleagues (1976) between superordinate concepts (for example, furniture), basic-level concepts (chair) and subordinate concepts (director's chair). This distinction turns out to be related to the previous factor; when Rosch and her associates had subjects list attributes for concepts at these three levels, they found hardly any common attributes for superordinate concepts, numerous common attributes for basic-level concepts, and even more common attributes for subordinate concepts. Putting these results together with our previous remarks about the distribution of properties, we are led to the following proposals: superordinate concepts are likely to be described by exemplar representations, whereas subordinate concepts are likely to be described by probabilistic representations (basic-level concepts may fall somewhere in between).[4]

Though this proposal seems to capture something important, it is likely too simple. Though superordinates probably have no common *perceptual* properties (as the listings from Rosch and colleagues indicate), they may well have common abstract or functional properties (which the listings are insensitive to). Thus a superordinate's perceptual properties may be represented in exemplar form (that is, shape is given separately for each exemplar), while its nonperceptual properties are described in probabilistic form (that is, as a summary representation). This amounts to positing a *mixed* representation.

Two Complications

In the course of trying to reconcile the probabilistic and exemplar views, we have implicitly been suggesting that a viable research program would consist of (1) first specifying facts that presumably would determine whether a concept will be stored as a probabilistic or an exemplar representation, and (2) then doing experiments that would ascertain if the factors work as hypothesized. There are complications involved in both of these steps. Step 1 presupposes that a concept is represented one way or the other. As we have noted, however, the representation of a single concept may be mixed in form. Such representations will be discussed in the next section.

Even if concepts are represented one way or the other, there can be difficulties in interpreting experimental results in the second step of the research program. The difficulties arise because probabilistic and exemplar models often make identical predictions. An example of this phenomenon is shown in Figure 36, which illustrates a hypothetical experiment on acquisition and transfer of concepts that is similar to many actual studies. In the acquisition phase of the experiment, subjects learn four instances of an artificial concept, each instance being described in terms of four binary dimensions. The figure shows two alternative representations of this concept, a

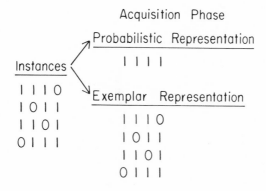

Acquisition Phase

Probabilistic Representation

Instances

1 1 1 1

1 1 1 0
1 0 1 1
1 1 0 1
0 1 1 1

Exemplar Representation

1 1 1 0
1 0 1 1
1 1 0 1
0 1 1 1

Transfer Phase

Distance from Concept Representation

Transfer Items	Probabilistic Concept	Exemplar Concept
1 1 1 1	0	1.0
1 1 1 0	1	1.5
1 1 0 0	2	2.0
1 0 0 0	3	2.5
0 0 0 0	4	3.0

Figure 36 *Hypothetical experiment showing difficulty of discriminating between probabilistic and exemplar representations*

probabilistic and an exemplar one. In the transfer phase, subjects must indicate their certainty that each of five transfer items fits in the learned concept. Presumably their degree of certainty, the data, will depend on the distance between the transfer item and the concept representation. But as indicated in Figure 36, the order of the transfer items in terms of distance from the learned concept is the same regardless of whether the concept is represented probabilistically or in exemplar form. (For the exemplar representation, we have calculated the average distance between a transfer item and every exemplar.)

The antidote to the above problem is the staple of experimental psychology: a consideration of alternative models and some experimental ingenuity. Given a prediction from a model based on one of the views, researchers need to consider whether plausible models based on an opposing view also can yield that prediction; if they can, one needs to devise a more diagnostic experiment.

Mixed Representations

We cannot ignore the possibility that the representation of a single concept can contain both probabilistic and exemplar components, that is, both a summary representation and exemplars. Earlier we suggested that such a mixed representation might be needed for superordinate concepts, such as furniture. Now we wish to point out that there is good reason to think that mixed representations may be needed with other kinds of concepts as well. Specifically, recall the developmental hypothesis that as one matures, one is more likely to represent a concept in probabilistic than in exemplar form. This suggests that children may initially represent concepts in terms of exemplars, and then later apply abstraction processes to these exemplars to yield a summary representation. As long as they do not discard the exemplars, mature learners would end up with both exemplars and a summary representation for the same concept. It is even possible that this developmental sequence occurs to some degree whenever adults learn a new concept — they first represent the concept in terms of exemplars, but with additional experience they form a summary representation as well.

For concepts believed to be represented in mixed form, there are new kinds of issues to confront. Thus, if a concept representation contains both a summary and exemplars, in some circumstances the summary may be more accessible (and hence the major determinant of categorization), while at other times the exemplars may be more accessible. If this is so, the research task becomes one of specifying what circumstances increase and decrease the accessibilities of summaries and exemplars.

Other issues involve possible interactions between the summary and exemplar components of a concept. To illustrate, consider how summary and exemplar information might interact in the process of learning or updating a concept. In particular, consider a child who has both summary and exemplar information about birds, with the summary containing the property of "flies." How should the child update his summary when confronted with one or two species of birds that do not fly? Clearly the new summary should be some combination of the old one and the new experiences, but the child needs some procedure for determining how much weight to attach to the new evidence. Such a procedure could be based on the stored exemplar information about birds: to the extent that the child can access many stored exemplars that fly, the old summary is based on substantial evidence and should be altered only minimally by the new evidence.[5]

In addition to this effect of old exemplars on the construction of a new summary, there may also be an effect of the old summary on the storage of new exemplars. Since the old summary specifies that most birds can fly, the fact that a newly encountered species does not is noteworthy, and hence should be encoded as a property of the new exemplars. In essence, the old summary provides the learner with a means of determining when to encode negative features in exemplar representations.

Although there are many other interesting issues concerning interactions between summary and exemplar information, we will not discuss them here. Our aim has been only to point out that we need to ask some new questions about concepts if a single concept representation contains both probabilistic and exemplar components.

Limits on the Present Work

The major conclusion to emerge from this book is that the facts about object categorization fit the probabilistic and exemplar views better than they do the classical view. The obvious question to ask is whether this conclusion can be generalized to domains other than object concepts. For most domains it is difficult to say, since research on these domains has rarely focused on a choice among views. One exception, however, is Keil's work (1979) on ontological concepts (for example, thing, event, physical object). Though this domain seems similar to the object domain we have concentrated on, Keil's analysis suggests that the facts about ontological concepts may fit the classical view quite well. If Keil is correct, we have hit upon an important limit to the generality of our conclusions. Given the importance of this, we will summarize Keil's case for the classical view in the first half of this section.

In the second half of this section we will consider another kind of limit on the present work. While we have shown that the probabilistic and exemplar views can yield satisfactory accounts of categorization, there are functions of concepts other than categorization, and the two views need to account for these other functions as well. We will discuss only one other function, conceptual combination, and argue that the present account of it in probabilistic or exemplar terms is inadequate. We do this not to end on a pessimistic note, but rather to point to research questions that seem most in need of future work.

Ontological Concepts and the Classical View

Background on Ontological Concepts

Keil (1979) takes ontological concepts to be the basic categories of existence. They include (among others) the concepts of thing, event, physical object, organism, functional artifact, animal, plant, and human. There is some overlap between these concepts and the object concepts we have considered (for example, animals and plants appear in both sets). There are also some differences: ontological concepts include things other than physical objects (such as events), and the set of ontological concepts makes fewer distinctions than our set of object concepts (for example, birds and fish would not be distinguished in the ontological set).

Keil's analysis of ontological concepts is based on philosophical work, particularly that of Sommers (1965). Rather than starting with the ontological concepts themselves, the analysis begins by focusing on a phenomenon that presumably reflects the knowledge contained in such concepts. The phenomenon, known as *predicability*, is that only certain predicates can combine with certain terms in any natural language. The predicate "is asleep," for example, can be applied sensibly to man and rabbit, but not to car and milk. What is particularly important about predicability is that it seems to involve hierarchical organization, as is shown in the tree diagram in Figure 37. The predicates are shown in uppercase letters and the terms in lowercase letters; the dashed lines indicate which predicates apply to which terms, while the solid lines indicate hierarchical relations between predicates. The predicate "is dead," for example, hierarchically dominates the predicate "is asleep" in that if the latter applies to a term then so does the former, but not vice

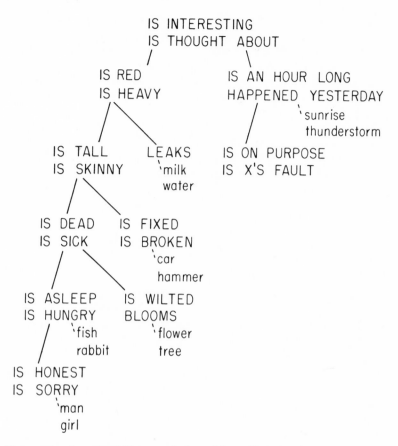

Figure 37   *A predicability tree (adapted from Keil, 1979)*

versa. More generally, a predicate applies to all those terms that every predicate below it applies to.

What exactly does this have to do with ontological concepts? Note that while a nonterminal node in Figure 37 explicitly represents a class of predicates, it implicitly represents a class of terms, namely the set of all terms under that node.[6] As an example, the node in Figure 37 that contains the predicates "is dead" and "is sick" also represents the set of all terms that can combine with either of these predicates or with the predicates dominated by them. The upshot is that each node represents a class of terms, with these terms denoting the members of an ontological concept, as is shown in Figure 38. This figure presents a hierarchy of ontological concepts that is isomorphic to the hierarchy of predicates in the previous figure.

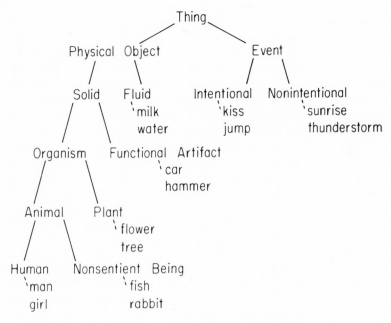

Figure 38   *An ontological tree (adapted from Keil, 1979)*

Compatibility with the Classical View

Now we can deal with the critical question, namely, what is Keil's evidence that the ontological concepts in Figure 38 conform to the classical view? First and foremost, Keil argues that ontological concepts *do* have necessary features (where predicates can be construed as features), and that these features may be sufficient as well. The concept of a solid object, for instance, has the necessary features of mass, volume, and a rigid structure. Keil's claim, then, is that what had been the most decimating problem for the classical view in our domain of object concepts will not be insurmountable in the domain of ontological concepts.[7]

Other problems associated with the classical view may disappear as well with ontological concepts. Consider the phenomenon of unclear cases. In the domain of object concepts, a lack of certainty about whether or not a test item is a subset of a target concept may often arise because the test item contains only some features of the target concept; that is, the feature sets of the two object concepts have an overlap relation rather than a subset relation. Such an overlap relation, however, cannot arise with the hierarchically organized features (predicates) of ontological concepts. As inspection of the trees in Figures 37 and 38 indicates, either two concepts have the identical set of features (predicates), or one has a proper subset of the other, or they share no features at all. This constraint follows directly from the structure of the trees, and it eliminates a major source of unclear cases. Now, we need evidence that the trees in question capture people's knowledge about predicability and ontological concepts. Keil tries to supply a good deal of such evidence by showing that the trees are compatible with subjects' judgments about: (1) sentence anomaly (for example, according to the tree in Figure 37, "The milk is dead" should be judged anomalous); (2) naturalness of concepts (according to the tree in Figure 38, animals and plants should form a more natural class than do animals and fluids); (3) naturalness of copredication (according to Figure 37, "is asleep" and "is broken" cannot apply to the same term); and (4) interconcept similarity (according to Figure 38, animal and plant should be judged more similar than animal and functional artifact).

The fourth finding provides Keil's most direct evidence for a classical-view representation of ontological concepts. In demonstrating that similarity judgments conform to a tree like that in Figure 38, Keil has shown that an ontological concept is consistently judged more similar to its immediate than its distant superordinate. This prediction from the classical view had, of course, proved troublesome when the view was applied to our set of object concepts.

The preceding summary by no means does justice to Keil's analysis. It should, however, suffice to convey some of the reasons for thinking that the classical view can provide a satisfactory account of ontological concepts. Of course, things could ultimately go badly for a classical view of ontological concepts — we still do not have detailed proposals about defining properties here. But at this point we have to concede that the probabilistic and exemplar views may be limited in their extension.

CONCEPTUAL COMBINATION AND THE PROBABILISTIC AND EXEMPLAR VIEWS

One function of concepts other than simple categorization is conceptual combination. It involves combining simple concepts into complex ones, such as when we combine the concepts of pet and fish into the conjunction pet-fish. How one approaches the study of conceptual combination depends as usual on one's view of concepts, and researchers who favor the probabilistic or exemplar views have routinely proposed that the principles of combination can be taken from *fuzzy-set* theory. Recently, Osherson and Smith (1981) have argued that this proposal is seriously flawed. If these arguments are correct, then a major sore point for the probabilistic and exemplar views is that they lack anything like a satisfactory account of conceptual combination.[8]

Fuzzy-Set Theory

As developed by Zadeh (for example, 1965), fuzzy-set theory is a branch of set theory designed for representing and manipulating concepts whose instances can manifest degrees of membership. Since "degrees of membership" is a hallmark of the probabilistic and exemplar views, fuzzy-set theory seems to be a natural complement to these views. And the reason for joining fuzzy-set theory to these views is that it supposedly gives them a way of accounting for conceptual combination (see Rosch and Mervis, 1975; Oden, 1977).

For our purposes the key set-theoretical construct is that of a *characteristic* function. A characteristic function of the fuzzy-set type maps entities into numbers in a way that indicates the degree to which the entity is a member of some set or concept. To illustrate, consider the characteristic function c_F, which measures degree of membership in the concept fish (F). When applied to any creature, $c_F(x)$ yields a number between 0 and 1, where:

The larger $c_F(x)$, the more x belongs to F;
the smaller $c_F(x)$, the less x belongs to F;
1 and 0 are limiting cases.

As an example, our pet guppy may not be a very typical fish, so it may be assigned a value of .80. Our pet dog will of course get a very low value, say .05 (we cannot give it a value of 0 since dog is more fish-like than most inanimate objects, and 0 must be reserved for the latter). If our concern switches to the concept of pets (P), then both our guppy and our dog will be assigned relatively high values, say .70 and .80 (with dog getting the larger value because it is the more typical pet).[9]

Problems in Representing Conceptual Combination

The issue of conceptual combination has often been reduced to the following question about characteristic functions: Given that concepts P and F combine to form complex concept P•F, how do we specify P•F's characteristic function on the basis of those of P and F? (This may seem a rather narrow question about conceptual combination, but it captures a good deal of what has been written on the issue.) To illustrate, given that the concepts of pet and fish combine to form the concept pet-fish (P•F), how can we express $c_{P \cdot F}(x)$ in terms of $c_P(x)$ and $c_F(x)$? The answer from fuzzy-set theory is that $c_{P \cdot F}(x)$ is the minimum of $c_P(x)$ and $c_F(x)$. More formally, for any domain, D,

$$(\forall x \epsilon D)\ c_{P \cdot F}(x) = \min(c_{P(x)},\ c_{F(x)}\ )$$

Applying this formula to our pet guppy, g, yields

$$c_{P \cdot F}(g) = \min(c_P(g),\ c_F(g)\ )$$
$$= \min(.70,\ .80) = .70$$

This says that our guppy is less typical of the concept pet-fish than it is of the concept fish, .70 versus .80; and therein lies a problem. For intuition strongly suggests that a guppy is more representative of the conjunction pet-fish than it is of either constituent — pet or fish. More generally, the formula has failed here because it requires an element to be less typical of a conjunction than of the maximum-valued conjunct. Osherson and Smith (1981) argue that this "guppy" example is just one of an indefinite number of cases where an instance is at least as typical of a conjunction as it is of its maximum-valued constituent; yet in each such case the formula given above will incorrectly declare the instance to be less typical of the conjunction.

The preceding case is only one difficulty that arises when fuzzy-set theory is joined to the probabilistic and exemplar views. Osherson and Smith (1981) detail several others. Thus, while intuition strongly suggests that the characteristic function for a logically empty concept should always be 0, often this will not be the case with characteristic functions of the fuzzy-set variety. For example, when the characteristic function for the logically empty concept "fish-and-not-a-fish" is applied to our pet guppy, it yields a number greater than 0,

$$c_{F \cdot \sim F}(g) = \min(c_F(g),\ c_{\sim F}(g)\ )$$
$$= \min(.80,\ .20) = .20$$

Some Implications

How damaging are the problems discussed above? Some might argue that these problems are not particularly serious because they are primarily a consequence of the specifics of Zadeh's fuzzy-set theory. Perhaps some other branch of set theory can be joined with the probabilistic and exemplar views to account satisfactorily for conceptual combination. This is possible, but as Osherson and Smith note, no obvious alternative to Zadeh's formulation has appeared on the horizon. What seems more plausible to us is that the above problems reflect a deep dilemma, namely, that one cannot specify the characteristic function of a complex concept on the basis of *only* the characteristic functions of the constituent concepts.

One may therefore need to consider other kinds of information in specifying the characteristic function of a complex concept, for example, the properties of the constituent concepts and rules for combining these properties. We know of no principled account along these lines. Attempts to develop such accounts within the boundaries of the probabilistic and exemplar views could be a particularly useful direction for future work. Such attempts not only might tell us something about conceptual combination, but also might produce some interesting constraints on the views themselves. For example, if only certain kinds of properties can be combined, then only these kinds of properties may appear in probabilistic and exemplar representations of concepts. More generally, we may have reached the point where a useful research strategy for studying concepts is to consider concurrently phenomena associated with different uses of concepts.

A Closing Comment

This section in particular, and this chapter in general, has made it clear that there will likely be no crucial experiments or analyses that will establish one view of concepts as correct and rule out all others irrevocably. Although the evidence we have sifted through in this book has generally been more favorable to the probabilistic and exemplar views than to the classical one, we think there are aspects of the classical view that will doubtless find their way into any comprehensive theory of concepts. In effect, then, what we have done in this book is to examine in detail some components of a comprehensive theory. The theory itself will take a little longer.

Notes
References
Index

Notes

1. Introduction

1. This was suggested to us by Amos Tversky.

2. Preliminary Issues

1. There is a major exception to this. When an object concept is represented as a point in a multidimensional space, that point is often assumed to be a holistic description of the concept, yet it is abstract in the sense that it results from combining the dimension values that characterize the object. We will have more to say about this in Chapter 5 when we take up dimensional representations of probabilistic concepts.

2. Our notion of a feature differs from that sometimes used in linguistics and anthropology, where a feature specifies a binary contrast. In phonetics, for example, one feature used to characterize speech sounds is *voiced* versus *unvoiced* (whether or not the vocal chords are vibrating during production of the sound). Here entities are as explicitly marked for the absence of a quality as they are for the presence of it, that is, *unvoiced* is as explicit a property as *voiced*. In our usage, we typically employ a feature to indicate only the presence of a quality.

3. There are exceptions to this general trend. Some successful uses of feature descriptions have employed only a few features that are relevant to most concepts in the domain. A prime example is the small set of articulatory features used to characterize speech sounds. Still, when it comes to object concepts like animals, plants, and artifacts, we think that feature descriptions will tend to contain more properties than dimensional descriptions, and that some of the features involved will be relevant to only a few concepts.

4. Though a feature set that exhausts all relations between concepts implies that the features are primitives, this implication is not bidirectional. One can posit a set of primitives for a domain that does not exhaust all possible relations.

5. Gibson (1966) suggests that some functional features are direct outputs from the perceptual system. However, the functional features that we consider in this book do not seem to us to be perceptually based.

6. The core may also play the major role in the functions of concepts that we noted earlier — conceptual combination, constructing propositional representations, and interrogating representations.

3. The Classical View

1. More recent philosophical work has, however, endeavored to deliver the death blow. In their attempts to devise a new theory of reference, Kripke (1971) and Putnam (1973) have argued that there is no property of an object that we refer to by the name X that the object must necessarily have in order for us to call it an X. Rather, in some cases, the reference of a name might be ultimately established by a kind of causal chain that started with someone initially dubbing the object an X, and continued with other people using X with the intent of referring to the same object (Kripke, 1972). Taken at face value, these arguments challenge the assumption that people's mental representations of concepts contain necessary features if we take "necessary" to mean "essential" rather than just "has a probability of 1.0." However, these philosophical arguments are sufficiently novel that their implications for psychology are still unsettled (Rey, 1978; Schwartz, 1979), and for this reason we will not dwell on them here.

2. In what follows, we use the phrase "X" is a member of Y" to mean the same as "X is a subset of Y"; both of these phrases contrast with "X is an instance of Y," since this last phrase applies to individuals.

3. Another strategy for demonstrating that simple typicality effects are not inconsistent with the classical view is to show that these effects occur even with concepts that apparently conform to the classical view. This is the strategy used by Armstrong, Gleitman, and Gleitman (forthcoming). One of the concepts they used was that of even number, which has the widely known defining feature of being divisible by 2. They showed that some even numbers were judged more typical of the concept than others, and that those numbers judged more typical were categorized as even numbers faster.

4. This is not to claim that the access-path approach has not proved valuable in the study of concepts. Indeed, the approach seems to be of indisputable value in research on concepts that tackles questions other than categorization. Thus the approach is perhaps the dominant one to the issue of how concepts are used in interrogating propositional representations (see Quillian, 1968; Fahlman, 1977; Brachman, 1980). Our real claim, then, is this: a set of assumptions designed to tackle a problem about one use of concepts (interrogating representations) cannot, without some refinements, be used to solve a problem about another use of concepts (categorization).

5. This was suggested to us by Dan Osherson.

4. The Probabilistic View: Featural Approach

1. The conditional probability that enters into the weight is to be taken as a subjective rather than an objective one. It is subjective because it need not be based on an unbiased estimate of how often a feature occurs with concept instances; it may be based, for example, mainly on certain significant instances, like those experienced during a critical acquisition period.

2. This is not to say that F_4–F_6 are definitely excluded from concept representation; rather, they are just less likely to be in that representation.

3. This explanation differs from that offered by Rosch and Mervis (1975). They assume that the typicality of an item is directly determined by the number of features that item shares with other members in the class, with no mention of a general concept mediating between the members and the determination of typicality. As we will see later, this interpretation fits better with an exemplar view of concepts than with the present probabilistic view.

4. In addition to featural evidence, Collins and Loftus consider other sources of information that a categorizer can use. One additional source consists of interconcept links (for example, a subset link between the concepts of bird and animal), like those we considered in one of our radical attempts to salvage the classical view. Another extra source includes the features of subsets of the target concept; for example, when asked if a stagecoach is an instance of "vehicle," a categorizer may compare the features of stagecoach to those of a more familiar subset of vehicle, say those of a coach car. Though this process involves features, it does so in a manner that is more consistent with the exemplar view than the probabilistic one. From the current perspective, then, the full Collins and Loftus model is a hybrid of the various views we are discussing.

5. Note that the problem of representing a correlation between features does not arise with the classical-view concepts; for example, if "sings" and "small" are defining features of bird they must occur in *all* subsets of bird, and hence there is no variability to base a correlation on. However, other relations between features are possible in classical-view concepts; for example, one feature might imply another. We did not tackle the problem of how to represent such relations because the classical view already had enough problems on its hands.

6. We have overlooked one problem here. In assuming the feature "wings" can itself have the feature "large," we acknowledge that "wings" is decomposable. Doesn't this violate our constraint that features not be decomposable, just as the conjunctive feature "sings-and-small" violated this constraint? We think there is a clear difference in the degree of violation between the two offending features, and perhaps a difference in kind as well. Not only does "sings-and-small" seem a more gross violation of the nondecomposability constraint, but the constituents into which it can be decomposed are manifest in the conjunctive feature itself. In contrast, the feature "large" is truly embedded within the feature of "wings." Thus to salvage the current labeled-relations approach while maintaining some constraints on features, we may have to tolerate decomposable features with an embedding structure, but not those with a simple conjunctive structure.

7. One bothersome aspect about Figure 15 is that we seem to have slipped some dimensional aspects into our supposedly featural representation. That is, the roles, "size" and "characteristic sound," seem to name dimensions, while the role fillers specify values on these dimensions. To the extent that this is so, it provides some rationale for incorporating both features and dimensions into a concept representation, a position we will later argue for explicitly.

8. It is possible that we are being too optimistic here. Perhaps necessary-but-not-sufficient features can readily be found for specific concepts when they involve artifacts, such as chair and jacket, but not when they involve natural kinds, such as dog and oak. This would be in line with the recent arguments against necessary features for natural kinds (for example, Putnam, 1973).

9. To the extent that certain context effects are problems for the probabilistic view, they may also be problems for the classical view. We did not raise these problems in the chapter on the classical view, since this might have taken our attention away from the view's more fundamental problems.

5. The Probabilistic View: Dimensional Approach

1. Like a subjective probability, a subjective average need not be based on an unbiased estimate of how frequently each dimension value occurs in instances; rather, it may be biased by particular values experienced during critical acquisition periods.

2. These properties are taken from Rosch et al., 1976, since Rosch and Mervis do not give the actual features listed in their studies.

3. It is possible that the difficulties just mentioned can be overcome by existent psychometric techniques, but this remains to be demonstrated.

4. We can be more precise about the sense in which unitary processing is suggested by the fact that similarity is captured by euclidean distance. Specifically: (1) There is some evidence from scaling studies with semantic concepts that a euclidean metric does a better job of fitting the data (usually similarity ratings) than the so-called city-block metric (for example, Rips, Shoben, and Smith, 1973); (2) unlike the case with the city-block metric, distance calculations with a euclidean metric do not proceed on a component-by-component basis; and in addition (3) prior work with perceptual concepts has shown that concepts requiring a euclidean metric in multidimensional scaling also tend to be processed as units in discrimination and selective-attention tasks.

5. Our criticisms here are a little unfair to Posner. Before ever using dot patterns to study concept acquisition, Posner, Goldsmith, and Welton (1967) did conduct psychophysical studies to try to determine the exact dimensions of such patterns. Their results showed, for example, that the judged similarity of a distortion to its prototype was systematically related to the difference between the corresponding dots in the two patterns. Such results are consistent with interpreting each prototype dot as a potential dimension, but they are also consistent with other dimensional interpretations of the dot patterns — for example, the dimensions may be the densities of dots in particular regions (see text).

6. The Probabilistic View: Holistic Approach

1. Since the metric representations discussed in the previous chapter seem capable of representing a concept by a single point, why are they not part of the present chapter? That is, can't the notion of a holistic property be instantiated by a point in a euclidean space? Though the question is a

difficult one, we think a negative answer can be defended. While metric models posit a level at which concepts may be represented holistically, they also seem to posit a level at which concepts are represented in terms of component dimension values. And it seems to be in the spirit of metric models to assume that people can decompose the point standing for a concept into its component dimension values.

2. If we had to spell out exactly what we mean by the isomorphic aspect of templates, we would probably opt for Kosslyn's description of an *abstract spatial isomorphism* (1980, pp. 33-34).

3. Note that this procedure for determining a concept template does not provide any means for updating a concept as new instances are experienced. Having determined that a particular cell in the concept template should be black because five of the initial six instances had this color in the relevant cells, what does one do when the next ten instances have white in the critical cell? The problem of updating concept representations is not unique to the template approach; similar difficulties arise in changing features and dimension values (and their weights) in other approaches.

4. In the preceding discussion, every cell of the instances was considered equally important in constructing a concept template. An alternative is that different cells may have different degrees of importance; for example, the exterior cells of an instance, which convey its overall shape, may be weighted most heavily.

5. Note that this simple matching process will not work if the concept template is determined by averaging color values of instances. For in this case, one cannot count matching cells, since all the instances' cells will be black or white while many of the concept's cells will be intermediate values.

7. The Exemplar View

1. While "your favorite pair of faded blue jeans" is something of an abstraction in that it abstracts over situations, it seems qualitatively less abstract than blue jeans in general, which abstracts over different entities.

8. Summary and Implications

1. For ease of exposition, we have omitted mention of the problems resulting from the metric assumption in the dimensional approach to the probabilistic view.

2. The argument that exemplar representations require more storage space than probabilistic ones applies to any *pure* exemplar model, that is, to any model in which a concept is represented by exemplars no matter what the level of the concept. As an alternative, one could assume that while generic concepts (for example, bird) are represented by their exemplars, more specific concepts (robin, sparrow) are represented in probabilistic form. In this kind of model, the representations of some specific concepts can be identical to exemplars in the representations of generic concepts; for example robin is both a specific concept and an exemplar in the concept of bird. To avoid redundancy, perhaps only one of these identical representations is stored, in which case the model would not necessarily re-

quire more storage space than a (pure) probabilistic model. We will say more about this kind of difference in levels later in the text.

3. Exceptions to this generalization may arise when the few properties on which the concept instances differ are extremely important. Thus if two instances of mushrooms differ only (1) in color and (2) in that one is poisonous and the other edible, then the two instances are unlikely to be amalgamated into a single probabilistic summary.

4. We should point out that here and elsewhere, what we are treating as changes from exemplar to probabilistic representations, and vice versa, can actually be handled by a single model, the context model. This is because the model permits strategy-based abstraction, wherein representations of different instances can be collapsed into one exemplar (see Chapter 7). We provide a fuller discussion of this point in Medin and Smith (1981).

5. In the event that the summary needs to be altered substantially by the new evidence, another issue arises — namely, should supersets of bird also be altered, for example, should the summary or exemplars (or both) associated with animal, or with living things, also be updated? This question arises whether concept representations are mixed or pure, probabilistic or exemplar. We know of no critical work on the issue.

6. Each nonterminal node in Figure 37 represents an indefinitely large class of predicates, only some of which are shown as examples.

7. If the concept of solid object has the necessary features of mass, volume, and a rigid structure, then so does the concept of animal, since the latter is hierarchically dominated by the former. But then why, in attribute listing studies, don't all subjects list these three features for animal? Because, according to Keil, subjects probably adopt a definition-giving convention that essentially says, "Start off with a general word that cues one into the relevant ontological category but . . . never go further to list the features of that ontological category or of more superordinate ones" (1979, p. 52).

8. Osherson and Smith (1981) treat the probabilistic and exemplar views as alternative versions of a single theory. Since nothing of consequence about conceptual combination seems to hinge on this condensation, we also will neglect distinctions between the two views in what follows.

9. A characteristic function value can be estimated by a typicality rating (or some transformation of the latter). A characteristic function value cannot be interpreted as a probability. Thus for the concept of fish, to say that guppy has a characteristic function value of .80 does not mean that we expect only 80 percent of guppies to be fish.

References

Anderson, J. R. 1976. *Language, memory, and thought.* Hillsdale, N.J.: Erlbaum.

Anderson, J. R., and G. H. Bower. 1973. *Human associative memory.* Washington, D. C.: Winston.

Anderson, R. C., and A. Ortony, 1975. On putting apples into bottles — a problem of polysemy. *Cognitive Psychology.* 7:167–180.

Anglin, J. M. 1977. *Word, object, and conceptual development.* New York: Norton.

Anisfeld, M. 1968. Disjunctive concepts. *Journal of General Psychology* 78:223–228.

Armstrong, S., L. R. Gleitman, and H. Gleitman (forthcoming). What most concepts are not.

Ashcraft, M. H. 1978. Property norms for typical and atypical items from 17 categories: A description and discussion. *Memory and Cognition* 6:227–232.

Atkinson, R. C., and W. K. Estes. 1963. Stimulus sampling theory. In *Handbook of mathematical psychology,* ed. R. D. Luce, R. R. Bush, and E. Galanter, vol. 2. New York: Wiley.

Banks, W. P. 1977. Encoding and processing of symbolic information in comparative judgements. In *The psychology of learning and motivation: Advances in research and theory,* ed. G. H. Bower, vol. 11. New York: Academic Press.

Barclay, J. R., J. D. Bransford, J. J. Franks, N. S. McCarrell, and K. Nitsch. 1974. Comprehension and semantic flexibility. *Journal of Verbal Learning and Verbal Behavior* 13:471–481.

Barresi, J., D. Robbins, and K. Shain. 1975. Role of distinctive features in the abstraction of related concepts. *Journal of Experimental Psychology: Human Learning and Memory* 1:360–368.

Barrett, M. D. 1977. Lexical development and overextension in child language. *Journal of Child Language* 5:205–219.

Beach, L. R. 1964. Cue probabilism and inference behavior. *Psychological Monographs* 78 (Whole no. 582).

Beals, R., D. H. Krantz, and A. Tversky. 1968. Foundations of multidimensional scaling. *Psychological Review* 75:127–142.

Bierwisch, M. 1970. Semantics. In *New horizons in linguistics*, ed. J. Lyons. Baltimore: Penguin Books.

Bledsoe, W. W., and I. Browning. 1959. Pattern recognition and reading by machine. *Proceedings of the Eastern Joint Computer Conference, 1959*, 225–232. (Reprinted in *Pattern recognition*, ed. L. Uhr. New York: Wiley, 1966.)

Bobrow, D. G., and T. Winograd. 1977. An overview of KRL, a knowledge representation language. *Cognitive Science* 3:3–46.

Bock, M. 1976. The influence of instructions on feature selection in semantic memory. *Journal of Verbal Learning and Verbal Behavior* 15:183–191.

Bolinger, D. L. 1975. *Aspects of language* (2nd ed.). New York: Harcourt Brace Jovanovich.

Bourne, L. E. 1966. *Human conceptual behavior*. Boston: Allyn and Bacon.

Bourne, L. E., Jr., R. L. Dominowski, and E. F. Loftus. 1979. *Cognitive processes*. Englewood Cliffs, N.J.: Prentice-Hall.

Brachman, R. J. 1980. An introduction to KL-ONE. In *Research in natural-language understanding: Annual report (1 Sept. 78–31 Aug. 79)*, ed. R. J. Brachman et al. Cambridge, Mass.: Bolt, Beranek, and Newman.

Bradshaw, M. 1976. An investigation of stimulus integrality in the perception of schematic faces (technical report 82). Baltimore: Johns Hopkins University, Department of Psychology.

Brooks, L. 1978. Nonanalytic concept formation and memory for instances. In *Cognition and categorization*, ed. E. Rosch and B. B. Lloyd. Hillsdale, N.J.: Erlbaum.

Brown, R. 1973. *A first language: The early stages*. Cambridge, Mass. Harvard University Press.

Bruner, J. S., J. Goodnow, and G. Austin. 1956. *A study of thinking*. New York: Wiley.

Cacoullos, T., ed. 1973. *Discriminant analysis and applications.* New York: Academic Press.

Caramazza, A., H. Hersch, and W. S. Torgerson. 1976. Subjective structures and operations in semantic memory. *Journal of Verbal Learning and Verbal Behavior* 15:103–118.

Cassirer, E. 1923. *Substance and function*. New York: Dover.

Charniak, E. 1977. A framed PAINTING: The representation of a common sense knowledge fragment. *Cognitive Science* 1:355–394.

Chen, C. H. 1973. *Statistical pattern recognition*. Rochelle Park, N.J.: Hayden Books.

Clark, E. V. 1973. What's in a word? On the child's acquisition of semantics in his first language. In *Cognitive development and the acquisition of language*, ed. T. E. Moore. New York: Academic Press.

Clark, H. H., and E. V. Clark. 1977. *Psychology and language*. New York: Harcourt Brace Jovanovich.

Collins, A. 1978. Fragments of a theory of human plausible reasoning. In

Proceedings of conference on theoretical issues in natural language processing 2, ed. D. Waltz. Urbana, Ill.: University of Illinois at Urbana-Champaign.

Collins, A., and E. F. Loftus. 1975. A spreading activation theory of semantic processing. *Psychological Review* 82:407–428.

Collins, A., and M. R. Quillian. 1969. Retrieval time from semantic memory. *Journal of Verbal Learning and Verbal Behavior* 8:240–247.

Crowder, R. G. (forthcoming). *The psychology of reading: A short survey.*

de Dombal, F. T., and F. Gremy, eds. 1976. *Decision making and medical care.* Amsterdam: North-Holland.

Dodwell, P. C. 1970. *Visual pattern recognition.* New York: Holt.

Fahlman, S. E. 1977. A system for representing and using real-world knowledge. Ph.D. diss., Massachusetts Institute of Technology.

Fakunaga, H. 1972. *Introduction to statistical pattern recognition.* London: Academic Press.

Fillmore, C. J. 1971. Verbs of judging: An exercise in semantic description. In *Studies in linguistic semantics*, ed. C. J. Fillmore and D. T. Langendoen. New York: Holt, Rinehart and Winston.

Fodor, J. A. 1975. *The language of thought.* New York: Crowell.

Fodor, J. A., T. G. Bever, and M. F. Garrett. 1974. *The psychology of language: An introduction to psycholinguistics and generative grammar.* New York: McGraw-Hill.

Franks, J. J. and J. D. Bransford 1971. Abstraction of visual patterns. *Journal of Experimental Psychology* 90:64–74.

Frege, G. 1892. On sense and reference. *Zeitschrift fur Philosophie und Philosophische Kritik* 100:25–50. (Reprinted in M. Black, *Translations from philosophical writings of G. Frege.* Oxford: Blackwell, 1960.)

Garner, W. R. 1974. *The processing of information and structure.* New York: Wiley.

————. 1976. Interaction of stimulus dimensions in concept and choice processes. *Cognitive Psychology* 8:98–123.

————. 1978. Aspects of a stimulus: Features, dimensions, and configurations. In *Cognition and categorization*, ed. E. Rosch and B. B. Lloyd. Hillsdale, N.J.: Erlbaum.

Garner, W. R., and G. L. Felfoldy. 1970. Integrality of stimulus dimensions in various types of information processing. *Cognitive Psychology* 1:225–241.

Gentner, D. 1978. What looks like a jiggy but acts like a zimbo? A study of early word meaning using artificial objects. *Papers and Reports on Child Language Development* 15:1–6.

Gibson, E. J. 1969. *Principles of perceptual learning and development.* New York: Appleton-Century-Crofts.

Gibson, J. J. 1966. *The senses considered as perceptual systems.* Boston: Houghton Mifflin.

Glass, A. L., and K. J. Holyoak. 1975. Alternative conceptions of semantic memory. *Cognition* 3:313–339.

Goldman, D., and D. Homa. 1977. Integrative and metric properties of abstracted information as a function of category discriminability, instance variability, and experience. *Journal of Experimental Psychology: Human Learning and Memory* 3:375–385.

Guenther, R. K., and R. L. Klatzky. 1977. Semantic classification of pictures and words. *Journal of Experimental Psychology* 3:498–514.

Hampton, J. A. 1979. Polymorphous concepts in semantic memory. *Journal of Verbal Learning and Verbal Behavior* 18:441–461.

Hayes-Roth, B., and F. Hayes-Roth. 1977. Concept learning and the recognition and classification of exemplars. *Journal of Verbal Learning and Verbal Behavior* 16:119–136.

Henle, N. 1969. A study of the semantics of animal terms. *Journal of Verbal Behavior* 8:176–184.

Hintzman, D. L., and G. Ludlam 1980. Differential forgetting of prototypes and old instances: Simulation by an exemplar-based classification model. *Memory and Cognition* 8:378–382.

Hirschfeld, S. L., W. M. Bart, and S. F. Hirschfeld. 1975. Visual abstraction in children and adults. *Journal of Genetic Psychology* 126:69–81.

Holland, J. H., and J. S. Reitman. 1978. Cognitive systems based on adaptive algorithms. In *Pattern directed inference systems*, ed. F. Hayes-Roth and D. Waterman. New York: Academic Press.

Holyoak, K. J. 1978. Comparative judgments with numerical reference points. *Cognitive Psychology* 10:203–243.

Holyoak, K. J. and A. L. Glass. 1975. The role of contradictions and counterexamples in the rejection of false sentences. *Journal of Verbal Learning and Verbal Behavior* 14:215–239.

Homa, D., J. Cross, D. Cornell, D. Goldman, and S. Shwartz. 1973. Prototype abstraction and classification of new instances as a function of number of instances defining the prototype. *Journal of Experimental Psychology* 101:116–122.

Homa, D., and R. Vosburgh. 1976. Category breadth and the abstraction of prototypical information. *Journal of Experimental Psychology: Human Learning and Memory* 2:322–330.

Hubel, D. H., and T. N. Wiesel. 1962. Receptive fields, binocular interaction and functional architecture in the cat's visual cortex. *Journal of Physiology* 160:106–154.

Hull, C. L. 1920. Quantitative aspects of the evolution of concepts. *Psychological monographs* (Whole no. 123).

Hunt, E. B., J. Marin, and P. Stone. 1966. *Experiments in induction.* New York: Academic Press.

Hutchinson, J. W., and G. R. Lockhead. 1977. Similarity as distance: A structural principle for semantic memory. *Journal of Experimental Psychology: Human Learning and Memory* 3:660–668.

Hyman, R., and N. H. Frost. 1975. Gradients and schema in pattern recognition. In *Attention and performance V*, ed. P. M. A. Rabbitt and S. Dornic. New York: Academic Press.

Kahneman, D., and A. Tversky. 1973. On the psychology of prediction. *Psychological Review* 80:237–251.

Katz, J. J. 1972. *Semantic theory.* New York: Harper & Row.

———. 1977. A proper theory of names. *Philosophical Studies* 31:1–80.

Katz, J. J., and J. A. Fodor. 1963. The structure of a semantic theory. *Language* 39:190–210.

Keil, F. C. 1979. *Semantic and conceptual development*. Cambridge, Mass.: Harvard University Press.

Kossan, N. E. 1978. Structure and strategy in concept acquisition. Ph.D. diss., Stanford University.

Kosslyn, S. M. 1980. *Image and mind*. Cambridge, Mass.: Harvard University Press.

Kripke, S. 1971. Identity and necessity. In *Identity and individuation*, ed. M. K. Munitz. New York: New York University Press.

———. 1972. Naming and necessity. In *Semantics of natural language*, ed. D. Davidson and G. Harman. Doedrecht, Holland: Reidel.

Krumhansl, C. 1978. Concerning the applicability of geometric models to similarity data: The interrelationship between similarity and spatial density. *Psychological Review* 85:445–463.

Labov, W. 1973. The boundaries of words and their meanings. In *New ways of analyzing variation in English*, ed. C. J. N. Bailey and R. W. Shuy, vol. 1. Washington, D.C.: Georgetown University Press.

Landauer, T. K., and J. L. Freedman. 1968. Information retrieval from long-term memory: Category size and recognition time. *Journal of Verbal Learning and Verbal Behavior* 7:291–295.

Lasky, R. E., and K. D. Kallio. 1978. Transformation rules in concept learning. *Memory and Cognition* 6:491–495.

Lindsay, P. H., and D. A. Norman. 1977. *Human information processing* (2nd ed.). New York: Academic Press.

Loftus, E. F., and W. Cole. 1974. Retrieving attribute and name information from semantic memory. *Journal of Experimental Psychology* 102:1116–1122.

Loftus, E. F., and R. W. Scheff. 1971. Categorization norms for 50 representative instances. *Journal of Experimental Psychology* 91:355–364.

Lyons, J. 1968. *Introduction to theoretical linguistics*. Cambridge: Cambridge University Press.

———. 1977. *Semantics* (2 vols.). Cambridge: Cambridge University Press.

Malt, B. C., and E. E. Smith. 1981a. The role of familiarity in determining typicality.

Malt, B. C., and E. E. Smith. 1981b. Correlational structure in semantic categories.

Markman, E. M. 1979. Classes and collections: Conceptual organization and numerical abilities. *Cognitive Psychology* 11:395–411.

Markman, E. M., and J. Siebert. 1976. Classes and collections: Internal organization and resulting holistic properties. *Cognitive Psychology* 8:561–577.

McCloskey, M. 1980. The stimulus familiarity problem in semantic memory research. *Journal of Verbal Learning and Verbal Behavior* 19:485–502.

McCloskey, M., and S. Glucksberg. 1978. Natural categories: Well defined or fuzzy sets? *Memory and Cognition* 6:462-472.

_____. 1979. Decision processes in verifying category membership statements: Implications for models of semantic memory. *Cognitive Psychology* 11:1–37.

Medin, D. L., and M. M. Schaffer. 1978. A context theory of classification learning. *Psychological Review* 85:207–238.

Medin, D. L., and P. J. Schwanenflugel (forthcoming). Linear separability and classification learning.

Medin, D. L., and E. E. Smith 1981. Strategies and classification learning. *Journal of Experimental Psychology: Human Learning and Memory.*

Mervis, C. B. 1980. Category structure and the development of categorization. In *Theoretical issues in reading comprehension,* ed. R. Spiro, B. C. Bruce and W. F. Brewer. Hillsdale, N.J.: Erlbaum.

Mervis, C. B., J. Catlin, and E. Rosch. 1976. Relationships among goodness-of-example, category norms, and word frequency. *Bulletin of the Psychonomic Society* 7:283–284.

Mervis, C. B., D. L. Medin, and E. Rosch (forthcoming). Salience of correlated attributes.

Meyer, D. E. 1970. On the representation and retrieval of stored semantic information. *Cognitive Psychology* 1:242–299.

Miller, G. A., and P. N. Johnson-Laird. 1976. *Language and perception.* Cambridge, Mass.: Harvard University Press.

Minsky, M. 1975. A framework for representing knowledge. In *The psychology of computer vision,* ed. P. H. Winston. New York: McGraw-Hill.

Neisser, U. 1967. *Cognitive psychology.* New York: Appleton-Century-Crofts.

Nelson, K. 1974. Concept, word, and sentence: Interrelations in acquisition and development. *Psychological Review* 81:267–285.

Neumann, P. G. 1974. An attribute frequency model for the abstraction of prototypes. *Memory and Cognition* 2:241–248.

_____. 1977. Visual prototype information with discontinuous representation of dimensions of variability. *Memory and Cognition* 5:187–197.

Nickerson, R. S. 1972. Binary-classification reaction time: A review of some studies of human information-processing capabilities. *Psychonomic Monograph Supplements* 4:275–317.

Norman, D. A., D. E. Rumelhart, and the LNR Research Group. 1975. *Explorations in cognition.* San Francisco: W. H. Freeman.

Oden, G. C. 1977. Integration of fuzzy logical information. *Journal of Experimental Psychology: Human Perception and Performance* 3:565–575.

Osherson, D. N., and E. E. Smith. 1981. On the adequacy of prototype theory as a theory of concepts. *Cognition* 9:35–58.

Palmer, S. E. 1978. Fundamental aspects of cognitive representation. In *Cognition and categorization,* ed. E. Rosch and B. B. Lloyd. Hillsdale, N.J.: Erlbaum.

Peterson, M. J., R. B. Meagher, Jr., H. Chait, and S. Gillie. 1973. The abstraction and generalization of dot patterns. *Cognitive Psychology* 4:378–398.

Pick, A. D. 1965. Improvement of visual and tactual form discrimination. *Journal of Experimental Psychology* 69:331–339.

Pittenger, J. B., and R. E. Shaw. 1975. Aging faces as visual-elastic events: Implications for a theory of non-rigid shape perception. *Journal of Experimental Psychology: Human Perception and Performance* 1:374–382.

Posner, M. I., R. Goldsmith and K. E. Welton, Jr. 1967. Perceived distance and the classification of distorted patterns. *Journal of Experimental Psychology* 73:28–38.

Posner, M. I., and S. W. Keele. 1968. On the genesis of abstract ideas. *Journal of Experimental Psychology* 77:353–363.

———. 1970. Retention of abstract ideas. *Journal of Experimental Psychology* 83:304–308.

Putnam, H. 1973. Meaning and reference. *Journal of Philosophy* 70:699–711.

Quillian, M. R. 1968. Semantic memory. In *Semantic information processing*, ed. M. Minsky. Cambridge, Mass.: MIT Press.

Reber, A. S. 1976. Implicit learning of synthetic languages: The role of instructional set. *Journal of Experimental Psychology: Human Memory and Learning* 2:88–94.

Reber, A. S., and R. Allen. 1978. Analogical and abstraction strategies in synthetic grammar learning: A functionalist interpretation. *Cognition* 6:189–221.

Reder, L. M., and J. R. Anderson. 1974. Negative judgements in and about semantic memory. *Journal of Verbal Learning and Verbal Behavior* 13:664–681.

Reed, S. K. 1972. Pattern recognition and categorization. *Cognitive Psychology* 3:382–407.

———. 1973. *Psychological processes in pattern recognition.* New York: Academic Press.

———. 1979. Schemes and theories of pattern recognition. In *Handbook of perception. IX: Perceptual processing*, ed. E. C. Carterette and M. P. Friedman. New York: Academic Press.

Rey, G. 1978. The possibility of psychology: Some preliminary remarks. Ph.D. diss. Harvard University.

Rips, L. J. 1975. Inductive judgements about natural categories. *Journal of Verbal Learning and Verbal Behavior* 14:665–681.

Rips, L. J., Shoben, E. J., and E. E. Smith. 1973. Semantic distance and the verification of semantic relations. *Journal of Verbal Learning and Verbal Behavior* 12:1–20.

Roberts, L. G. 1960. Pattern recognition with adaptive network. *IRE Convention Records* 8:66–70.

Rodwan, A. S., and H. W. Hake. 1964. The discriminant function as a model for perception. *American Journal of Psychology* 77:380–392.

Rosch, E. 1973. On the internal structure of perceptual and semantic categories. In *Cognitive development and the acquisition of language*, ed. T. E. Moore. New York: Academic Press.

———. 1974. Universals and cultural specifics in human categorization. In

Cross-cultural perspectives on learning, ed. R. Breslin, W. Lonner, and S. Bochner. London: Sage Press.

————. 1975. Cognitive representations of semantic categories. *Journal of Experimental Psychology: General* 104:192–233.

————. 1978. Principles of categorization. In *Cognition and categorization,* ed. E. Rosch and B. B. Lloyd. Hillsdale, N.J.: Erlbaum.

Rosch, E., and C. B. Mervis. 1975. Family resemblance studies in the internal structure of categories. *Cognitive Psychology* 7:573–605.

Rosch, E., C. B. Mervis, W. Gray, D. Johnson, and P. Boyes-Braem. 1976. Basic objects in natural categories. *Cognitive Psychology* 3:382–439.

Rosch, E. H., C. Simpson and R. S. Miller. 1976. Structural bases of typicality effects. *Journal of Experimental Psychology: Human Perception and Performance* 2:491–502.

Roth, E. H., and E. J. Shoben. 1980. Unpublished data, University of Illinois-Champaign.

Rumelhart, D. E., and P. Siple. 1974. Process of recognizing tachistoscopically presented words. *Psychological Review* 81:99–118.

Sattath, S., and A. Tversky. 1977. Additive similarity trees. *Psychometrika* 42:319–345.

Schwartz, S. P. 1979. Natural kind terms. *Cognition* 7:301–315.

Shepard, R. N. 1964. Attention and the metric structure of the stimulus space. *Journal of Mathematical Psychology* 1:54–87.

————. 1974. Representation of structure in similarity data: Problems and prospects. *Psychometrika* 39:373–421.

Shepard, R. N., and P. Arabie. 1979. Additive clustering: Representation of similarities as combinations of discrete overlapping properties. *Psychological Review* 86:87–123.

Shepard, R. N., and J. J. Chang. 1963. Stimulus generalization in the learning of classifications. *Journal of Experimental Psychology* 65:94–102.

Shepard, R. N., C. I. Hoveland and H. M. Jenkins. 1961. Learning and memorization of classifications. *Psychological Monographs* 75 (Whole no. 517).

Shoben, E. J. 1976. The verification of semantic relations in a Same-Difference paradigm: An asymmetry in semantic memory. *Journal of Verbal Learning and Verbal Behavior* 15:365–381.

Simpson, G. G. 1961. *Principles of animal taxonomy.* New York: Columbia University Press.

Smith, E. E. 1978. Theories of semantic memory. In *Handbook of learning and cognitive processes,* ed. W. K. Estes, vol. 6. Potomac, Md.: Erlbaum.

Smith, E. E., and G. J. Balzano. 1977. Concepts and prototypes. Paper presented at Harvard University.

Smith, E. E., G. J. Balzano, and J. H. Walker. 1978. Nominal and semantic processes in picture categorization. In *Semantic factors in cognition,* ed. J. Cotton and R. Klatzky. Potomac, Md.: Erlbaum.

Smith, E. E., E. J. Shoben, and L. J. Rips. 1974. Structure and process in semantic memory: A featural model for semantic decisions. *Psychological Review* 81:214–241.

Smith, L. B. and D. G. Kemler. 1978. Levels of experienced dimensionality in children and adults. *Cognitive Psychology* 10:502–532.

Sokal, R. R. 1974. Classification: Purposes, principles, progress, prospects. *Science* 185:1115–1123.

Sommers, F. 1965. Predicability. In *Philosophy in America,* ed. M. Black. Ithaca, N.Y.: Cornell University Press.

Townsend, J. T., and F. G. Ashby. 1976. Toward a theory of letter recognition: Testing contemporary feature models. Paper presented at the Midwestern Psychological Association Meetings, Chicago, May 1976.

Tulving, E. 1974. Cue dependent forgetting. *American Scientist* 62:74–82.

Tversky, A. 1977. Features of similarity. *Psychological Review* 84: 327–352.

Tversky, A., and D. Kahneman. 1973. Availability: A heuristic for judging frequency and probability. *Cognitive Psychology* 5:207–232.

Tversky, A., and E. E. Smith (forthcoming). A centrality effect in similarity ratings.

Uhr, L., ed. 1966. *Pattern recognition.* New York: Wiley.

Walker, J. H. 1975. Real-world variability, reasonableness judgments, and memory representations for concepts. *Journal of Verbal Learning and Verbal Behavior* 14:241–252.

Watanabe, N., ed. 1972. *Frontiers of pattern recognition.* New York: Academic Press.

Winograd, T. 1972. *Understanding natural language.* New York: Academic Press.

Winston, P. H., ed. 1975. *The psychology of computer vision.* New York: McGraw-Hill.

Wittgenstein, L. 1953. *Philosophical investigations,* G. E. M. Anscombe. Oxford: Blackwell.

Woods, W. A. 1981. Procedural semantics as a theory of meaning. In *Computational aspects of linguistic structure and discourse setting,* ed. A. Joshi, I. Sag, and B. Webber. Cambridge: Cambridge University Press.

Zadeh, L. 1965. Fuzzy sets. *Information and control* 8:338–353.

Index